Germaine Greer is one of the world's most famous celebrity feminists, a fact confirmed by her voluminous archive of reader (and viewer) correspondence. Following her lengthy immersion in this extraordinary archive, Anthea Taylor has emerged with a rich and insightful account of the relationship between Greer and her many audiences.

Michelle Arrow, author of *The Seventies: The Personal, The Political and the Making of Modern Australia,* Macquarie University

Using previously unavailable archival materials, Anthea Taylor's groundbreaking study explores the complex relationships between feminism, celebrity and the public through an insightful and carefully nuanced analysis of the close management of those relationships by that most public of celebrity feminists, Germaine Greer.

Graeme Turner, author of *Understanding Celebrity,* University of Queensland

GERMAINE GREER, CELEBRITY FEMINISM AND THE ARCHIVE

Germaine Greer, Celebrity Feminism and the Archive, the first scholarly book on this internationally renowned feminist, draws upon Greer's largely unexplored archive to demonstrate her impact on readers and viewers since the 1970s.

Across many decades in the limelight and through multiple media forms, the provocative Greer has worked to shape audience understandings of gender, sexuality, and feminism. Through deep engagement with archival material, Anthea Taylor offers a compelling reassessment of Greer's celebrity feminist labour and its effects over time. Examining archived letters from fans, anti-fans, and those in between, this innovative volume shows how and why readers and viewers have come to affectively invest – or disinvest – in this iconoclastic feminist.

Advancing debates about the social and political function of celebrity, *Germaine Greer, Celebrity Feminism and the Archive* is essential reading for scholars in Gender Studies, History, Archival Studies, and Media and Cultural Studies.

Anthea Taylor is an Associate Professor and Chair of Gender and Cultural Studies at the University of Sydney, Australia. She is the author of four books in feminist cultural studies, including *Celebrity and the Feminist Blockbuster* (2016).

GERMAINE GREER, CELEBRITY FEMINISM AND THE ARCHIVE

Anthea Taylor

LONDON AND NEW YORK

Designed cover image: Soydar, Getty Images

First published 2025
by Routledge
4 Park Square, Milton Park, Abingdon, Oxon OX14 4RN

and by Routledge
605 Third Avenue, New York, NY 10158

Routledge is an imprint of the Taylor & Francis Group, an informa business

© 2025 Anthea Taylor

The right of Anthea Taylor to be identified as author of this work has been asserted in accordance with sections 77 and 78 of the Copyright, Designs and Patents Act 1988.

All rights reserved. No part of this book may be reprinted or reproduced or utilised in any form or by any electronic, mechanical, or other means, now known or hereafter invented, including photocopying and recording, or in any information storage or retrieval system, without permission in writing from the publishers.

Trademark notice: Product or corporate names may be trademarks or registered trademarks, and are used only for identification and explanation without intent to infringe.

British Library Cataloguing-in-Publication Data
A catalogue record for this book is available from the British Library

Library of Congress Cataloging-in-Publication Data
Names: Taylor, Anthea, 1972- author.
Title: Germaine Greer, celebrity feminism and the archive / Anthea Taylor.
Description: Abingdon, Oxon ; New York, NY : Routledge, 2025. |
Includes bibliographical references and index.
Identifiers: LCCN 2024025497 (print) | LCCN 2024025498 (ebook) |
ISBN 9781138894693 (hardback) | ISBN 9781138894716 (paperback) |
ISBN 9781315179841 (ebook)
Subjects: LCSH: Greer, Germaine, 1939- | Greer, Germaine, 1939---Archives. |
Feminists--Australia--Biography. | Fan mail--Australia. |
Feminism in the press--Australia. | Feminism on television.
Classification: LCC HQ1822.5.G74 T39 2025 (print) |
LCC HQ1822.5.G74 (ebook) | DDC 305.42092 [B]--dc23/eng/20240826
LC record available at https://lccn.loc.gov/2024025497
LC ebook record available at https://lccn.loc.gov/2024025498

ISBN: 978-1-138-89469-3 (hbk)
ISBN: 978-1-138-89471-6 (pbk)
ISBN: 978-1-315-17984-1 (ebk)

DOI: 10.4324/9781315179841

Typeset in Sabon
by SPi Technologies India Pvt Ltd (Straive)

*In memoriam, Owen Maurice Taylor (1969–2019).
To O, the best big brother I could have ever
wished for.*

CONTENTS

Acknowledgements	*x*
Introduction: 'For their sake I must keep at it': Celebrity, Audiences, and Archived Letters	1
1 'The archive will put matters right, for posterity': Greer's Curatorial Labour	23
2 'You are the twentieth century messiah!': Blockbuster Fan Mail	45
3 'The best thing to happen to night-time television': Consuming the Televisual Greer	73
4 'Greer has done it again!': Reader-writers and Feminist Journalism	102
5 'Miss Greer is the most pathetic eunuch of all': Anti-fandom and *McCall's* Magazine	129
6 'Steve is twice the Aussie icon you will ever be': Nationalistic Misogyny and the Irwin Hate Email	153
Conclusion: 'Messages in a bottle': Reframing Greer's Legacy	177
Index	*187*

ACKNOWLEDGEMENTS

This book is based on research funded by the Australian Research Council (Discovery Grant: DP170100755), and I am grateful for the support which enabled me to immerse myself in the Greer archive and produce this work.

I have built upon and expanded some previously published material, including '"Steve is twice the Aussie icon you will ever be": Germaine Greer, The Crocodile Hunter's Death, and Nationalistic Misogyny', *European Journal of Cultural Studies* (2019, vol. 22, no.5–6: 630–645); '"The most revolting ideas I've read in a woman's magazine": *The Female Eunuch*, Affective (dis)investments, and *McCall's* Reader-writers' , *Australian Feminist Studies* (vol. 35, no. 1: 20–36); and 'Archiving Greer/Greer Archiving: Germaine Greer's Curatorial Labour, Feminist Celebrity Studies and Archival Methodologies', *Celebrity Studies* (vol. 15. no. 3: 320–335). I thank the editors of these publications for their permission to draw upon some of that material here.

I am thoroughly indebted to archival staff at the University of Melbourne for all their assistance and support as well as those in the Ballieu Library Reading Room, especially Chen Chen and Leanne McCredden. My deep gratitude to Dr Rachel Buchanan and all the archivists who have worked on the Greer collection, particularly Lachlan Glanville.

I wish to thank the Research Assistants who have supported me across this project, including Dr Alexa Appel, Dr Grace Sharkey, Darby Judd, and most recently Dr Nathan Jackson, especially for proofreading chapters. I would also like to acknowledge Stephen Poole for his thoughtful copyediting.

Thanks also to staff at Routledge, including Alexandra MacGregor, who initially commissioned this book. This project was considerably delayed by the COVID-19 pandemic, which made access to the Greer archive impossible

Acknowledgements **xi**

for extended periods of time. Thank you to Routledge for their patience and understanding, particularly most recently Dr Jodie Collins.

I am extremely lucky to have a lovely group of women friends who are also fabulous feminist scholars and who, in addition to discussing these ideas with me over many years, read and provided invaluable feedback on various chapters (often within tight timeframes). For their generosity and cheerleading, my heartfelt thanks go to Dr Hannah Hamad, Associate Professor Margaret Henderson, Dr Joanna McIntyre, and Dr Kate O'Halloran. Margaret deserves special thanks for coming to the rescue when I couldn't see the wood for the (archival) trees. My sincere thanks also to Dr Rebecca Sheehan, a fellow Greer scholar who generously offered to read some of this work in the final hours and reassured me that I was doing justice to this formidable figure and her audiences.

Thanks to my colleagues and friends in Gender and Cultural Studies at the University of Sydney, especially Professor Elspeth Probyn and Dr Shawna Tang, for their support, wisdom, and comradery.

My wonderful family, as always, have helped make this book possible. My endlessly supportive parents, Rose and Maurice, my brother, Owen, and sister-in-law, Kirsty, and their three incredible daughters, Isabella, Olivia, and Amelie (I am so proud of the loving, fierce young women you have become), and my partner, Eoin. My deepest love and gratitude to them all, especially my dearly missed brother, Owen, who made my life – and me – better.

INTRODUCTION

'For their sake I must keep at it': Celebrity, Audiences, and Archived Letters

In 1972, during the height of what became known as Western feminism's 'second wave', a woman from Gulargambone in central west New South Wales wrote to ask feminist superstar Germaine Greer if she felt all her media efforts were having the desired impact on audiences: 'Do you think it's worth it? Are people listening?' (M.T., 23 March). A few months later – a common delay given the amount of mail Greer was receiving in response to her bestselling feminist polemic, *The Female Eunuch* (1970) – she replied:

> I myself wonder if I'm not utterly masochistic in the way in which I overwork and tangle myself up trying to do all sorts of things at once. You are right to ask me if it's worth it, and if people are listening. But I have always had the notion that somewhere, someone, perhaps shy and self-effacing, is turning on to what's going on, and for their sake I must keep at it.
>
> (19 June 1972, 2014.0042.00888)

In her typed response to her countrywoman, Greer suggested she laboured for that imagined addressee, whom she believed needed to be 'turned on to' women's liberation. These letters are just a few of many to and from Greer now in her extensive and hitherto underexplored archive.

Germaine Greer, Celebrity Feminism and the Archive is the first scholarly monograph on this iconic feminist figure, and uses Greer's own archival material to reframe her lengthy celebrity career – primarily by looking into its effects.[1] Through deep engagement with the archive, this book explores how audiences, over decades, have made sense of, negotiated with, and responded

DOI: 10.4324/9781315179841-1

2 Germaine Greer, Celebrity Feminism and the Archive

(either publicly or privately) to Greer and her feminism. To sustain their cultural authority, celebrity feminists, like all famous figures, rely upon audiences. The Greer archive is brimming with letters from diverse readers and viewers that provide fascinating insights into how her work as a popular author, television host and performer, print journalist, and celebrity persona profoundly mediated their understandings of gender, sexuality, and feminism. As I argue, such letters underscore the intense affective investments – or, conversely, disinvestments – that audiences have made in this iconic feminist across time and space. Working with these rich archival sources and seeking to recuperate Greer's at times troubled feminist legacy, this book foregrounds the impact of her extensive feminist creative labour on audiences, revealing much about the social and political function of celebrity in various historical and cultural contexts.

* * *

Germaine Greer, who has been described as a 'pioneer in the celebrity zone' (Lilburn et al. 2000, p. 335) and 'the star feminism had to have' (Wallace 1997, p. 207), is one of the Western world's most enduring celebrity feminists.[2] Although Greer's renown initially stemmed from the publication of her first 'feminist blockbuster' (Rowlands and Henderson 1996; Lilburn et al. 2000; Taylor 2016), *The Female Eunuch* (1970), the iconoclastic feminist has consistently worked to maintain her public visibility across myriad literary and media forms and genres,[3] from further feminist bestsellers to reality television, with significant cultural and political effects (and indeed affects) that are illuminated by archived audience letters. Greer's feminism, which I argue is a decidedly radical form, continues to reverberate culturally – for better or worse. Through her anti-trans commentary, as well as her criticisms of the #MeToo movement and attacks on other women celebrities such as Australia's first woman Prime Minister Julia Gillard, Greer has become an increasingly divisive figure for feminism.[4] Often courting controversy, she has sustained, developed, and leveraged her 'attention capital' – defined as the 'accumulation and distribution of attention' (Van Krieken 2012, p. 55) – in service of political goals since the late 1960s. Given her broader cultural impact and legacy, however, scholarly attention has been relatively scant (Taylor et al. 2016). As well as intervening in ongoing debates about celebrity and popular feminisms, and archival studies and feminist historiography, this book uses the opportunity provided by Greer's enormous archive to lay the foundations for further feminist work in Greer studies.

The archival material examined throughout this book – carefully collected, curated, and even sourced by the famous feminist since her teens – shows for the first time how, over many years, international audiences have responded to Greer in ways that seek to reinforce, extend, complicate, or undermine this feminist fame – and this feminism. As I argue, it has been Greer's cross-media

Introduction **3**

celebrity feminism that has enabled her to reach such wide and varied audiences across her protracted career. Precisely *how* is something about which we have, until now, known little. The archive underscores that Greer is not just a bestselling author, she is an accomplished professional journalist, television host and performer, and indeed archivist (Buchanan 2018). In this respect, the archive's capacity to expand and 'unsettle what we think know' (Buchanan 2018, p. 34; see also Stead 2021) about Greer and her wider cultural resonance makes it especially valuable to a project of this nature. The extensive Greer collection – sold to the University of Melbourne in 2013 and, apart from extended closures during the COVID-19 pandemic, fully accessible to researchers since 2017 – contains copious letters, research material, book drafts, diaries, photographs, press clippings, and thousands of hours of radio and television appearances. These artefacts individually and collectively can shed new light on a figure who occupies an ambivalent position within feminist history – and its present. The Greer archive currently consists of 32 series; I say 'currently' as the collection continues to grow, as those of living celebrities invariably do.[5]

However, the archive is not simply where we *find* knowledge about Greer (or any other figure) but a site of and for knowledge production itself; there is no singular, authentic 'voice' awaiting its unearthing or retrieval (Milthorpe 2019, pp. 8–9). But it is certainly the case that through the archive, its collection, curation, cataloguing, and conditions of access, Greer seeks – within, of course, very material limits – to author herself in significant ways, often directing the researcher's gaze towards specific material (Buchanan 2018; Glanville 2018). Indeed, most of the letters analysed here are those to which Greer, through her archival labour, draws our attention. As Elizabeth Yale astutely observes, 'scholars who rely on archives, do well to understand the histories that have shaped them: these histories constrain the kinds of stories that can be written from any particular archive' (2015, p. 332). Accordingly, in the first chapter I turn to Greer's curatorial practices and how they shape the kinds of 'Greers' I have been able to write into being. This book also places celebrity studies and archival studies in dialogue to help better tease out the possibilities of archival methodologies for historical studies of celebrity and fandom.

Audience letters in the Greer archive

In her public commentary on the archive, Greer repeatedly asserts that it is not about her but about the 'ordinary' people it features – especially in its thousands and thousands of unsolicited letters. Letters in the Greer archive appear across all its major series, with the largest featured in the strategically alphabetised General Correspondence series – a gesture that Greer frames as one of democratisation (Glanville 2017), as I discuss further in the first

4 Germaine Greer, Celebrity Feminism and the Archive

chapter. It is this series, along with others such as Early Years, Major Works, Print Journalism, and Television, that contains most of the material used here. As we will see, there are different forms of reader and viewer letters analysed across the course of this book: seemingly 'private' letters addressed to Greer; 'public' letters to the editor addressed to various magazines and newspapers, and through which readers themselves become writers (Farrell 1998); letters to agents, publicists, and producers; and, in more recent instances, emails addressed to both Greer and her representatives. Many were sent to Greer in batches, and kept together, especially those addressed to third parties, while those sent directly to Greer are usually (though not always) filed alphabetically in the General Correspondence series. Spanning over four decades, these letters are significant longitudinally, indicating shifts in understandings of gender, sexuality, feminism, and Greer herself over an extended period of time. Although the Greer archive is filled with many types of documents that might help us reposition her in popular and intellectual feminist history, the audience correspondence captured in this archive helps make clear the stakes of such a project; that is, why it matters.

The uses I make of such letters, as will become evident, is informed by my position as a feminist celebrity studies scholar. I draw upon these epistolary texts primarily as a form of historical audience research, to help give some insights into how Greer-as-celebrity became 'folded into audience ways of making sense of the world' (Turner et al. 2000, p. 15), incorporating a feminist politics into the everyday (or, in some cases, refusing to do so). Not all correspondents can be constituted (or constitute themselves) fans or anti-fans, but where relevant to do so, I conceptualise these letters as acts of fandom and, conversely, anti-fandom. Many letter writers, however, exist between these two extremes. Some are just curious consumers who wish to reflect further on an issue, episode, argument, or comment in epistolary form. Others seek to offer alternative perspectives on the kind of feminism Greer prosecutes and to engage in debate with her or those who have given her voice (such as newspaper or magazine editors). This book addresses all these different levels of engagement with Greer and her celebrity feminism.

In terms of the archived letters in the Greer collection, others have written about her correspondence with well-known feminists such as civil rights and feminist activist Florynce Kennedy (Sheehan 2019) and Indigenous rights activist Roberta Sykes (Sheehan 2024), and others still on her letters to famous men with whom she was romantically involved (Simons 2015). This book, in contrast, focuses predominantly on the voices of everyday readers and viewers who did not personally know Greer – though her public persona created the sense they did, such is the work of celebrity culture (Rojek 2015; Coffin 2020). Given that celebrity is always intertextual (Dyer 1979), letter writers are responding not just to the 'Greer' they might see on television or read in her newspaper columns but to the celebrity persona established across all these forms: 'Rare is the person who can pick up a book by Germaine Greer and profess to reading it with no perceived opinion about the writer and her work' (Munford 1984, p. 16).

These letters, of course, reveal much about the periods in which they were composed and particularly how women (and, to a lesser extent, men) negotiate their being as gendered subjects at various points in history (Grasso 2013, p. 26). Whether they explicitly discussed or identified with feminism depends largely, though not solely, on when they were written. For some, such identification is politically significant; for others, it is either taken for granted or something to be resisted. In many instances, as I will further explore, Greer has clearly acted as a 'consciousness-raiser', offering a feminist interpretive framework through which readers and viewers could imagine alternative futures. Such letters therefore tell us about how feminism, through Greer, circulated and resonated with audiences – that is, the role she played in fostering feminist attachments (Ahmed 2004). This archived correspondence is especially important given that 'the role of ordinary women in the history of second-wave feminism has been silenced by the histories that focus on the radicals and activists' (Le Masurier 2016, p. 211; see also Sheehan 2016, p. 74).[6] Although my own study of this one iconic feminist could, in some respect, reinscribe this limited focus, my attention to Greer's audiences enables me to re-centre such 'ordinary' figures. That Greer retained this mail and included it in her archive also implies that she values such epistolary communication, as her often generous replies confirm (Glanville 2017).

Alongside those of admiration, gratitude, excitement, relief, and hope, feelings of disdain, hatred, anger, and resentment circulate across these letters, revealing the complex 'affective circuitry' (Waters 2016) around this internationally renowned feminist. Such epistolary texts give a sense of how audiences affectively responded to, and sought to intimately connect with, Greer and how communities of disparate fans and anti-fans came into being around her star persona, books, television, and journalism. For some critics, such insights are thought to have become available only with the advent of digital media. Sharon Marcus (2015, p. 4), for example, has suggested that scholars interested in fan behaviour have 'often lacked evidence of what fans felt and thought', adding that it is social media that has brought 'affect to the fore'. However, like others (Thomas 2014; Fuller-Seeley 2018; Steuer 2019), I am interested in challenging this presumption of 'new-ness' through showing that archived letters *do* provide such 'evidence' and are thus crucial sources in understanding historical audiences and their emotional attachments to celebrities and, importantly, to their politics. There is – as the Greer archive illustrates – also a more extensive history of audiences actively negotiating with and responding to popular and celebrity feminisms, including via the letter form (Farrell 1998; Le Masurier 2009), than is sometimes acknowledged. This is likewise underscored by the archives of other celebrity feminists, such as those of Betty Friedan (Taylor 2016) and Gloria Steinem (Taylor 2023).

6 Germaine Greer, Celebrity Feminism and the Archive

These reader and viewer letters represent an 'archive within an archive' (Groeneveld 2018), giving a sense not just of what feminism (and one of its key public figures) may have meant to correspondents but how it *felt* across different cultural and historical moments (Hesford 2013). In this respect, the Greer fonds are an 'archive of feelings', defined by Ann Cvetkovich as 'repositories of feelings and emotions, which are encoded not only in the content of the texts themselves but in the practices that surround their production and reception' (2003, p. 7). When these letters are read together, it is possible to see the ways in which emotional responses to feminism and its celebrities can be collectively experienced (Ahmed 2004). The letters and their revelations were even invoked by Greer in media coverage to justify her feminist labour. As she told *Tribune* journalists, 'the letters I get from women saying "I've done this and done that and I've decided that I won't let my husband get away with it any more, I'm leaving", make it all worthwhile' (Aarons and Ryan 1972, as cited in Arrow 2019, p. 45). Much of this correspondence therefore, even perhaps from those who were more resistant, reassured Greer that the feminist work she was doing in the mediasphere was meaningful and worth continuing – despite the immense cost to her personally.

Throughout her public career, Greer has received so much unsolicited mail that she even reflected upon it in a few of her newspaper columns. Although Greer's replies are not my primary focus here, apart from some brief consideration in Chapter 2, she found writing responses to such audience letters so labour-intensive that she even pleaded with readers of her 'Country Notebook' column in the UK's *Daily Telegraph* (1999b) to desist: 'Dear reader, if you have any regard for my mental and physical health, any respect for me as a fellow human being, please do not write to me EVER'. Similarly, her article in the *Independent*, 'Germaine Greer on Strangers in the Mail' (1992), gives some sense of the toll exacted by this form of affective labour, as she melodramatically claims that 'letters from strangers are ruining my life'. While Greer may have viewed them as strangers, this is not how her correspondents saw themselves, as we will see.

Greer's lifelong 'media pragmatism'

Early in her career, Greer adopted a form of what Bernadette Barker-Plummer calls 'media pragmatism', conceptualising mainstream media as a 'powerful movement resource' that could be wielded strategically for feminist ends (1995, p. 312). Consistent with such an approach, Greer has always seen celebrity as a vital consciousness-raising tool and acted accordingly. In a disingenuous disavowal of celebrity culture commonly performed by Greer (Taylor 2016), and in recognition that many feminists viewed celebrity to be fundamentally at odds with the women's movement's anti-hierarchal, collectivist principles (Gever 2003; Whelehan 2005), she self-reflexively remarked: "'I'm against the cult of personality, too, but I think we have to use whatever weapons we've got. And I have always been a personality'" (Lehrmann 1972, p. 64). Many Anglo-American second-wave feminists, however, did dismiss these interventions into the mainstream media and commercial publishing as 'selling-out' (Dreifus 1971). Viewing Greer as an 'outsider' in terms of the women's movement, they denounced her personal lack of grassroots activism and what they saw as a misguided privileging of the individual over the collective (Wallace 1997; Lake 2016; Sheehan 2019).[7] They also argued that, with *The Female Eunuch*, she had failed to offer a practical manifesto that could be used by women to improve their lives (Goodman 1971) – a point with which readers patently disagreed, as Chapter 2 illustrates. Greer-the-celebrity, these feminists argued, was not doing feminism 'correctly' (Taylor 2016; Sheehan 2019).

In response to these harsh second-wave feminist judgements about her self-commodification[8] and their failure to concede that her media work was a crucial form of 'discursive activism' (Young 1997), Greer repeatedly defended her media strategy to journalists. In 'The Greering of the Press' (1971), for example, at the height of her post-*Eunuch* fame, the feminist iconoclast told *Washington Post* journalist Sally Quinn:

> I'm a complete media freak…And the only reason I ever submitted to the commercialization of Germaine Greer is to help women in the home, to raise the self-image of women, to spread the movement on the widest possible base. My aim is to demonstrate that everything could be otherwise and joyously otherwise.

This is not to suggest that Greer was unaware of the limits of her media pragmatism – for example, she complained to another journalist (Allison 1971) about *Life* magazine's infamous characterisation of her as 'the saucy feminist even men like' (Bonfante 1971) – or that such narratives were not themselves strategic persona-building gestures, mobilised to stave off these feminist critiques (Taylor 2016). Rather, it is to highlight that through her deployment of various forms of media to reach as wide an audience as possible, she was arguably more sanguine than many 1970s feminists who rejected media engagement wholesale. As Rebecca Sheehan argues, Greer 'stepped into a space they [other women's liberationists] refused to inhabit' (2019, p. 80), securing her a prolonged form of international fame experienced by few feminists (Wallace 1997).

This lifelong strategy of media pragmatism, however, has not simply been about making herself available to journalists as a source or interviewee. Greer, most importantly, has not just been represented by the media, she *was/is* the media (Buchanan 2018). In Australia, the US, and the UK, Greer has often been a pioneer in her media work, hosting television programs and obtaining regular newspaper columns when to do so as a woman let alone as

8 Germaine Greer, Celebrity Feminism and the Archive

a feminist was exceptionally rare (while the archive reveals her efforts to create screen content were at times stymied [Taylor 2022]). In the later stages of her career, though she has continued to publish books and write for newspapers and magazines, British television is where she has been most active (Taylor 2014). The fact that Greer has made a career out of her feminism – though not an especially lucrative one if we are to believe her audio diaries, discussed in the following chapter – makes her a problematic figure for many feminists. However, as I argue, Greer did not use feminism to further her career, she used her career to further feminism – and she has sparked and shaped debate, dialogue, and public response to it for decades.

Despite the fears of both second-wave feminists and later scholars (Spongberg 1993; Bradley 2003; Murray 2004), Greer's strategic media intervention and fame have *not* diluted or evacuated her feminist critique of its oppositional potential (Taylor 2016). In fact, from her elevated speaking position as media maker and celebrity feminist, she has always prosecuted a much more radical form of feminism than is usually found in mass-mediated versions of feminisms (Dow 1996; Henderson 2006).[9] Greer has persistently rejected the reformism of equality feminism, preferring a more revolutionary mode, regularly dismissing equality as '"a profoundly conservative goal"' (Davey 2017). While Greer's feminism may not easily fit into dominant ways of categorising feminism, she has critiqued patriarchal capitalism and commodity culture; underscored the limits of marriage and the nuclear family itself (both of which she urged women to reject); advocated for a more expansive definition of sexual assault (most recently in *On Rape* [2018]); and, as one of the earliest 'sex positive' feminists (Gerhard 2000), promoted the reclamation and celebration of women's sexuality and bodily autonomy, including through her 'cunt power' writing (Le Masurier 2016) wherein she tested many of the ideas further outlined in *The Female Eunuch*. Though Greer may not have necessarily articulated a 'coherent political platform', she has always sought 'to inspire women to revolt' (Le Masurier 2016, p. 37).

Greer has, then, for decades problematised the critical narrative that it is only the most palatable forms of feminism (typically reformist or liberal) that have been elevated in the mainstream media (Casey and Watson 2023). That said, across this book, I attend to the white, heterosexual, middle-class privilege embodied by Greer (not least in terms of the immense institutional support she has received for her archive). These are intersecting advantages that celebrity problematically relies upon and reinforces and that some of her correspondents themselves critique. This is important, for, as Sara Ahmed observes, 'Where we find feminism matters; from whom we find feminism matters' (2017, p. 5). As a voice elevated 'above others' (Marshall 1997, p. xi), Greer has been given the space not just to *speak* but to be *heard*. And despite claims to the contrary (Faludi 1991), her uncompromising feminist voice has been remarkably consistent across her media career – especially on issues such as rape (Bueskens 2020). Moreover, although Greer is a crucial figure in terms of the second wave's collective memory (Henderson 2006), I demonstrate here that she is by no means a figure from/of the past. Greer's ongoing public visibility as a feminist, in a way that itself troubles the dominant wave model of feminist historiography (Henry 2004), is one of the most extraordinary things about her (Dux 2010; Taylor 2016; Bueskens 2020).[10] But this presence is not happenstance: it is the product of her strategic and persistent feminist labour.

The labour and function of celebrity feminism

While there have been multiple definitions, celebrities can be classified as 'distinguishably high-profile mediated public figures addressing substantial audiences' (Drake 2018, p. 282); or, in Chris Rojek's rendering, 'celebrity = impact upon public consciousness' (2001, p. 101). In these respects, and as audience letters make clear, Greer's status as a celebrity is irrefutable. Given her decades of celebrity feminism, the Greer archive offers unique insights into the evolution of this complicated activist phenomenon, foregrounding its generative capacities (Brady 2016). Notably, Greer is a celebrity *feminist* – a feminist who has been celebrified (i.e., her publicly articulated feminism is the source of her fame) – not a *celebrity* feminist, someone whose celebrity emerges from their achievements in a particular field but who later adds feminism to their brand (Taylor 2016), a category that has increased markedly over the past decade or so (Hamad and Taylor 2015).[11] This is an important distinction given how it affects Greer's relationship both to the media industries and to her audiences.

Following other feminist scholars (Wicke 1994; Lilburn et al. 2000; Henderson 2006), I have previously argued (Taylor 2016) that celebrity feminism cannot be dismissed as merely a lesser, compromised, or 'inauthentic' form of commodified activism, a position that other critics have since further developed (Hobson 2017; Brady 2021; Chidgey 2021; Casey and Watson 2023; Lawson 2023; Majic 2023). Rather than being something 'done to' reluctant feminists, celebrity is a 'performative practice' (Marwick and boyd 2011) – something they actively and strategically '*do* for decidedly political ends' (Taylor 2016, p. 5, original emphasis). Celebrity, as opposed to being a distraction from 'real' feminist work, is how they perform their activism (Brady 2021), making it a crucial political resource that requires a more nuanced approach. Celebrity feminism – like popular feminism more broadly – also has a much longer history than scholars writing about intensified feminist identification by celebrities concede (Gill 2016; Banet-Weiser 2018; Zielser 2017). Archival material allows us to see the extent of the visibility work that Greer has had to undertake across her career to remain in the spotlight, emphasising that she has *done* her celebrity through multiple media forms.

Although under the broader umbrella of celebrity feminism, and as I establish here, Greer is several forms of celebrity at once: bestselling author,

10 Germaine Greer, Celebrity Feminism and the Archive

television host and performer, and print journalist. Her celebrity is sustained, or rather *she* agentically works to sustain her celebrity, in and through various platforms, genres, and cultural contexts – notwithstanding the cultural intermediaries (agents, publicists, and assistants) who all play crucial roles in the maintenance of renown (Gamson 1994; Turner et al. 2000; York 2013). As material in the archive makes clear, Greer's celebrity feminism is the result of creative media work on her part: 'As a professional communicator whose major theme was feminism, she helped breathe life into that now prevalent public persona, the multi-media cultural commentator' (Nolan 1999, p. 168). Greer, as I have suggested, sought to make feminism accessible to those 'into whose lives it may not otherwise have flowed' (Taylor 2016, p. 4; see also Arrow 2019). That is, she was explicit that her priority was to speak to those outside the women's movement, and this cross-media strategy was crucial to reaching wider audiences; if Greer did not reach them in one form, she would reach them in another, as many letters explicitly suggest. In this regard, her media work constitutes an important form of feminist praxis. As she asserted, underscoring the labour of celebrity, '"my life's work is to make the feminist position comprehensible to more and more people"' (Lehrmann 1972, p. 82). Moreover, as a celebrity figure upon whose 'unruliness' I have previously remarked (Taylor 2016), Greer has publicly embodied a different way of doing womanhood (single, childfree, bold, assertive, and uncompromising), to which geographically dispersed women and men eagerly responded.

This mapping of the considerable labour Greer expended to ensure that her feminism was publicly legible does not, however, downplay the place of other key actors in the overdetermined practices of celebrification. Indeed, by drawing primarily upon audience letters, I am foregrounding the role of publics in such processes. As Marcus argues of 'publics, media producers, and stars themselves', each has 'partial, contested, but real agency', and it is their interactions that produce celebrity (2019, p. 217). As she notes, 'None has perfect power; none is perfectly powerless' (Marcus 2019, p. 4). This study, therefore, addresses all these key players, to varying degrees. Here, I am primarily concerned not with how Greer has been *represented* by the media (though there is undoubtedly much more to be said in that regard) but with the public life of her feminist ideas and especially how they have (or have not) gathered traction – a process in which celebrity culture is central. As Graeme Turner (2010, p. 14) has emphasised, it is essential that scholars further attend to celebrity as a 'cultural formation that has a social function' (see also 2004). Celebrities help shape who we become, our aspirations, fantasies, and desires (Mendick et al. 2018), embodying alternative possibilities that may not have been otherwise imaginable – which was especially crucial during feminism's second wave but also beyond. We therefore need 'a more capacious understanding of celebrity as a cultural aspect of worldmaking' (Flood 2019, p. 424).

Introduction **11**

While it is common to suggest that women like Greer help influence identity formation and wider understandings of political issues and social movements, 'there is no agreement on exactly how that occurs, or to what effect' (Turner 2016, p. 110). There has been intensified critical interest in celebrity feminism, but surprisingly little work exists on how celebrities mediate audience understandings of feminism (notable exceptions include Keller and Ringrose 2015; Lonie 2019; Jackson 2021). In terms of how such processes have operated historically, these letters are a useful if imperfect proxy for this kind of audience research (Collins 1997). They are crucial in revealing how audiences in concrete terms have negotiated with and given meaning not just to Greer-as-celebrity but to feminism more broadly. Readers and viewers, as will become clear, have not just passively imbibed Greer's feminism (Sheehan 2016); they have actively worked to make it meaningful in the context of their everyday lives.

Affect, epistolarity, and audiences

These letters offer, amongst other things, insights into the complicated ways in which Greer, her texts, and her feminism have come to matter – individually and collectively. While the relationship between affect and emotions continues to exercise many critics, with some conceptualising the former as bodily and pre-discursive, here I follow feminist theorist Sara Ahmed, who refuses the strict demarcation advocated by others. As she asserts, in everyday life affect and emotions 'are contiguous; they slide into each other; they stick, and cohere, even when they are separated' (Ahmed 2008, p. 33). For my purposes, the concept of 'affective investments' (or dis-investments) is especially efficacious for understanding audiences and how they may connect with a particular celebrity. As cultural studies theorist Lawrence Grossberg argues, in terms of any popular text (and I would include a star text), 'People are constantly struggling, not merely to figure out what a text means, but to make it mean something that connects to their own lives, experiences, needs and desires' (1992, pp. 582–83). Affect both operates within and produces 'mattering maps' which govern our relations to texts and events, 'tell[ing] us where and how we can become absorbed – not into the self but into the world – as potential locations for our self-identifications, and with what intensities' (Grossberg 1992, p. 583). Following such work, I am preoccupied not just with what Greer does as a celebrity but with what the audience *does* with the celebrity 'Greer', something these archived letters bring into sharp relief.

Women and girls have long turned to life writing genres such as letters and diaries to 'disrupt and renegotiate dominant discourses' (Douglas and Poletti 2016, p. 121), as the Greer archive makes abundantly clear (though men too did write). The self-representational possibilities of such forms are

12 Germaine Greer, Celebrity Feminism and the Archive

vital in a feminist sense. The political and affective role of letters in feminist history is also canvassed by Margaretta Jolly (2008); she outlines how crucial letters and the epistolary relationships they sustained were to the women's movement. New selves and new modes of intimacy and political alliances, as she argues, are brought into being in and through epistolary networks. Furthermore, preserved letters, as Judith Coffin remarks of those written to French philosopher and feminist blockbuster author Simone de Beauvoir, 'constitute a remarkable archive of interior lives' (2010, p. 1065), making them important sources in the history of emotions (Borges 2020). However, we must be mindful that they are also epistolary acts of self-construction, produced in specific historical and cultural contexts, and always written for distinct purposes. As Maryanne Dever et al. note, such archived letters are 'occasions for the projection of "ideal selves", fleeting – or flirting – masks adopted according to the demands of the recipient and circumstances, opportunities to fashion and perform a particular self for a chosen audience' (2009, p. 49). They also invoke a particular 'Greer' as their addressee, or as the subject of their epistolary texts.

As a method to help us gain some insight into the function of celebrity feminism in the lives of audiences, such letters are crucial but there are limits to them as historical sources. In this regard, Kate Douglas and Anna Poletti observe in their examination of letters from the Riot Grrrl archive: 'What letter writing can be said to represent, and what kind information it can tell us about the past—the moment of writing, the person who wrote them or the more general milieu in which they circulated—must be acknowledged as limited' (2016, p. 127). These are methodological limits of which I am mindful, and critically engage with, throughout this book. Ethically, moreover, there is a need to reflect upon the writers of such correspondence, who perhaps never imagined their often confessional texts would come to form part of a publicly available archive. In response to the ethical issues of drawing upon these 'private lives made public by virtue of their preservation within an archive' (Dever et al. 2009, p. 120), across this book I de-identify reader and viewer letters, using just initials, date, and location to differentiate them.

From this extensive correspondence, like that of Beauvoir (Coffin 2020), Greer's fan (and indeed anti-fan) base appears diverse in terms of age, gender, sexuality, education, race, class, politics, and geographical locations. Nuns, aspiring writers, university students, housewives, teachers, and activists all took up their pens to share intimate details of their personal circumstances with Greer, underscoring the role she has played in their understandings of gender and sexuality. That is, Greer's letter writers are far from homogeneous but represent a significant cross-section of communities across both time and space. As Greer herself notes, 'I can discern from it [her mail] that not all people who understand are middleclass, educated and young and female, though, and that is a comfort' (1972, 2014.0044.00198). Whereas some make

Introduction **13**

explicit their racial positioning, many others are silent on this, implying that an unmarked whiteness dominates this audience archive, a limitation of which we must be conscious (Moreton-Robinson 2000). On average, letters are between one and two pages, though some are considerably longer (or indeed shorter as with some of those effusively praising her hosting of *The Dick Cavett Show*). Letters come from various parts of the globe, but the majority that I engage with here were produced in response to American, Australian, or British texts and/or appearances, across about a 40-year period.

While 'fan practices may be occurring even when people do not self-describe as fans' (Hills 2018, p. 477), many of these correspondents *do* explicitly identify as Greer 'fans' – a self-identificatory gesture that it is important for us to understand. Letter writers who identify as fans are not just fans of Greer's writing or media performances but the politicised worldview they help precipitate (i.e., they are fans of Greer *and* her feminism). Engaging with such mail, I seek to reaffirm the 'fan letter as a non-standard archival object worthy of sustained scholarly attention' (Stead 2021, p. 129). The relationship between celebrities and fans has been predominantly framed as one of parasociality (Horton and Wohl 1956); it is, however, often more complicated than such presumption of a one-sided fan activity and attachment permits. In addition, although there have been some recent attempts to theorise feminist fans and fandoms (Yodovich 2022; Hannell 2023), there has been little critical engagement with fans *of* celebrity feminists and certainly none in terms of historical fandoms around such figures (Fuller-Seeley 2018). This critical elision is perhaps because the inherently unequal fan–celebrity relationship, and the sense of idolatry it implies, is not considered to be consistent with feminism. Notwithstanding its constructed-ness, fan mail to celebrity feminists illuminates these affective processes, as I argue especially in Chapter 2. (In addition to often gushing letters, other common forms of fan behaviour are evident in the archive, including multiple requests for autographed pictures.[12])

In contrast to the mail that comes from self-professed fans, some use the epistolary genre – including outward-facing forms such as letters to the editor – to solidify and publicly circulate their anti-feminist sentiments. Across this book, but especially in the final two chapters, I therefore examine what we might dub Greer's 'anti-fans' (Gray 2003), as they reveal as much about the impact of her feminist media work as fans. In addition to those analysed here, the General Correspondence series contains four folders, somewhat problematically labelled 'Nutters 1–4', overflowing with letters, many of which remain unopened (2014.00042.00629–32). For women in the public spotlight, and particularly celebrity feminists, hostile letters are unfortunately all too common.[13] In the past few decades, of course, as I will argue in Chapter 6, digital media – including email – has only seen such antagonisms intensify.

14 Germaine Greer, Celebrity Feminism and the Archive

Pathways through the archive

Archival methodologies, as I demonstrate, are vital for coming to terms with the historical impact of celebrities and how celebrity capital is established and maintained. Each chapter therefore reflects on the archival material upon which it draws and what it makes possible in a study of this nature. In Chapter 1, '"The archive will put matters right, for posterity": Greer's Curatorial Labour', I make clear that while the Greer archive offers insights into her fame and its reverberations, it also evidences the extensive persona-building labour in which she has engaged across her career. Given her central role in both its creation and curation, Greer's archive is a form of renown maintenance and extension in and of itself, which can be figured as a feminist practice consistent with her own recuperative feminist scholarship. Placing archival studies and celebrity studies in a much-needed dialogue, this chapter considers Greer's own curatorial practices and how they seek to shape the way the archive is consumed, the uses to which it is being put, and the kind of 'Greers' it seeks (not necessarily with success) to render visible.

Former Greer archivist Rachel Buchanan (2018) argues that Greer in many ways needs to be 'liberated' from *The Female Eunuch*, a laudable goal which I too seek to pursue here. Nevertheless, I find myself returning to it repeatedly in this book, not least because the archive, including through Greer's correspondents, does so. In Chapter 2, '"You are the twentieth century women's messiah!": Blockbuster Fan Mail', I examine archived letters from readers of Greer's popular feminist books, especially *The Female Eunuch* and *The Change*, to reveal the deep affective investments that audiences have made in this iconic figure and her writing over many decades. This chapter therefore reflects upon what constitutes a feminist fan, as in a fan of a celebrity feminist. In often intimate epistolary exchanges, many suggest that Greer's bestsellers are transformational, offering them the tools to envisage and enact alternative futures – for which they express their enormous gratitude. Given Greer's public embodiment of the gendered subjectivities promoted in her books, fan mail authors perceive her to be an inspirational figure worthy of emulation. For many women, she confirms that their discontentment with normative gender roles is not an individual complaint but a collectively experienced one, a revelation which brings great relief. Though sometimes ambivalent about identifying as fans, they see themselves as part of an imagined feminist community from which they gather hope and strength.

In Chapter 3, '"The best thing to happen to night-time television": Consuming the Televisual Greer', I demonstrate how Greer's appearances on television have always represented important forms of feminist labour that enable her to reach diverse audiences. In this way, television is not just where Greer and her feminism are represented, it is where her activist work is itself done across decades. Greer's archive, containing myriad recordings of her television work which she actively sourced, as well as a written series covering this labour, provides the opportunity to revisit the role of television in the maintenance of her renown. On talk and reality television, where she is seen to just 'be herself' (Bennett 2010), her embodied celebrity offers the sense of an 'authentic' Greer obscured by other media platforms. Her varied work as a television personality led to significant forms of audience investment not just in her but in her feminism. Letters analysed in this chapter are those sent in response to her role as guest host of *The Dick Cavett Show* in the US (1971), as the presenter of the BBC series *The Last Word* (1994), and as a housemate on *Celebrity Big Brother* (2005). These letters, like others, also bear witness to a sophisticated media and feminist literacy, especially in terms of the intersectional feminist readings that self-identified Greer fans offered of *The Last Word*.

As Chapter 4 – '"Greer has done it again!": Reader-writers and Feminist Journalism' – makes clear, Greer, in contrast to some second-wave feminists who viewed the media with intense suspicion, worked to develop a viable career as a professional journalist. Greer's celebrity ensured she was granted newspaper and magazine column space, and her journalistic writing secured and expanded this fame. This chapter focuses on a series of letters to the editor in response to Greer's journalism; as a form which is addressed to wider publics and which seeks to intervene in public debates, such letters are significantly different from some of the more intimate letters considered in other chapters. The readers who responded to the three pieces examined in this chapter – in *Playboy* ('Seduction is a Four-Letter Word'), *The Sunday Times* ('Germaine Greer on why the Abortion Act is a calamity'), and *Harper's* ('McGovern, The Big Tease'), each of which engages with key feminist issues (rape, abortion, and feminist political interventions) in the early 1970s – span the full spectrum, from fans to anti-fans and those located affectively somewhere in between. While Greer did transform how some readers conceptualised feminism, and gender and sexuality more broadly, other readers were resistant to her style of feminist journalism and used the letter to the editor form to contest her growing cultural authority.

There are two instances in the archive where such contestations become more heavily pronounced. In Chapters 5 and 6, I turn to more hostile responses to this provocative figure. In the former, '"Miss Greer is the most pathetic eunuch of all": Anti-fandom and *McCall's* Magazine', I analyse letters to the editor of American women's magazine, *McCall's*, after it published an extract from *The Female Eunuch*, as an instance of intense 'anti-fandom'. Its readers, largely white, middle-class housewives, took Greer to task for discrediting their mode of being, by criticising her way of embodying femininity and revaluing marriage and motherhood through a feminist-inspired rhetoric of 'choice'. Reader-writers also denounced *McCall's* editors for giving space in their favourite magazine to such a contentious voice. Similarly dealing with anti-fans, Chapter 6, '"Steve is twice the Aussie icon you will ever be": Nationalistic

16 Germaine Greer, Celebrity Feminism and the Archive

Misogyny and the Irwin Hate Email', focuses on the deeply misogynistic emails to Greer's agents following her *Guardian* article on the death of celebrity environmentalist Steve Irwin, printed and filed alongside the piece itself, in a curatorial gesture that departs from her usual practice (Buchanan 2018). Again, correspondents attack Greer for calling into question their own ideological assumptions about gender and, in this case, nation. Both these chapters foreground the affective dis-investments of audiences in Greer and her purportedly objectionable 'brand' of feminism. As I argue, anti-fandom reveals as much about the cultural reverberations of this at times controversial figure as fandom.

Finally, summarising the book's key findings, the conclusion reflects upon some of the dominant ways that audiences have responded to Greer and her feminism across her career. It also identifies areas in need of further scholarly attention, in both Greer studies and feminist celebrity studies more broadly. The conclusion considers celebrity feminism as a phenomenon working to mobilise audiences in the present, including via digital media, and its potential to precipitate legislative and policy alongside attitudinal change. The chapter finishes with the hope that further scholarly engagements with the extensive Greer archive will secure her place in feminist intellectual and popular history. In the first chapter, though, I consider Greer's role as the curator of her archive in more depth, shaping and reshaping the stories we are able to tell about her and her myriad correspondents.

Notes

1 There have been two unauthorised biographies, Christine Wallace's *Germaine Greer: Untamed Shrew* (1997) and Elizabeth Kleinhenz's *Germaine: The Life of Germaine Greer* (2018), with the latter engaging with the Greer archive, but no scholarly monographs to date.
2 This is perhaps rivalled only by the US's Gloria Steinem.
3 While it was Greer's first international 'feminist blockbuster' (Rowlands and Henderson 1996), *The Female Eunuch* (1970), that brought her widespread attention, the Australian expatriate feminist has since worked to maintain her public visibility through many forms of cultural production: television (talk shows, documentary, sitcoms, quiz, variety, and reality) and radio; print journalism; and further non-fiction bestsellers, including *Sex and Destiny* (1984), *The Change* (1991), and *The Whole Woman* (1999a), as well as biographies (*Daddy, We Hardly Knew You* [1989]) and an environmental polemic, *White Beech* (2013). In terms of the last of these, see Lara Stevens' 2018 work on Greer's environmentalism.
4 In 2012, on the ABC's *Q&A* television program, Greer criticised Gillard's fashion sense and in particular her favouring of short suit jackets that exposed her 'fat arse' ('Greer defends "fat arse" PM comment', 2012). Furthermore, Greer made transphobic comments in a 2015 BBC interview, leading to an unsuccessful campaign at Cardiff University, where she was due speak, to 'no platform' her (Morris 2015). In relation to complaints of sexual assault against Hollywood movie producer Harvey Weinstein, Greer remarked: "'if you spread your legs because he said be nice to me and 'I'll give you a job in a movie' then I'm afraid that's tantamount to consent, and it's too late now to start whingeing about that"' (Flood 2018). Kate Edwards and Emma Nagouse (2018) argue that with these more recent controversies, which they suggest she courts to sell books, Greer has moved from 'feminist firebrand to professional troll'.

Introduction **17**

5 The archive website notes 'The University of Melbourne Archives is working with Germaine Greer to manage further deposits', https://library.unimelb.edu.au/asc/collections/highlights/collections/germainegreer/about-the-collection.

6 Throughout I use 'ordinary' in Le Masurier's sense, 'to describe those women who did not identify as women's liberationists or as feminists, who did not share the privileges of class and education that characterised most of the women involved in the movement, and those who found radical feminism's critique of the family, the state, and men alienating' (2016, p. 29).

7 For example, in *The Female Eunuch*, she notes: '[the housewife] could begin by not by changing the world, but by re-assessing herself' (1970, p. 161).

8 Debates which have been reanimated more recently (Zielser 2017; Banet-Weiser 2018).

9 Indeed, this book is consistent with wider efforts to reassess the second wave's more radical thinkers, such as Valerie Solanas (Fahs 2014), Shulamith Firestone (Margree 2018), and Andrea Dworkin (Serisier 2013).

10 For a consideration of women's stardom and why it may or may not endure, see Bolton and Wright's collection, *Lasting Stars* (2016).

11 Most recent scholarship, apart from my own, focuses on this latter form of celebrity feminism. In addition, this is not a strict binary, as the boundaries between these categories can be porous.

12 In response to one of these correspondents, Greer writes (W.B., 1 June 1972, Nottingham, 2014.0044.00197), reiterating her common refrain about her disdain for fame: 'I am afraid I am not in the habit of distributing photographs of myself to people for any use at all. My reasons for this are not all personal. Some of them are political and relate to my own distaste for the personality cult'. This practice does seem to have varied, however, with others at different points having had their requests fulfilled.

13 In this vein, Maryanne Dever (2014) discusses hate mail received by Australian feminist activist Merle Thornton after she and a colleague chained themselves to the bar of Brisbane hotel, The Regatta, in protest of its prohibition against women drinkers.

References

Ahmed, S. (2004) *The Cultural Politics of Emotion*, London: Routledge.

Ahmed, S. (2008) 'Creating Disturbance: Feminism, Happiness and Affective Differences', in Marianne Liljeström and Susanna Paasonen (eds.) *Working with Affect in Feminist Readings: Disturbing Differences*, London: Routledge, pp. 31–44.

Ahmed, S. (2017) *Living a Feminist Life*, Durham: Duke University Press.

Allison, J. (1971) 'Marriage contract? Refuse to sign it', *The Indianapolis News*, 2 June, Germaine Greer Archive, Early Years, 2014.0044.00171, University of Melbourne.

Arrow, M. (2019) *The Seventies: The Personal, the Political and The Making of Modern Australia*, Sydney: New South Press.

Banet-Weiser, S. (2018) *Empowered: Popular Feminism and Popular Misogyny*, Durham: Duke University Press.

Barker-Plummer, B. (1995) 'News as a Political Resource: Media strategies and Political Identity in the U. S. Women's Movement, 1966–1975', *Critical Studies in Mass Communication*, vol. 12, no. 3: 306–324.

Bennett, J. (2010) *Television Personalities: Stardom and The Small Screen*, London: Routledge.

Bolton, L and Wright, J.L. (eds.) (2016) *Lasting Screen Stars: Images that Fade and Personas That Endure*, London: Palgrave Macmillan.

Bonfante, J. (1971) 'Saucy Feminist Even Men Like', 7 May, *Life*, pp. 30–32.

Borges, M.J. (2020) 'Narratives of the Self', in K. Barclay, S. Crozier-de Rosa, and P.N. Stearns (eds.), *Sources for the History of Emotions: A Guide*, London: Routledge, pp. 99–113.

Bradley, P. (2003) *Mass Media and the Shaping of American Feminism*, Mississippi: University of Mississippi.

Brady, A. (2016) '"Taking Time Between G-String Changes to Educate Ourselves": Sinead O'Connor, Miley Cyrus, and Celebrity Feminism', *Feminist Media Studies*, vol. 16, no. 3: 429–444.

Brady, A. (2021) 'Clementine Ford, Online Misogyny, and the Labour of Celebrity Feminism', in A. Taylor and J. McIntyre (eds.), *Gender and Australian Celebrity Culture*, London: Routledge, pp. 91–108.

Buchanan, R. (2018) 'Foreign Correspondence: Journalism in the Germaine Greer Archive', *Archives and Manuscripts*, vol. 46, no. 1: 18–39.

Bueskens, P. (2020) 'Germaine Greer's *On Rape* Revisited: Clarifying the Long-standing Relationship Between Rape and Heterosexual Pleasure in Greer's Work', *Hecate*, vol. 45, no. 1–2: 268–288.

Casey, S. and Watson, J. (2023) *Hashtag Feminisms: Australian Media Feminists, Activism, and Digital Campaigns*, Bern: Peter Lang.

Chidgey, R. (2021) 'Postfeminism™: Celebrity Feminism, Branding and the Performance of Activist Capital', *Feminist Media Studies*, vol. 21, no. 7: 1055–1071.

Coffin, J. (2010) 'Sex, Love, and Letters: Writing Simone de Beauvoir, 1949–1963', *American Historical Review*, October: 1061–1088.

Coffin, J. (2020) *Sex, Love, and Letters: Writing Simone de Beauvoir*, New York: Cornell University Press.

Collins, C. (1997) 'Viewer Letters as Audience Research: The Case of *Murphy Brown*', *Journal of Broadcasting and Electronic Media*, vol. 41, no. 1: 109–131.

Cvetkovich, A. (2003) *An Archive of Feelings: Trauma, Sexuality, and Lesbian Public Cultures*, Durham: Duke University Press.

Davey, M. (2017) 'Equality is a "profoundly conservative goal" for women, Germaine Greer says', *The Guardian*, 8 March, accessed via: www.theguardian.com/books/2017/mar/09/equality-is-a-profoundly-conservative-goal-for-women-germaine-greer-says

Dever, M. (2014) 'Archiving Feminism: Papers, Politics, Posterity', *Archivaria*, vol. 77: 25–42.

Dever, M., Newman, S., and Vickery, A. (2009) *The Intimate Archive: Journeys Through Private Papers*, Canberra: National Library of Australia.

Douglas, K. and Poletti, A. (2016) *Life Narratives and Youth Culture Representation, Agency and Participation*, London: Palgrave Macmillan.

Dow, B.J. (1996) *Prime-time Feminism: Television, Media Culture, and The Women's Movement Since 1970*, Philadelphia: University of Pennsylvania Press.

Drake, P. (2018) 'Celebrity, Reputational Capital and the Media Industries', in A. Elliott (ed.) *Routledge Handbook of Celebrity Studies*, London: Routledge, pp. 271–284.

Dreifus, C. (1971) 'The Selling of a Feminist', *Notes From the Third Year: Women's Liberation*: 100–101.

Dux, M. (2010) 'Temple of *The Female Eunuch*: Germaine Greer Forty Years On', *Kill Your Darlings*, vol. 2: 8–17.

Dyer, R. (1979) *Stars*, London: Routledge.

Edwards, K. and Nagouse, E. (2018) 'Germaine Greer: from feminist firebrand to professional troll', *The Conversation*, 7 June, accessed via: https://theconversation.com/germaine-greer-from-feminist-firebrand-to-professional-troll-97645.

Fahs, B. (2014) *Valerie Solanas: The Defiant Life of the Woman Who Wrote SCUM (and Shot Andy Warhol)*, New York: The Feminist Press.

Faludi, S. (1991) *Backlash: The Undeclared War Against Women*, New York: Viking.

Farrell, A.E. (1998) *Yours in Sisterhood: Ms Magazine and The Making of Popular Feminism*, Chapel Hill: University of North Carolina Press.

Flood, A. (2018) 'Germaine Greer criticises "whingeing" #MeToo movement', *The Guardian*, 23 January, accessed via: https://www.theguardian.com/books/2018/jan/23/germaine-greer-criticises-whingeing-metoo-movement

Flood, M. (2019) 'Intersectionality and Celebrity Culture', *Women's Studies in Communication*, vol. 42, no. 4: 422–426.

Fuller-Selley, K. (2018) 'Archaeologies of Fandom: Using Historical Methods to Explore Fan Cultures of the Past', in M. Click and S. Scott (eds.) *The Routledge Companion to Media Fandom*, London: Routledge, pp.27–35.

Gamson, J. (1994) *Claims to Fame*, Los Angeles: University of California Press.

Germaine Greer Archive. Early Years, 2014.0044, University of Melbourne.

Germaine Greer Archive. General Correspondence, 2014.0042, University of Melbourne.

Germaine Greer Archive. Major Works, 2014.0045, University of Melbourne.

Germaine Greer Archive. Print Journalism, 2014.0446, University of Melbourne.

Germaine Greer Archive. Television, 2017.0002, University of Melbourne.

Gerhard, J. (2000) '"The Myth of the Vaginal Orgasm": The Female Orgasm in American Sexual Thought and Second Wave Feminism', *Feminist Studies*, vol. 26, no. 2: 449–476.

Gever, M. (2003) *Entertaining Lesbians: Celebrity, Sexuality, and Self-invention*, New York: Routledge.

Gill, R. (2016) 'Post-postfeminism?: New Feminist Visibilities in Postfeminist Times', *Feminist Media Studies*, vol. 16, no. 4: 610–630.

Glanville, L. (2017) 'Friday Essay: Reading Germaine Greer's Mail', *The Conversation*, 24 March, accessed via: https://theconversation.com/friday-essay-reading-germaine-greers-mail-74693

Glanville, L. (2018) 'The End of Reckoning – Archival Silences in the Germaine Greer Archive', *Archives and Manuscripts*, vol. 46, no. 1: 45–48.

Goodman, E. (1971) 'Greer on Lib: Talk, No Tactics', *The Boston Globe*, 'Press clippings about GG', Germaine Greer Archive, Print Journalism, 2014.0046.00171, University of Melbourne.

Grasso, L.M. (2013) '"You are no stranger to me": Georgia O'Keeffe's Fan Mail', *Reception: Texts, Readers, Audiences, History*, vol. 5 no. 1: 24–40.

Gray, J. (2003) 'New audiences, New Textualities: Anti-fans and Non-fans', *International Journal of Cultural Studies*, vol. 6, no. 1: 64–81.

Greer, G. (1970) *The Female Eunuch*, London: Paladin.

Greer, G. (1972) 'Australian press conference notes', Germaine Greer Archive, Print Journalism, 2014.0044.00198, University of Melbourne.

Greer, G. (1984) *Sex and Destiny*, New York: Harper and Row.

Greer, G. (1989) *Daddy, We Hardly Knew You*, New York: Random House.

Greer, G. (1991) *The Change*, London: Hamish Hamilton.

Greer, G. (1992) 'Germaine Greer on Strangers in the Mail', *The Independent*, 4 April, Germaine Greer Archive, Print Journalism, 2014.0046.00287, University of Melbourne.

Greer, G. (1999a) *The Whole Woman*, London: Doubleday.

Greer, G. (1999b) 'The postman always knocks far too many times', *Daily Telegraph*, 10 July, Germaine Greer Archive, Print Journalism, 2014.0046.0499, University of Melbourne.

Greer, G. (2013) *White Beech*, London: Bloomsbury.

Greer, G. (2018) *On Rape*, Melbourne: University of Melbourne Press.

'Greer defends "fat arse" PM comment' (2012), *Sydney Morning Herald*, 28 August, accessed via: https://www.smh.com.au/politics/federal/greer-defends-fat-arse-pm-comment-20120828-24x5i.html

Groeneveld, E. (2018) 'Letters to the Editor as "Archives of Feeling": *On Our Backs* Magazine and the Sex Wars', *American Periodical Studies*, vol. 28, no. 2: 53–167.

Grossberg, L. (1992) 'Is There a Fan in the House? The Affective Sensibility of Fandom', in L. Lewis (ed.), *The Adoring Audience: Fan Culture and Popular Media*, New York: Routledge, pp. 50–68.

Hamad, H. and Taylor, A. (2015) 'Introduction: Feminism and Celebrity Culture', *Celebrity Studies*, vol. 6, no. 1: 124–127.

Hannell, B. (2023) *Feminist Fandom: Media Fandom, Digital Feminisms, and Tumblr*, London: Bloomsbury Academic.

Henderson, M. (2006) *Marking Feminist Times: Remembering the Longest Revolution in Australia*, Bern: Peter Lang.

Henry, A. (2004) *Not My Mother's Sister: Generational Conflict and Third Wave Feminism*, Bloomington: Indiana University Press.

Hesford, V. (2013) *Feeling Women's Liberation*, Durham: Duke University Press.

Hills, M. (2018) 'Implicit Fandom in the Fields of Theatre, Art, and Literature: Studying "Fans" Beyond Fan Discourses', in P. Booth (ed.), *Companion to Media Fandom and Fan Studies*, London: Wiley, pp. 477–494.

Hobson, J. (2017) 'Celebrity Feminism: More than a Gateway', *Signs: Journal of Women in Culture and Society*, vol. 42, no. 4: 999–1007.

Horton, D. and Wohl, R.R. (1956) 'Mass Communication and Para-social Interaction: Observations on Intimacy at a Distance', *Psychiatry*, vol. 19: 215–229.

Jackson, S. (2021) '"A very basic view of feminism": Feminist Girls and Meanings of (Celebrity) Feminism', *Feminist Media Studies*, vol. 21, no. 7: 1072–1090.

Jolly, M. (2008) *In Love and Struggle: Letters in Contemporary Feminism*, New York: Columbia University Press.

Keller, J. and Ringrose, J. (2015) 'But then feminism goes out the window!': Exploring Teenage Girls' Critical Response to Celebrity Feminism', *Celebrity Studies*, vol. 6, no. 1: 132–135.

Kleinhenz, E. (2018) *Germaine: The Life of Germaine Greer*, North Sydney: Knopf.

Lake, M. (2016) '"Revolution for the hell of it": The Transatlantic Genesis and Serial Provocations of *The Female Eunuch*', *Australian Feminist Studies*, vol. 31, no. 87: 7–21.

Lawson, C. (2023) *Just Like Us: Digital Debates on Feminism and Fame*, New Brunswick, NJ: Rutgers University Press.

Lehrmann, N. (1972) 'Germaine Greer: A Candid Conversation with the Ballsy Author of "The Female Eunuch"', *Playboy*, January: 61–82.

Le Masurier (2009) 'Desiring the (Popular Feminist) Reader: Letters to CLEO during the Second Wave', *Media International Australia*, vol. 131. no. 1: 106–116.

Le Masurier, M. (2016) 'Resurrecting Germaine's Theory of Cuntpower', *Australian Feminist Studies*, vol. 31, no. 87: 28–42.

Lilburn, S., Magarey, S., and Sheridan, S. (2000) 'Celebrity Feminism as Synthesis: Germaine Greer, *The Female Eunuch* and the Australian Print Media', *Continuum*, vol. 14, no. 3: 335–348.

Lonie, K. (2019) 'Hillary, Hashtags and Hermione: Young Women's Political Engagement, Celebrity and the New Media Landscape', unpublished doctoral thesis, USyd.

Majic, S. (2023) *Lights, Camera, Feminism: Celebrities and Anti-trafficking Politics*, Berkeley: California University Press.

Marcus, S. (2015) 'Celebrity, Past and Present', *Public Culture*, vol. 27, no. 75: 1–5.

Marcus, S. (2019) *The Drama of Celebrity*, Princeton, NJ: Princeton University.

Margree, V. (2018) *Neglected or Misunderstood: The Radical Feminism of Shulamith Firestone*, New York: Zero Books.

Marshall, P.D. (1997) *Celebrity and Power*, Minneapolis: University of Minnesota Press.

Marwick, A. and boyd, d. (2011) 'To See and Be Seen: Celebrity Practice on Twitter', *Convergence*, vol. 17, no. 2: 139–158.

Mendick, H., Ahmad, A., Allen, K. and Harvey, L. (2018) *Celebrity, Aspiration and Contemporary Youth: Education and Inequality in an Era of Austerity*, London: Bloomsbury.

Milthorpe, N. (2019) 'Archives, Authority, Aura: Modernism's Archival Turn', *Papers on Language & Literature*, vol. 55, no. 1: 3–15.

Moreton-Robinson, A. (2000) *Talkin' Up to the White Woman*, Brisbane: University of Queensland Press.

Morris, S (2015) 'Germaine Greer gives university lecture despite campaign to silence her', *The Guardian*, 19 November, accessed via: https://www.theguardian.com/books/2015/nov/18/transgender-activists-protest-germaine-greer-lecture-cardiff-university

Munford, T. (1984) 'Fertility and the new imperialism', *Canberra Times*, 2 June, p. 16.

Murray, S. (2004) *Mixed Media: Feminism and Publishing Politics*, London: Pluto.

Nolan, S. (1999) 'Tabloid Women', *Meanjin*, vol. 58, no. 2: 165–177.

Quinn, S. (1971) 'The Greering of the press', *The Washington Post*, 19 May, Germaine Greer Archive, Early Years, 2014.0044.00159, University of Melbourne.

Rojek, C. (2001) *Celebrity*, London: Reaktion.

Rojek, C. (2015) *Presuming Intimacy: Parasocial Interaction in Media, Society and Celebrity Culture*, London: Polity.

Rowlands, S. and Henderson, M. (1996) 'Damned Bores and Slick Sisters: The Selling of Blockbuster Feminism in Australia', *Australian Feminist Studies*, vol. 11, no. 23: 9–16.

Serisier, T. (2013) 'Who Was Andrea? Writing Oneself as a Feminist Icon', *Women: a Cultural Review*, vol. 24, no. 1: 26–44.

Sheehan, R.J. (2016) '"If we had more like her we would no longer be the unheard majority": Germaine Greer's Reception in the United States', *Australian Feminist Studies*, vol. 31, no. 87: 62–77.

Sheehan, R.J. (2019) 'Intersectional Feminist Friendship: Restoring Colour to the Second-wave through the Letters of Florynce Kennedy and Germaine Greer', *Lilith*, vol. 25: 76–92.

Sheehan, R. (2024) 'Settler Colonialism in Black and White: Roberta Sykes, Germaine Greer, and the Different Embodied Experiences of Womanhood, Rape, and Sovereignty', *Signs: Journal of Women in Culture and Society*, vol. 49, no. 4: 731–754.

Simons, M. (2015) 'The Long Letter to a Short Love, or...', *Meanjin*, Summer, accessed via: https://meanjin.com.au/essays/the-long-letter-to-a-short-love-or/

Spongberg, M. (1993) '"If she's so great, how come so many pigs dig her?": Germaine Greer and the Malestream Press', *Women's History Review*, vol. 2, no. 3: 407–419.

Stead, L. (2021) *Reframing Vivien Leigh: Stardom, Gender, and the Archive*, Oxford: Oxford University Press.

Steuer, L. (2019) 'Structural Affects of Soap Opera Fan Correspondence, 1970s–80s', *Transformative Works*, no. 30, accessed via: https://journal.transformativeworks.org/index.php/twc/article/download/1735/2209?inline=1

Stevens, L. (2018) '"Mother? Nature?": Germaine Greer, Contemporary Feminisms and New Materialisms', *Hecate*, vol. 44, no. 1: 156–170.

Taylor, A. (2014) 'Germaine Greer's Adaptable Celebrity: Feminism, Unruliness, and Humour on the British Small Screen', *Feminist Media Studies*, vol. 14, no. 5: 759–774.

Taylor, A. (2016) *Celebrity and The Feminist Blockbuster*, Basingstoke: Palgrave Macmillan.

Taylor, A. (2022) 'Germaine Greer's Story of Human Reproduction, the Dismissal, and Feminist "Unproduction Studies"', unpublished conference paper, Cultural Studies Association of Australasia, 28–30 June, Edith Cowan University.

Taylor, A. (2023) '"My consciousness has certainly been raised": Gloria Steinem's celebrity, *The Phil Donahue Show* and Feminist Fan Mail', unpublished conference paper, Console-ing Passions, 22–24 June, University of Calgary.

Taylor, A., Dever, M., and Adkins, L. (2016) 'Greer Now: Editorial', *Australian Feminist Studies*, vol. 31, no. 87: 1–6.

Thomas, S. (2014) 'Celebrity in the "Twitterverse": History, Authenticity and the Multiplicity of Stardom: Situating the 'newness' of Twitter', *Celebrity Studies*, vol. 5, no. 3, pp. 242–255.

Turner, G. (2004) *Understanding Celebrity*, London: Sage.

Turner, G. (2010) 'Approaching Celebrity Studies', *Celebrity Studies*, vol. 1, no. 1: 11–20.

Turner, G. (2016) 'Celebrity, Participation, and the Public', in S. Redmond and P.D. Marshall (eds.), *A Companion to Celebrity*, London: Sage, pp. 83–97.

Turner, G., Bonner, F. and Marshall, P.D. (2000) *Fame Games: The Production of Celebrity in Australia*, Sydney: Cambridge University Press.

Van Krieken, R. (2012) *Celebrity Society*, London: Routledge.

Wallace, C. (1997) *Germaine Greer: Untamed Shrew*, Melbourne: PanMacMillan.

Waters, M. (2016) '"Yours in Struggle": Bad Feelings and Revolutionary Politics in *Spare Rib*', *Women: A Cultural Review*, vol. 27, no. 4: 446–465.

Whelehan, I. (2005) *The Feminist Bestseller: From Sex and the Single Girl to Sex and the City*, London: Palgrave Macmillan.

Wicke, J. (1994) 'Celebrity Material: Materialist Feminism and the Culture of Celebrity', *South Atlantic Quarterly*, vol. 93, no. 4: 751–778.

Yale, E. (2015) 'The History of Archives: The State of the Discipline', *Book History*, vol. 18: 332–359.

Yodovich, N. (2022) *Women Negotiating Feminism and Science Fiction Fandom*, London: Palgrave Macmillan.

York, L. (2013) *Margaret Atwood and The Labour of Literary Celebrity*, Toronto: University of Toronto Press.

Young, S. (1997) *Changing the Wor(l)d: Discourse, Politics, and the Feminist Movement*, New York: Routledge.

Zielser, A. (2017) *We Were Feminists Once: From Riot Grrrl to CoverGirl®, the Buying and Selling of a Political Movement*, New York: PublicAffairs.

1

'THE ARCHIVE WILL PUT MATTERS RIGHT, FOR POSTERITY'

Greer's Curatorial Labour

Introduction

The University of Melbourne's 2013 acquisition of Greer's vast personal and professional records – comprising over 500 boxes, dating from the 1950s and into the 2010s – enables a mapping of the wider cultural reverberations of her celebrity feminism. Greer has actively worked to craft her public persona over many decades, including via her own archival practices. The archive includes – in addition to drafts of her writing, print and audio diaries, contracts, publisher correspondence, proofs, press clippings, project budgets, photographs, ephemera, and audiovisual material – myriad responses from audiences around the world outlining how Greer and her cross-media feminism have impacted them, raising their consciousness or, in other cases, provoking their ire. The Greer archive, therefore, offers much evidence of the considerable labour underpinning public visibility and its effects. As Lisa Stead argues, celebrity archives – in both content and composition – can 'offer alternative ways of reflecting on *stardom as process and creative labor rather than stardom primarily as image*' (2021, p. 5, emphasis added). I draw upon and extend these insights to suggest that, in addition to specific material contained in the archive, it is the living celebrity's status as an archivist (and particularly their formative role in the archive's existence, arrangement and cataloguing, and conditions of access) that enables this reorientation. In the case of Greer, and other comparable figures, the archive does not just *tell* us about the various forms of celebrity feminist labour in which she has engaged across her public career, it is also the product of this labour (Stead 2020). Greer's own curatorial practices seek (perhaps impossibly) to shape the kinds of stories we may come to tell about her and her celebrity feminism.

DOI: 10.4324/9781315179841-2

24 Germaine Greer, Celebrity Feminism and the Archive

Here, then, I argue that archival methodologies are important to feminist celebrity studies, not simply for revelations about their subject and their impact but for insights into women's active persona-building and reputation management and their effects. However, I wish not to overstate the role of the celebrity in overdetermined processes of celebrification, or indeed in archival practices, but to offer a way to think through the 'situated agency' (Moran 2000) exercised by living iconic figures whose curatorial efforts have significant political, material, intellectual, and institutional impacts. This book seeks, amongst other things, to bring feminist celebrity studies into conversation with archival studies. From archival scholarship, I deploy the concept of the 'archiving "I"' to help theorise Greer's active role in the constitution of her archive (Douglas and MacNeil 2009; Douglas 2015, 2018) – something that critical commentary from archivists who have worked on the Greer collection helps to further tease out.

Former Greer archivist Rachel Buchanan remarks, 'there is much more scholarly work to be done on Greer's efforts to construct, keep and sell such a large archive, and her arrangement and description of the records' (2018, p. 22). This chapter responds to Buchanan's prescient call for further critical attention to Greer's archival work, work she argues (2018, p. 22) is just as important as the celebrity feminist's myriad other professional roles (academic, bestselling author, television performer, journalist, and conservationist). In this chapter, I also contemplate my own attempts to navigate this vast archive and discuss how its arrangement has helped shape my own research practices in very material ways. Moreover, I conceptualise Greer's archival work as part of her wider, lifelong feminist practice, a practice that has involved the strategic cultivation of various modes of public visibility for feminist purposes. Given that archives, as Giselda Pollock (1993, p. 12) argues, are 'shaped according to the interests and needs of certain groups', their inherent 'interestedness' comes into sharp relief when the subject herself is so heavily implicated in such processes (as Greer has been). As Robert McGill notes in his work on living authors and archives, 'she or he has the potential to irrupt in the research process as a subject who has legal rights over archival materials and personal preferences about their use' (2009, p. 129). This is certainly the case with Greer's archive.

Despite the second-wave concerns identified here in the Introduction, Greer's strategic media intervention and fame did not evacuate her feminist critique of its oppositional potential, and she has brought often diverse audiences a much more radical form of feminism than is commonly found in the mainstream media (Dow 1996, 2014; Henderson 2006). This is not to elide the contradictions and ambivalences in her thought or practices; like Clare Hemmings in her work on anarchist Emma Goldman, I am interested in 'what it means to include [Greer] in a feminist history without wanting to *clean her up first*' (2018, p. 6, emphasis added). Relatedly, Greer's own archival micro-managing should not imply that this is a 'sanitised' or a censored self. As I will show, through both archival scholarship on her archive and my own experiences working with it, she does not seek to 'clean herself up' either. As Buchanan remarks, speaking specifically of Greer's journalistic labour (see Chapter 4 here), 'The grime, the bad behaviour, the insults, the ferocity, the high-handedness, even sometimes the hate – Greer's, editors, readers – all of that has been preserved' (2018, p. 33). I am especially interested in Greer's curatorial processes and how they have shaped the 'Greers' that I am able to bring into being through my writing from the archive.

Following Stead (2020, 2021), I am concerned with how we might further reflect upon archival research as a core methodology for feminist studies of celebrity. As Stead makes clear, while archival material provides insights into how renowned women as 'professionals navigated their working lives and identities' (2020, p. 21), archiving – as in the preservation, collection, and curation of specific materials – is itself a crucial form of star labour, which represents an attempt by the celebrity to exercise their agency and self-fashion in important ways (2021). The archive, as I have previously argued, 'especially when sold to an institution prior to the celebrity's death', is invariably shaped by its creator, 'representing another obvious attempt to control the public meanings of their lives, their texts, and their public selves' (Taylor 2016, pp. 46–47). In particular, we must acknowledge the maintenance of attention capital as work (York 2013a; Brady 2021) and, in this instance, as specifically feminist work. That is, celebrity is 'something a person does, rather than something a person is' (Marwick 2016, p. 334; see also Marwick and boyd 2011; Taylor 2016; Yelin 2021), something which is 'done' in and through institutional spaces like archives, including by feminists, for the purpose of raising awareness (or consciousness-raising) about ongoing feminist issues. In this respect, celebrity – as Richard Dyer remarked – *and* the archive are 'both labour and the thing that labour produces' (1986, p. 5). Furthermore, Greer did not just collect material for the archive, she *created* for it (Glanville 2018; Hodgetts 2018), adding another layer to the kind of archival labour that Stead maps in her study. Nevertheless, the question of agency, within both celebrity studies and archival studies, remains a fraught one.

Celebrity feminism, agency, and the archive

Celebrity and feminism may seem antithetical to some, but following scholars like Jennifer Wicke (1994), I have argued that celebrity has been a significant political resource for the women's movement (Taylor 2016; see also Hamad and Taylor 2015; Brady 2016; Hobson 2017). Indeed, fame remains vital to securing widespread support for various feminist issues, as more recent celebrity feminist activism suggests (Chidgey 2021; Casey and Watson 2023; Lawson 2023; Majic 2023). Greer's archive – like those of American celebrity feminists Gloria Steinem, Betty Friedan, and Helen Gurley Brown (Taylor 2016) – contains extensive evidence of the feminist labour that undergirds her renown; that is, the considerable work she had to do to ensure her voice was heard. Furthermore, through the inclusion of print journalism copy or televisual material that otherwise may have been lost (Buchanan 2018, p. 20), the archive itself preserves that voice (along with the voices of her interlocutors). In collecting and curating the records of her own personal and professional lives, Greer both evidences and further exercises her feminist agency.

As many scholars have shown, celebrity relies upon a vast array of cultural intermediaries for its maintenance (Marshall 1997; Rojek 2001; Turner 2004 York 2013a; Marcus 2019), but the performer herself has often been overlooked, not least because of the difficulties of theorising her agency (York 2013b; Stead 2020). However, famous figures have always 'actively negotiate[d] their own celebrity rather than having it imposed upon them' (Moran 2000, p. 10) – a statement apposite to all forms of renown, including feminist (Taylor 2016). As these comments imply, the celebrity herself is a crucial actor in these overdetermined processes of celebrification, but precisely how and with what effects are less addressed; agency, that is, has been a problem for studies of celebrity. Lorraine York has identified an 'impasse' when it comes to thinking through the renowned figure's role in her celebrification: 'When agency has been attributed to celebrities in individual instances, it is often conceived negatively, as an opting out of the workings of production or consumption that are otherwise understood to be definitive' (2013b, p. 1135, original emphasis).

One of the fields that has negotiated this terrain most successfully is literary studies, with critics foregrounding the 'situated agency' of celebrity authors (Moran 2000) and emphasising that they operate 'alongside and within structural forces and constraints' (York 2013b, p. 1339) – including in relation to gender. Such scholarship, augmented by more recent work in digital media and persona studies (Marshall et al. 2019; Barbour 2023), is especially important in a feminist sense, ensuring that we do not see women as merely passive victims of celebrification (Weber 2012) nor as entirely unconstrained actors in these processes. In this vein, recent studies of women's celebrity memoir have enabled a rethinking of gendered fame and self-fashioning: 'a celebrity is one of many agents in the production of the life story. They may not act freely, but they do act' (Yelin 2020, p. 27; see also Lee 2020). This includes feminists, whose relationship to fame (particularly in terms of its active cultivation) has been especially fraught, as I made clear in the introductory chapter.

As I further explore, the same 'problem' regarding how – or whether – to theorise the role of the individual creator has marred archival studies. As Jennifer Douglas (2018, pp. 35–36) asserts, 'Although notions of impartiality

'The archive will put matters right, for posterity' **27**

and naturalness are now regularly critiqued, there is still relatively little attention paid to the creator's active role in fashioning her archive'. Where personal papers exist, they provide the opportunity for the celebrified figure to be re-centred, especially when they donate or sell their papers while still living (McGill 2009). As in Greer's case, they provide insights into the visibility labour (Abidin 2016) – successful or otherwise (Taylor 2022) – that she has undertaken across her career: the negotiations with publishers, editors, television producers, journalistic copy, intimate correspondence with fans, and the refusals (especially around television appearances or requests for journalistic copy sought without renumeration). But, as I argue here, what is included and how it is organised, including the creator's instructions on how material should be catalogued and the restrictions placed on access, are themselves crucial parts of such feminist fame work.

These claims about Greer's considered interventions are not merely speculative, however. There is much evidence, including within the archive, as well as public meta-commentary from University of Melbourne archivists and Greer herself, of this celebrity feminist's pronounced curatorial control. Greer's celebrity has helped make the usually obscured labour of archivists publicly visible, as they critically reflect upon the archive at public events, in journal special issues (*Archives and Manuscripts*), and articles in popular outlets like *The Conversation*. Greer's notoriety has ensured audiences for such material, which itself further buttresses this fame. As Buchanan observes:

> Greer's hand is on thousands of records in the form of scribbled instructions on where to file the item. Greer also wrote succinct scope and content notes, the production or commissioning of at least four inventories, placing in folders, naming and arranging thousands of files and the supervision of assistants who wrote notes for individual series and included these in drafts of documents designed to entice buyers for the archive, notably a five-page fragment called "The Greer Archive", that archivists found inside a black notebook in the Major Works series. In time, Greer's work as an archivist may have an impact equal to that of her other achievements.
>
> (2018, p. 19, emphasis added; see also Glanville 2018)

As I argue throughout, and as Buchanan here makes clear, Greer has laboured considerably to shape her archive in ways that deserve deeper critical reflection. In a further attempt to circumscribe how the archive is used, Greer herself publicly tells a particular tale about its content and its research potentialities, with which I engage here.

It is also worth reflecting on what I was seeking from this archive and how my own research goals may have been helped or hindered by my subject's interventions. Maryanne Dever et al. argue that

28 Germaine Greer, Celebrity Feminism and the Archive

the very processes of preserving (or destroying), gathering, selecting and ordering archival records represent mediating acts: acts that shape the archive as we find it and inevitably transform the possible meanings of those artefacts and the historical narratives they might sponsor.

(2009, p. 105)

I am acutely aware of how researchers (myself included) are, as Dever et al. remark, necessarily 'shaping the archive in our own image and according to our own research priorities' (2009, p. 17; see also Douglas and Mills 2018, p. 262). My own theoretical and methodological commitments as a feminist celebrity studies scholar mean that what I sought, the folders I ordered on my multiple archival trips to the University of Melbourne, were those that enabled me to construct a particular narrative about Greer's feminist renown, its maintenance, and its effects.

Given that such encounters with the archive are always-already subjective, I inevitably mined it for my own scholarly purposes, searching for 'evidence' to help answer my own research questions, skimming over that which would not (the archive's vastness, as well as Greer's strict prohibition on photographing the material, required such pragmatism). With a special interest in fandom and audience affective investments and the performed intimacy of epistolary exchanges, my heart raced when I caught a glimpse of the flimsy yellow or pink paper on which Greer's type-written letters appear in the 1970s, hoping for a reply to a fan letter or a rebuttal of a criticism about *The Female Eunuch* (Greer 1970), which I often did find – what Antoinette Burton dubs the 'archival "pay dirt" moment' (2006, p. 8). Reflecting upon such processes in her study of Canadian author Alice Munro's archive, JoAnn McCaig (2002, p. 15) notes: 'I am making it produce interesting information, I am extracting data, but at the same time the author and archivist through their omissions, restrictions, and selections manipulate me'. Via my engagements with this archive, I have constructed a particular 'Greer,' who in turn has publicly constructed a particular 'Greer' (or indeed 'Greers') – neither of us has been disinterested in these endeavours, and neither of us was (or could ever be) entirely in control (Scott 2011, p. 146). So how did the Greer archive come into being and why does it matter?

The Greer archive's origin story

Kate Eichhorn argues that 'sometimes an archive's story may be as important as its contents' (2013, p. 43), and with Greer, this story dates back many decades. Buchanan notes that Greer began the practice of 'keeping things' when she was an 18-year-old undergraduate student at the University of Melbourne in the mid to late 1950s. Buchanan further observes that, although she moved often, 'Greer's papers and other things were not lost, destroyed, damaged or

'The archive will put matters right, for posterity' **29**

dispersed in all these moves. She considered her hoard worth protecting and did so. The effort must have been considerable' (2016, p. 22). This is remarkable, for women writers, as Elizabeth Meese argues, 'have a tendency to destroy their unpublished papers and work, often viewing this material as private and irrelevant' (1982, p. 41, as cited in Dever et al. 2009, p. 107). Greer's motivation for amassing such a vast collection over such a lengthy period, or at least the public narrative she offers about it, will be considered shortly.

Rather than being innocent 'repositories', archives are now widely acknowledged to be spaces of privilege and exclusion, sites of knowledge formation bound up in and constitutive of complex relations of power (Schwartz and Cook 2002). Any engagement with archives raises questions around whose lives come to be preserved, which lives come to matter, and the politics of this for feminism are necessarily fraught (Schwartz and Cook 2002; Butler 2009; Eichhorn 2013; Cifor and Wood 2017). Celebrity archives themselves inevitably reinscribe the limitations of celebrity feminism more broadly, especially in their promotion and authorisation of the lives and voices of already highly privileged women. Fame elevates quotidian documents and objects, reifying them and imbuing them with an aura of authenticity and intimacy, deeming them 'archivable' in the way the personal papers of more marginalised subjects are not.

The fact that Greer's voice has been elevated over those of other women and particularly other feminists has caused much contention, with the archive and its public availability securing and indeed extending this privilege in important ways (not to mention that, as archival researchers, focusing our critical gaze on select famous figures, we are part of the apparatus of renown-maintenance itself). Nevertheless, archives 'retain a sustained gravitational pull on feminist researchers. We experience them as sites of promise and desire, even as we recognise they are also sites of power and privilege that have long been implicated in acts of violence and erasure' (Dever 2017, p. 1). Moreover, Greer's immense contributions to both popular feminist history and feminist intellectual history remain under-examined, and the archive not only provides the opportunity to revisit this iconic figure but also offers new ways to think about Greer's accumulation and sustenance of this long-enduring attention capital and its effects.

As audio diary entries contained in the collection indicate, the archive also represented a commercial opportunity for Greer when she was experiencing financial difficulties, with her anxieties about money suggesting the limits of the kinds of freelancing work on which she appeared to be focusing around this time (mid-1990s). Here, we see that being a precarious cultural worker certainly has its downsides. On 29 June 1996, she says, 'money-wise, we've got to finish the archive'. She continues, making explicit that this will require sustained labour: 'I've really got to organise my life…I've got to work, say, one hour a day on the archive' (2014.0040.00103, at 00.03:56).

30 Germaine Greer, Celebrity Feminism and the Archive

Similarly, on 27 March 1997, while walking outside with her dogs early in the morning, wind whistling loudly in the background, she remarks with concern: 'The discovery of the week is that we're very short of money, and I'm spending like a drunken sailor as usual' (2014.0040.00099). Her solution again is to focus on selling her collection: 'I think we are going to have to concentrate on the sale of the archive, just get it moving' (00.04:27). Later in the same diary, she returns to this issue, once again foregrounding the collection's potential commercial value: 'Money, money, money...well, I'll just have to sell the archive' (00.15.39). Of course, as we now know, Greer did not actually sell her archive until 2013, and it is unclear if she or anyone on her behalf initiated any negotiations in the late 1990s regarding its sale. (I found no material to that effect in her papers.) Nevertheless, these comments reveal that it was not only 'posterity', as she had noted on the tapes (Hodgetts 2018, p. 40) and as cited in this chapter title (2014.0040.00103), that was motivating Greer's archival labour but very material factors too.

The carefully crafted collection was eventually purchased by her undergraduate alma mater, the University of Melbourne, for AU$3million; the majority of proceeds went to her conservation charity, The Friends of Gondwana Rainforest. Indicative of its creator's celebrity capital, the sale itself was considered newsworthy, both locally and internationally (Dean 2013; Gough 2013; Schuessler 2013; Simons 2013), and at least one journalist singled out the correspondence upon which this book focuses: 'Germaine Greer sells letters to Melbourne University for £1.8m' (Marks 2013). Archivist Katrina Dean travelled to Greer's Essex home in 2014 to bring the enormous collection back to Australia (Buchanan 2016). As Greer remarked during the move, presumably referring to both the archive and its contents, '"Looking at all this, anyone can see I worked very hard"' (McColl 2017). Notably, she was able to safeguard her papers in ways that perhaps other women could not, with the archival material 'stored at Greer's three and a half acre property in Essex in her purpose-built office above a garage' (Simons 2013). Once it arrived, the University of Melbourne reportedly employed up to ten people between 2016 and 2018 to work on the collection (Burn 2020, p. 142) – a fact that is indivisible from its creator's celebrity and her privilege as a white, highly educated, middle-class woman.

Briefly open in 2015 when I first saw the material, the archive was closed for cataloguing in 2016 and re-opened in March 2017. Across 2020–2021, it was completely inaccessible for extended periods, as Melbourne underwent a series of prolonged lockdowns during the COVID-19 pandemic. This was followed by considerably restricted access because of ongoing social distance measures which continued until early 2023. Compounding these accessibility issues, very few items have been digitised and researchers, even after signing a compulsory deed of undertaking, are prohibited from photographing material. It currently stands at over 500 archive boxes – the largest collection of any woman in Australia – housed at a repository in the inner-city Victorian suburb of

'The archive will put matters right, for posterity' **31**

Brunswick. As one of the archivists who worked on the Greer collection, Lachlan Glanville (2017), notes, 'Greer once stated that her archive "will take five years of genuine commitment to read"'. He concludes that this is a 'conservative estimate', and, after years working with it, I certainly concur.

Greer herself has been self-reflexive about her archival and cataloguing practices for many years, and in a very meta gesture, this material itself is contained in the archive. She provided the University of Melbourne with a 230-page document, 'Catalogue of works of Germaine Greer by the author, including selected correspondence 1957–1997' (Greer 1997). This document, kept in the Major Works series (2014.0045), advises: 'The archive is useful not only as a guide to feminism, but, because of the 20,000 letters etc. from the general public, to the evolution of social attitudes in the latter half of the century.' Of her curatorial practices, she notes therein: 'Before I relinquish possession of this material, I will check off all items and annotate them, giving dates and context or cross reference, to assist eventual cataloguer' (Greer 1997) – which she most certainly did (Buchanan 2018, p. 19). Though under the guise of simply being 'helpful' to the institution where this material would eventually land, she clearly sought (and indeed seeks) to provide the interpretive framework for this material, and subsequent public commentary on it serves as a kind of paratext seeking to delimit its meanings (Genette 1997), a point to which I shortly return.

Not only did Greer 'keep everything', she went out of her way to augment the collection, hiring staff to remedy its absences, including copies of her television appearances (Glanville 2018). Indicative of her active curatorial labour, Greer sought to 'complete the record' of 'her work in the public domain' (Glanville 2018, p. 46) – not always successfully, as Chapter 3 further explores. However, the inclusion of countless hours of television in the archive (2014.0041), as well as related print records and correspondence in the Television series (2017.0002), allows me to suggest that this mode (particularly through her deft movement across genres) was, and remains, crucial to Greer's public feminism and thus her stardom, offering a much fuller rendering of her career than has perhaps hitherto been possible. This is clearly Greer-the-curator actively shaping the archive, and her public self, in important ways.

'Setting the record straight': Greer as the 'archiving "I"'

Although Greer was not/is not merely an innocent 'collector', she nevertheless attributes an immense power to the archive, especially in terms of its supposed truth-telling capacity. When reflecting upon the archive and its potential uses, Greer commonly deploys the phrase 'setting the record straight' (Glanville 2017, 2018, p. 45; see also Hodgetts 2018, p. 42). For Greer, the archive's purpose is 'to combat the myths born from [her] celebrity status' (Glanville 2018, p. 47), purportedly offering access to the 'real' Greer

32 Germaine Greer, Celebrity Feminism and the Archive

(impossible though that may be). Referring to what she sees as the distortion of her image in print media interviews, she remarked at the 'Germaine Greer Meets the Archivists' event (discussed further below) that 'this falsification can't continue'. She added, in a frustrated tone, 'I've lived in this atmosphere of fiction-making about me personally' (Greer 2017). According to Greer, the archive is her response to this lack of veracity. She figures archival material as a corrective to decades of 'misrepresentation': Greer's archive is full of complaints about how she has been made-to-mean in the mainstream media – leading to her refusal to undertake print media interviews – as well as how her work has been edited in ways she did not approve, such as legally motivated editorial changes to her 1971 *Esquire* piece on Norman Mailer about which she was not consulted (to J.G., 20 July 1971, New York, 2014.0042.0240).

Greer reassures us that this is an authorised life, a position that Buchanan not unproblematically affirms when she sees Greer's archival practices as akin to autobiography (2018, p. 28). The iconic feminist has publicly suggested many times that she will never write an autobiography or indeed support a biography, even deeming biographer Christine Wallace a 'parasite' (Greer 1994). Accordingly, the famous author and media performer's attempts to so carefully manage the 'Greers' that emerge from the archive perhaps take on an even greater significance as part of a self-representational process that will not be staged elsewhere (as Stead argues of Vivien Leigh [2021]). Citing Greer's diary cassette tapes (2014.0041), which Greer appeared to create for the archive, archivist Kate Hodgetts writes, 'while she insists that she would never write an autobiography in an effort to defend her side of the story, *she understands that the archive does just that*' (2018, p. 42, emphasis added). From within the archive itself, Greer tells us – literally in her own voice – how she wishes us to approach her materials. Whether we comply is another question.

Despite Greer's encouragement, however, there is a danger in viewing the archive of the living author as autobiography. As Catherine Hobbs (2001, p. 132) astutely observes,

> the personal record should not be treated as if it contained only straightforward evidence, but as the site of multiple constructs – of a person upholding and struggling with ideas, of self and of others, while simultaneously contradicting, convincing, and contriving.

In this vein, the concept of 'the archiving "I"' (Douglas and MacNeil 2009), which helps to underscore the constructed-ness of archival selves, can mitigate such risks and allow for greater circumspection when confronted with the subject's claims of transparency and authenticity: 'The archiving "I" is the "I" who makes decisions about what will represent the "real" or historical "I" as part of her archive' (Douglas 2015, p. 55). The work done by this 'archiving "I"' in turn produces the archived "I", defined as 'another

'The archive will put matters right, for posterity' **33**

completely textual "I" and the result of the archiving "I"'s acts of selection, retention, and representation' (Douglas 2015, p. 55). However, as in celebrity studies, the subject-as-creator remains a problem in archival theory, wherein the creator is portrayed 'as a passive accumulator of records' (Douglas 2018, p. 36) – a portrayal that has particular implications for women's and feminists' archives.

Douglas (2018, p. 36) underscores that greater critical attention needs to be directed towards 'the creator's active archiving role,' a gesture which will enable researchers to 'make more informed interpretations of [the archive].' As she (2018, p. 35) demonstrates through her study of Canadian author archives, the level of curation varies considerably between women writers, ranging from simply haphazardly gathering material in boxes to providing strict instructions about arrangement and cataloguing (as in the case of Greer). Douglas argues that, as a concept, the 'archiving "I"' foregrounds that the creation of archives 'involves deliberate decision-making and archiving activities associated with a range of motivations on the part of the person who creates, uses, organizes and keeps records' (2018, pp. 128–29). Greer's archive, as well as public and scholarly commentary from those involved in its cataloguing, contains many traces of such a calculated approach to these fonds.

An example of the ways that Greer appears to use the archive as a corrective to forms of representation with which she disagrees is its inclusion of her marked-up copy of Anne Coombs's *Sex and Anarchy* (1996, 2014.0056.00089), a history of the Sydney Push – a libertarian, counter-cultural group of which Greer was a prominent member. Greer's archived annotated copy of the book contains many amendments to Coombs's account. For example, challenging Coombs's narrative about Greer moving to Sydney in 1959, the latter scribbles: 'Wrong. I was still an undergraduate' (Coombs 1996, p. 113). Of Push women, Coombs notes, 'they could operate on the same wavelength of detachment as the men. Germaine Greer was a case in point' (p. 205). Greer underlines the second sentence, pencilling 'Where is the evidence for this?' in the margins. In response to claims that Greer wrote for the University of New South Wales student magazine *Tharunka*, Greer queries: 'When?' (p. 250) – she even corrects typographical errors and dates. Regarding Coombs's claims that Greer 'gave one of the first, controversial, papers on the clitoral orgasm (delivered to elicit maximum laughs)' to a group of Push members, Greer writes: 'Surely not – no recollection, nothing in the archive' (p. 183). This comment suggests that Greer herself views the archive as a site of authority. Using this marginalia to contest the truth-claims made in Coombs's text, Greer offers a kind of counter-history (Stead 2021), another instance where she seeks to very literally *rewrite* the 'Greer' to which the public – including those consuming her archive – has access.

Without doubt, as in the above example, in Greer's collection we see the 'archiving "I" at work' (Douglas 2015, p. 71). That said, Greer is certainly

34 Germaine Greer, Celebrity Feminism and the Archive

not the only actor engaged in such labour; there are 'multiple layers of agency implicated in the construction of archival fonds' (MacNeil 2019, p. 47) – as there are in the construction and maintenance of celebrity. To account for this, and to ensure that we do not exaggerate the role of the creator or the celebrity in these complicated processes, Douglas and Heather MacNeil argue that the archive should be conceptualised as a 'social and collaborative text' (2009, p. 39) – again, also a useful way of theorising celebrity. Much more could also be said about the Greer archivists' custodial roles in preserving the creator's original ordering and arrangement, which we can see as a form of feminist archival practice much like Greer's own. Indeed, Glanville speaks self-reflexively of archivists who have worked on the collection being 'complicit' in the 'counter-narrative' Greer aims to construct (2018, p. 47). Similarly, Sarah Brown – who worked on the 'Publications By, Contributed To, or About Greer' (2014.0056) series (containing 124 books which Greer either used for research or in which she features as a subject) – suggests: 'Our approach throughout this project has been deliberately non-interventionist, respectful of provenance and original order and the relationship of the creator to her archive' (2018, p. 10). Greer's professed desires have clearly been taken into account by those she entrusted to care for and manage her archive, once again revealing her immense privilege in this regard. Here, though, my focus is on Greer's work in curating her archive in ways that are consonant with the other forms of persona-building labour, as well as feminist activism, in which she has engaged across her lengthy career.

Celebrity disavowal and narratives of democratisation: Greer on the archive

As briefly mentioned, Greer has publicly invoked a particular narrative about the archive and the uses to which she believes it should be put. Of the archive, Greer, perhaps rather disingenuously and consistent with her own public meta-commentary on her celebrification over many years (Taylor 2016), seeks to downplay her own presence therein (clearly contradicting her other claims about its functioning as a corrective to her misrepresentation). The archive, she has repeatedly told audiences and journalists, is not about *her* (Hodgetts 2018). One such occasion which I attended was the 'Germaine Greer Meets the Archivists' event at the University of Melbourne on 8 March 2017, to mark International Women's Day and the reopening of the archive. Such public events are the result of, and help sustain, Greer's extensive attention capital. At the event, Greer and a panel of archivists involved with her collection discussed the process of constituting the archive. Greer (2017) spoke at length, defining the archive in terms of what it is not: 'The archive is not meant to serve any kind of personality cult...The archive is not about me but about the moment'. She continues, 'if you use the archive at any length,

'The archive will put matters right, for posterity' **35**

you will be puzzled by my absence from it. At least that's, in a way, what I hope for'. She also explicitly disavows her fame, a common if strategic gesture for women (York forthcoming), pronouncing 'I have never been a celebrity' and reductively equating fame with appearing 'on the red carpet'. This reinforces a narrative articulated earlier, at 'Protest! Archives from the University of Melbourne', where she remarked: 'I am probably the least interesting part of my archive' (Greer 2013). Although Greer effectively tells us she is a 'reluctant celebrity' (York 2018), her actions – including the very public sale of her archive – clearly complicate this carefully crafted narrative.

Publicly, then, Greer professes a desire to decentre herself in discussions on and engagements with her archival material. This is a case of Greer, like one of the Shakespearean characters she has so extensively studied, protesting too much. Apart from anything, what if the archive *is* about her? Women, as Brenda Weber has argued, are rendered suspicious and judged harshly if they are seen to actively cultivate renown (2012, p. 18; see also Taylor 2016; York forthcoming) – including by other feminists, who see fame as fundamentally inequitable and hierarchal, which, of course, it is (not least because of the white, heterosexual, cisgender privilege enjoyed by those in this space [Phipps 2020]). This is clearly part of the wider, ongoing 'problem' of the individual for feminism (Downing 2019) which continues to be rehearsed in debates about celebrity and popular feminisms, especially given the dominance of neoliberal cultural logics (Rottenberg 2014; Banet-Weiser 2018).

Greer becomes illegible if she is seen to be too deeply invested in the self (Downing 2019), so she must locate the archive's value elsewhere (i.e., in the 'ordinary' correspondents or in what it reveals about the 'moment', as she puts it). Moreover, in deeply gendered and ageist ways, Greer is regularly positioned as a publicity-seeking narcissist (Nowra 2010), and her 2005 *Celebrity Big Brother* appearance (discussed in Chapter 3) is often invoked as evidence of this. Her public framing of the archive as 'not about her' represents an attempt to reject such positioning. She does this not by embracing her iconicity but by constructing a narrative about its undesirability and relatedly performing its disavowal – as she, like others such as Steinem (Bradley 2003), has done at various points in her career (Taylor 2016). As Stella Tillyard (1999) puts it, the famous feminist is in a bind:

> Greer remains resolutely uneasy about her stardom and that makes us question it, too…So while inviting us to consume her as a celebrity, she demands in her written work and her recorded remarks that we understand this to be false and limiting.

This is an apt rendering of Greer's paradoxical approach to public visibility.

As we have seen, Greer repeatedly mobilises a narrative of democratisation about the archive, which some of her so-called egalitarian curatorial practices, such as the alphabetisation of (some) reader and viewer correspondence, do support (Glanville 2017). The archivist responsible for the General Correspondence series, Lachlan Glanville (2017), reaffirms Greer's narrative about its apparent equalisation of voices: 'I like to imagine that the arrangement also has a touch of the diehard Marxist, giving equal prominence to noted author Margaret Atwood and Joe Public from Manchester.' Greer's archival practices seek to direct us away from privileged voices, such as male celebrities and paramours like Martin Amis, Warren Beatty, or Frederico Fellini, and towards 'ordinary' correspondents. In this respect, Greer's curatorial labour aids (or perhaps fosters) my own research preoccupations, particularly in relation to the fan mail contained in this series. Through this alphabetisation, Greer attempts to ensure that we engage with these more diverse voices, but this is not her only strategy for focusing the researcher's gaze towards her audiences. There are other instances where, by keeping letters together with other relevant documentation (as opposed to organising them alphabetically), 'Greer is subtly directing us to look' (Glanville 2018, p. 47) – as with responses to her television appearances on *The Dick Cavett Show* and *The Last Word* (Chapter 3), along with letters to various editors (Chapters 4 and 5).

In addition to the inclusion of copious fan mail, the archive features much material that can be classified anti-fandom (Taylor 2020; see also Gray 2003) – as later chapters emphasise. While critics have argued that letters preserved in archives tend to be those that paint the creator in a positive light (Ryan and Johanningsmeier 2013, pp. 4–5), thereby providing a one-sided account of their reception, Greer does not seek to censor or mask these more negative responses. The inclusion of hate mail in the archive is clearly an important feminist gesture, illuminating the misogyny with which women celebrities, and especially feminists, are invariably confronted (Jane 2016; Ging and Siapera 2019; Brady 2021). This is certainly the case with the anti-fan email sent in the wake of her controversial comments on the death of Australia's iconic 'Crocodile Hunter,' Steve Irwin: Rather than filing the printed emails alphabetically with other correspondence, Greer took the unusual curatorial step of placing the *Guardian* article to which readers were responding with the responses themselves (2014.0046.01067). As Buchanan notes, Greer 'arranged the Irwin records like this as a red flag to researchers that this small essay had touched a large national nerve' (2018, p. 26; see also Glanville 2018, p. 3); this material is analysed here in Chapter 6.

To the extent that there is a cacophony of voices in the archive, not least those who attribute their feminist awakening to Greer, and those who ask her for advice on how to make their lives otherwise, or even those who find her views abhorrent, her point that the archive is about them is perhaps sustainable. Indeed, my emphasis in this book on how Greer has impacted audiences may appear to reinforce this position. But no matter how zealous the disavowals, it is indeed Greer's extant attention capital that made her archive

'The archive will put matters right, for posterity' **37**

institutionally preservable, saleable, and consumable in ways that those of more marginalised subjects simply are not. In terms of its content and arrangement, Greer is undoubtedly *everywhere* in this archive (Buchanan 2016), despite her repeated claims that it is 'not a portrait of me' (Greer 2017). Here, I mean not to invoke an essential, singular, or unchangeable identity emerging from the aggregation of its many sources but rather to underscore that this live archive is part of the 'performative practice' and labour in which all famous figures engage (Marwick and boyd 2011) as well as containing evidence of such work.

The archive, that is, does not simply *tell* us about Greer's fame and the activities that were its source, it is in and of itself a form of renown maintenance and extension, which moreover can be figured as a feminist practice consistent with Greer's own feminist scholarship. Greer's academic work, especially on forgotten women painters (1979), poets (1995), and even on Shakespeare's wife, Anne Hathaway (2007), has involved the feminist act of retrieval, putting women's voices in and on the record – the kind of work we might associate with second-wave feminist literary critics such as Sandra Gilbert and Susan Gubar (1979) or Dale Spender (1982). Though, of course, such processes themselves produce knowledge (rather than simply 'recover' it), the sale and availability of her archive ensure that future feminist scholars will not have to perform such recuperative gestures on her behalf, rendering it not just an archive of a feminist but itself a feminist archive. Greer's archival efforts then, like her performative practice as a celebrity, are part of her public feminism. We can see Greer's fonds, therefore, as 'offering a space that not only legitimates her papers and her career, but also extends the activism she pursued in her lifetime' (Morra 2004, p. 111).

Celebrity archives, institutionally supported and sanctioned, appear to exist in opposition to community-based and -led archives. Such 'memory collecting' is itself a vital form of activism for local feminist organisations, 'redress[ing] the marginalization of women in the archival record' (Sadler and Cox 2018, p. 158). Archives like Greer's are, of course, considerably different from those produced by such collectives. But rather than dismissing such collection and curation as self-interested or selfish (and, by extension, 'unfeminist') – the dominant discursive framework for making sense of women's focus on the self (Downing 2019) – we can see Greer's curatorial labours as part of 'larger trends in the history of 1970s-era feminists and their attempts to self-fashion their historical legacies' (O'Donnell 2020, p. 91). That is, part of the same feminist 'memory work' in which community archivists are also engaged. As Kelly O'Donnell remarks, 'When they came to see themselves as historically significant, they also realized that if the personal was political, then so were personal papers' (2020, p. 94). Although Greer's archive-building commenced well before the second wave, it certainly intensified over this period. That said, the archive – and Greer's feminism – far exceeds that period of heightened feminist

38 Germaine Greer, Celebrity Feminism and the Archive

activism, and indeed it continues to expand, as those of living subjects invariably do. While often contentious, Greer is a remarkable woman, who has lived a remarkable feminist life – much of it in the spotlight. Her meticulously arranged archive enables us to revisit this impactful figure and to reflect critically on the methodologies we deploy to make sense of modes of public visibility, their maintenance, and how they come to resonate with audiences over time.

Across the archive, however, there are significant absences of which we should also be conscious, especially given that they 'might be just as significant as the surviving material' (Dever et al. 2009, p. 111). Greer's archive draws attention to these omissions with the multiple flags it has in place; it is common to find A4 sheets of papers noting 'pages have been removed from this file', ranging between 2 and 41 pages, and these enforced silences, too, are significant and further evidence of Greer's management of the files (Glanville 2018, p. 47). Such movement also suggests the 'liveness' of the Greer archive, which can be reshaped in response to its uses; for example, following Margaret Simons's (2015) lengthy article on Greer's intimate correspondence with author Martin Amis (what she characterises as a '30,000 word love letter'), the publication of which garnered significant international media coverage (Shea 2015), the material was removed from the collection. These instances reveal not only that the living Greer crafted and moulded the material before it was deposited but that she continues to exercise control over it and the uses to which it can be put. We can imagine that such oversight on Greer's part will persist for as long as she is able.

Conclusion

Approaching the archive as a site of renown-building labour, as I do here, is an important political gesture, which works to unsettle troublesome narratives of women as passive victims of celebrification. In my work on this iconic figure, I conceptualise the archive as part of the processes of self-construction in which Greer has always been heavily invested as well as evidence of the extensive labour that fame necessitates (York 2013a; Stead 2020) – including, even if problematically, for feminists. Public visibility requires considerable work, as recent scholarship in both digital media and persona studies has underscored (Abidin 2016; Marshall et al. 2019), arguably even more so for those – like celebrity feminists – who deploy such visibility to disrupt dominant assumptions around gender and sexuality (Taylor 2016; Brady 2021). In particular, the living celebrity's archive can offer important insights into the ongoing work of constructing a viable self for public consumption – as well as demonstrating the effects of this consumption on diverse audiences, my key preoccupation throughout this book.

Through the specific example of Greer's archive, I have argued that celebrity archives both reveal and extend this work, in ways that necessitate deeper critical reflection. This is not to elide the role of other key intermediaries or

'The archive will put matters right, for posterity' **39**

to overstate the role of celebrities in the meaning-making processes in which they are implicated. It is, however, to emphasise that the inclusion, and conversely the active exclusion, and strategic arrangement of certain materials in personal fonds invariably steer our research in particular directions – in enabling and/or constraining ways, as my personal negotiations with the Greer material reveal. This is something about which those of us who use archival methodologies in our work on celebrity should be self-reflexive. In this particular case, Greer's work as an archivist is indisputable, and I wholeheartedly concur with Buchanan (2018) that we need to add this to her myriad professional roles. Such curation, as I have argued, aligns with Greer's own way of 'doing celebrity' (Yelin 2021) over decades as well as her own intellectual and political commitment to ensuring that women's voices (including her own) are firmly placed on the historical record. However, the concepts of the 'archiving and archived "I"' (Douglas and MacNeil 2009) help ensure that we do not look to such material to find some essential truths about our celebrity subjects; instead, we can see the archive as but one site for the constitution of celebrity selves.

This chapter has argued that both feminist celebrity studies and archival studies need to further critically think through the kinds of curatorial interventions mapped here and their active role in shaping what we (are able to) do as researchers of renown. While there are many actors involved in the cultivation and maintenance of fame, as there are in archival spaces, acknowledging and analysing the formative role of figures like Greer as curators can (re)centre them in the knotty processes of both celebrification and archivisation. Beyond this specific archive, feminist celebrity studies scholars can and should continue to move much further beyond the mere analysis of celebrity signs or star texts. Instead, celebrities like Greer should be repositioned as agentic subjects who attempt – though, of course, not always successfully and always within discursive, material, political, and institutional limits – to shape how they come to be framed and consumed, including through reconceptualising the archive as a site of feminist fame work. As shown throughout this book, archival material permits a deeper critical reflection on the work that Greer-as-celebrity does in the world, in terms of precipitating feminist refigurations of gender and sexuality and mobilising audiences, individually and collectively. In the next chapter, I offer a sustained analysis of the copious amounts of fan mail sent to Greer following the publication of *The Female Eunuch* and, to a lesser extent, her subsequent blockbusters.

References

Abidin, C. (2016) 'Visibility Labour: Engaging with Influencers' Fashion Brands and #OOTDadvertorial Campaigns on Instagram', *Media International Australia*, vol. 161, no. 1: 86–100.

40 Germaine Greer, Celebrity Feminism and the Archive

Banet-Weiser, S. (2018) *Empowered: Popular Feminism and Popular Misogyny*, Durham, NC: Duke University Press.

Barbour, K. (2023) *Women and Persona Performance*, London: Palgrave Macmillan.

Bradley, P. (2003) *Mass Media and the Shaping of American Feminism, 1963–1975*, Jackson: University of Mississippi Press.

Brady, A. (2016) 'Taking Time Between G-string Changes to Educate Ourselves: Sinéad O'Connor, Miley Cyrus, and Celebrity Feminism', *Feminist Media Studies*, vol. 16, no. 3: 429–444.

Brady, A. (2021) 'Clementine Ford, Online Misogyny, and the Labour of Celebrity Feminism', in A. Taylor and J. McIntyre (eds.), *Gender and Australian Celebrity Culture*, London: Routledge, pp. 91–108.

Brown, S. (2018) 'Books as Archival Objects', *Archives and Manuscripts*, vol. 46, no. 1: 49–58.

Buchanan, R. (2016) 'The Record Keeper', *Australian Feminist Studies*, vol. 31, no. 87: 22–27.

Buchanan, R. (2018) 'Foreign Correspondence: Journalism in the Germaine Greer Archive', *Archives and Manuscripts*, vol. 46, no. 1: 18–39.

Burn, M. (2020) 'Overwhelmed by the Archive? Considering the Biographies of Germaine Greer', *Australian Journal of Biography and History*, vol. 3, accessed via: https://press-files.anu.edu.au/downloads/press/n6404/html/review_article01.xhtml

Burton, A. (2006) *Archive Stories: Facts, Fictions, and the Writing of History*, Durham: Duke University Press.

Butler, J. (2009) *Frames of War: When is Live Grieveable*, London: Verso.

Casey, S. and Watson, J. (2023) *Hashtag Feminisms: Australian Media Feminists, Activism, and Digital Campaigns*, Bern: Peter Lang.

Chidgey, R. (2021) 'Postfeminism™: Celebrity Feminism, Branding and the Performance of Activist Capital', *Feminist Media Studies*, vol. 21, no. 7: 1055–1071.

Cifor, M. and Wood, S. (2017) 'Critical Feminism in the Archives', *Journal of Critical Library, and Information Studies*, vol. 1, no. 2: 1–27.

Coombs, A. (1996) *Sex and Anarchy: The Life and Death of the Sydney Push*, London: Viking, Germaine Greer Archive, Publications by, contributed or about Germaine Greer, 2014.0056.00089, University of Melbourne.

Dean, K. (2013) 'Why Germaine Greer's life in letters is one for the archives', *The Conversation*, 1 November, accessed via: https://theconversation.com/why-germaine-greers-life-in-letters-is-one-for-the-archives-19625

Dever, M. (2017) 'Archives and New Modes of Feminist Research', *Australian Feminist Studies*, vol. 32, no. 91–92: 1–4.

Dever, M., Newman, S., and Vickery, A. (2009) *The Intimate Archive: Journeys Through Private Papers*, Canberra: National Library of Australia.

Douglas, J. (2015) 'The Archiving "I": A Closer Look in the Archives of Writers', *Archivaria*, vol. 79, April: 53–89.

Douglas, J. (2018) 'A all to Rethink Archival Creation: Exploring Types of Creation in Personal Archives', *Archival Science*, vol. 18, no. 1: 29–49.

Douglas, J. and MacNeil, H. (2009) 'Arranging the Self: Literary and Archival Perspectives on Writers' Archives', *Archivaria*, vol. 67: 25–39.

Douglas, J. and Mills, A. (2018) 'From the Sidelines to the Center: Reconsidering the Potential of the Personal in Archives', *Archival Science*, vol. 18, no. 3: 257–277.

Dow, B.J. (1996) *Prime-time Feminism: Television, Media Culture, and the Women's Movement since 1970*, Philadelphia: University of Pennsylvania Press.

'The archive will put matters right, for posterity' **41**

Dow, B.J. (2014) *Watching Women's Liberation 1970: Feminism's Pivotal Year on the Network News*, Urbana: University of Illinois.

Downing, L. (2019) *Selfish Women*, London: Routledge.

Dyer, R. (1986) *Heavenly Bodies: Film Stars and Society*, London: Routledge.

Eichhorn, K. (2013) *The Archival Turn in Feminism: Outrage in Order*, Philadelphia: Temple University Press.

Genette, J. (1997) *Paratexts: Thresholds of Interpretation*, Cambridge: Cambridge University Press.

Germaine Greer Archives. Audio series, 2014.0040, University of Melbourne.

Germaine Greer Archive. Audiovisual Recordings Produced and Received by Greer, 2014.0041, University of Melbourne.

Germaine Greer Archive. General Correspondence, 2014.0042, University of Melbourne.

Germaine Greer Archive. Major Works c.1969–2014. 2014.0045, University of Melbourne.

Germaine Greer Archive. Print Journalism, 2014.0046, University of Melbourne.

Germaine Greer Archive. Publications By, Contributed to, or About Germaine Greer, 2014.0056, University of Melbourne.

Germaine Greer Archive. Audio series, 2014.0040, University of Melbourne.

Gilbert, S. and Gubar, S. (1979) *The Madwoman in the Attic: The Woman Writer and the Nineteenth-century Literary Imagination*, New Haven: Yale University Press.

Ging, D. and Siapera, E. eds. (2019) *Gender Hate Online: Understanding the New Anti-Feminism*, London: Palgrave Macmillan.

Glanville, L. (2017) 'Friday Essay: Reading Germaine Greer's Mail', *The Conversation*, 24 March, accessed via: https://theconversation.com/friday-essay-reading-germaine-greers-mail-74693

Glanville, L. (2018) 'The End of Reckoning – Archival Silences in the Germaine Greer Archive', *Archives and Manuscripts*, vol. 46, no. 1: 45–48.

Gough, D. (2013) 'Germaine Greer Sells Her Archive to Melbourne University', *The Age*, 28 October, accessed via: https://www.theage.com.au/national/victoria/germaine-greer-sells-archive-to-melbourne-university-20131028-2wbho.html

Gray, J. (2003) 'New Audiences, New Textualities: Anti-fans and Non-fans', *International Journal of Cultural Studies*, vol. 6, no. 1: 64–81.

Greer, G. (1970) *The Female Eunuch*, London: Paladin.

Greer, G. (1979) *The Obstacle Race: The Fortunes of Women Painters and Their Work*, New York: Farrer, Strauss and Giroux.

Greer, G. (1994) 'Me, My Work, My Friends, and My Parasite', *The Guardian*, 31 October, Germaine Greer Archive, 2014.0042.00974, University of Melbourne.

Greer, G. (1995) *Slip-shod Sibyls: Recognition, Rejection and the Woman Poet*, London: Viking.

Greer, G. (1997) 'Catalogue of works of Germaine Greer by the author, including selected correspondence 1957–1997', Major Works c.1969–2014, 2014.0045.00603, Germaine Greer Archive, University of Melbourne.

Greer, G. (2007) *Shakespeare's Wife*, London: Bloomsbury.

Greer, G. (2013) 'Protest! Archives from the University of Melbourne', 28 October, YouTube, accessed via: https://www.youtube.com/watch?v=ppRX1XuCO8w

Greer, G. (2017) 'Germaine Greer meets the Archivists', 9 March, YouTube, accessed via: https://www.youtube.com/watch?v=LOcMazsj6OQ

Hamad, H. and Taylor, A. (2015) 'Introduction: Feminism and Contemporary Celebrity Culture', *Celebrity Studies*, vol. 6, no. 1: 124–127.

42 Germaine Greer, Celebrity Feminism and the Archive

Hemmings, C. (2018) *Reconsidering Emma Goldman*, Durham: Duke University Press.

Henderson, M. (2006) *Marking Feminist Times: Remembering the Longest Revolution in Australia*, Bern: Peter Lang.

Hobbs, C. (2001) 'The Character of Personal Archives: Reflections on the Value of Records of Individuals', *Archivaria*, vol. 52: 126–135.

Hobson, J. (2017) 'Celebrity Feminism: More than a Gateway', *Signs: Journal of Women in Culture and Society*, vol. 42, no. 4: 999–1007.

Hodgetts, K. (2018) 'Hear Greer: Voices in the Archive', *Archives and Manuscripts*, vol. 46, no. 1: 40–44.

Jane, E. (2016) *A Short History of Misogyny*, London: Sage.

Lawson, C. (2023) *Just Like Us: Digital Debates on Feminism and Fame*, New Brunswick, NJ: Rutgers University Press.

Lee, K. (2020) *Limelight: Canadian Women and the Rise of Autobiography*, Toronto: Wilfred Laurier Press.

MacNeil, H. (2019) 'Understanding the Archival Fonds as Autobiographical Text through Three Discourses', *JLIS.It*, vol. 10, no. 3: 47–58.

Majic, S. (2023) *Lights, Camera, Feminism: Celebrities and Anti-trafficking Politics*, Berkeley: California University Press.

Marcus, S. (2019) *The Drama of Celebrity*, Princeton, NJ: Princeton University Press.

Marks, K. (2013) 'Germaine Greer sells letters to Melbourne University for £1.8m', *The Independent*, 28 October, accessed via: https://www.independent.co.uk/news/world/australasia/germaine-greer-sells-letters-to-melbourne-university-for-ps1-8m-8909489.html

Marshall, P.D. (1997) *Celebrity and Power*, Minneapolis: University of Minnesota Press.

Marshall, P.D., Moore, C., and Barbour, K. (2019) *Persona Studies: An Introduction*, London: Wiley.

Marwick, A.E. (2016) '"You may know me from YouTube": (Micro-)Celebrity in Social Media', in P.D. Marshall and S. Redmond (eds), *A Companion to Celebrity*, London: Wiley Blackwell, pp. 333–350.

Marwick, A. and boyd, d. (2011) 'To See and Be Seen: Celebrity Practice on Twitter', *Convergence*, vol. 17, no. 2: 139–158.

McCaig, J. (2002) *Reading In: Alice Munro's Archives*, Ontario: Wilfred Laurier University Press.

McColl, G. (2017) 'International Women's Day 2017: Secrets Revealed in Germaine Greer's Archives', *The Age*, 24 February, accessed via: https://www.theage.com.au/national/victoria/international-womens-day-2017-secrets-revealed-in-germaine-greers-archives-20170224-gukbyv.html

McGill, R. (2009) 'Biographical Desire and the Archives of Living Authors, *a/b: Auto/Biography Studies*, vol, 24, no. 1: 129–145.

Moran, J., (2000) *Star Authors: Literary Celebrity in America*, London: Pluto.

Morra, L.M. (2004) *Unarrested Archives: Case Studies in Twentieth-Century Canadian Women's Authorship*, Toronto: University of Toronto Press.

Nowra, L. (2010) 'The Better Self? Germaine Greer and *The Female Eunuch*', *The Monthly*, March: 40–46.

O'Donnell, K. (2020) 'The Activist Archive: Feminism, Personal-political Papers, and Recent Women's History', *Journal of Women's History*, vol. 32, no. 4: 88–109.

Phipps, A. (2020) *Me, Not You: The Trouble with Mainstream Feminism*, Manchester: Manchester University Press.

Rojek, C. (2001) *Celebrity*, London: Reaktion.

Rottenberg, C. (2014) 'The Rise of Neoliberal Feminism', *Cultural Studies*, vol. 28, no. 3: 418–437.

Ryan, B. and Johanningsmeier, C. (2013) 'Guest Editors' Introduction: Fans and the Objects of Their Devotion', *Reception*, vol. 5: 3–8.

Sadler, R. and Cox, A.M. (2018) '"Civil disobedience" in the Archive: Documenting Women's Activism and Experience through the Sheffield Feminist Archive', *Archives and Records*, vol. 39, no. 2: 158–173.

Schuessler, J. (2013) 'Germaine Greer's Archives are sold to the University of Melbourne', *New York Times*, 28 October, accessed via: https://archive.nytimes. com/artsbeat.blogs.nytimes.com/2013/10/28/germaine-greers-archives-are-sold-to-the-university-of-melbourne/

Schwartz, J.M. and Cook, T. (2002) 'Archives, Records, and Power: The Making of Modern Memory', *Archival Science*, vol. 2, no. 1–2: 1–19.

Scott, J. (2011) *The Fantasy of Feminist History*, Durham: Duke University Press.

Shea, C.D. (2015) 'Greer Love Letter to Amis Sheds Light on Relationship', *New York Times*, 17 November, accessed via: https://archive.nytimes.com/artsbeat. blogs.nytimes.com/2015/11/17/greer-love-letter-to-amis-sheds-light-on-relationship/

Simons, M. (2013) 'Germaine Greer sells archive to University of Melbourne', *The Guardian*, 28 October, accessed via: https://www.theguardian.com/books/2013/oct/28/germaine-greer-sells-archive-to-university-of-melbourne

Simons, M. (2015) '"The Long Letter to a Short Love, or…', *Meanjin*, Summer, accessed via: https://meanjin.com.au/essays/the-long-letter-to-a-short-love-or/

Spender, D. (1982) *Women of Ideas and What Men Have one to Them: From Aphra Behn to Adrienne Rich*, London: Routledge.

Stead, L. (2020) 'Archiving Star Labour: (Re)framing Vivien Leigh', *Women's History Review*, vol. 29, no. 5: 860–874.

Stead, L. (2021) *Reframing Vivien Leigh: Stardom, Gender, and the Archive*, Oxford: Oxford University Press.

Taylor, A. (2016) *Celebrity and the Feminist Blockbuster*, London: Palgrave Macmillan.

Taylor, A. (2020) '"The Most Revolting Ideas I've Read in a Woman's Magazine": *The Female Eunuch*, Affective (dis)investments, and *McCall's* Reader-writers', *Australian Feminist Studies*, vol. 35, no. 103: 20–36.

Taylor, A. (2022) 'Germaine Greer's Story of Human Reproduction, The Dismissal, and Feminist "Unproduction Studies"', unpublished conference paper, Cultural Studies Association of Australasia Conference, 28–30 June, Edith Cowan University.

Tillyard, S. (1999) 'Germaine Greer', *Prospect Magazine*, 20 April, accessed via: https://www.prospectmagazine.co.uk/magazine/germainegreerWallace

Turner, G. (2004) *Understanding Celebrity*, London: Sage.

Weber, B. (2012) *Women and Literary Celebrity in the Nineteenth Century: The Transatlantic Production of Fame and Gender*, London: Ashgate.

Wicke, J. (1994) 'Celebrity Material: Materialist Feminism and the Culture of Celebrity', *The South Atlantic Quarterly*, vol. 93, no. 4: 751–778.

Yelin, H. (2020) *Celebrity Memoirs: From Ghostwriting to Gender Politics*, London: Palgrave Macmillan.

Yelin, H. (2021) '"I am the centre of fame": Doing Celebrity, Performing Fame and Navigating Cultural Hierarchies in Grace Jones,' *I'll Never Write my Memoirs*', *Celebrity Studies*, vol. 12, no. 1: 119–131.

York, L. (2013a) *Margaret Atwood and The Labour of Literary Celebrity*, Toronto: University of Toronto Press.

York, L. (2013b) 'Star Turn: The Challenges of Theorizing Celebrity Agency', *Journal of Popular Culture*, vol. 46, no. 6: 1330–1347.

York, L. (2018) *Reluctant Celebrity: Affect and Privilege in Contemporary Stardom*, London: Palgrave Macmillan.

York, L. (forthcoming) 'Unseemly Affects: Gender, Celebrity, and The Policing of Fame Hunger', in J. McIntyre and A. Taylor. (eds.), *The Routledge Companion to Gender and Celebrity*, London: Routledge.

2

'YOU ARE THE TWENTIETH CENTURY MESSIAH!'

Blockbuster Fan Mail

Introduction

The Germaine Greer archive's 'General Correspondence' series, as the previous chapter has shown, is shaped by Greer's own curatorial practices. Through alphabetising this material, she seeks to turn the researcher's gaze towards a wider range of correspondents, equalising celebrity voices and those of 'ordinary' citizens who write to tell her of the impact she has had upon them (Glanville 2017). Feminist blockbusters (and their celebrity feminist authors) are overwhelmingly transformational (Taylor 2016), as the myriad letters in this series attest. This book aims to establish that Greer is much more than just the author of *The Female Eunuch*, but certainly in terms of letters from readers, it is her first groundbreaking polemic that dominates. *The Change* (1991), her bestseller critiquing dominant discourses around menopause, prompts the next largest amount of reader correspondence. The sheer number of letters from readers preserved in the Greer archive is itself remarkable and is especially valuable to my efforts to further our understandings of how Greer shaped affective engagements with feminism. 'Personal letters', as Marcelo Borges observes when reflecting upon the history of emotions as an interdisciplinary field, are 'promising sources to explore the emotion work of individuals in historical context' (2020, p. 101), particularly in periods of social and political upheaval, like the 1970s.

Here, I consider these epistolary texts addressed to Greer as important forms of feminist life writing, marked by recurrent self-representational strategies, tropes and metaphors, and rhetorical techniques. These letters exhibit what Elspeth Probyn (1993) characterises as 'feminist reflexivity' and the sense of 'affective dissonance' (Hemmings 2012) that is crucial to feminist politics.

DOI: 10.4324/9781315179841-3

46 Germaine Greer, Celebrity Feminism and the Archive

They are also significant as attempts to perform certain modes of intimacy to interpersonally connect with Greer-as-celebrity, and reveal much about the role of recognition in reading – and indeed fan – practices. This chapter, focusing on fan mail to the iconic feminist author, reflects upon what constitutes a feminist fan – as in a fan of a feminist. These letter writers are not just fans of Greer, they are fans of (her) feminism, enabling me to consider how attachments to feminism are made and sustained (Ahmed 2004). Further, these correspondents likely never met each other, nor Greer, but clearly conceive of themselves as part of a community from which they gather strength, solace, hope, and inspiration. While the sense of 'like-minded-ness' has been seen to be central to online fan communities (Hannell 2023, p. 67), it is also important to the imagined feminist community of readers who responded to Greer's books in remarkably similar ways (Le Masurier 2009).

Greer's first 'feminist blockbuster' and consciousness-raising

Drawing upon Shane Rowlands and Margaret Henderson's (1996) work, I have previously established that *The Female Eunuch* is the quintessential 'feminist blockbuster' (Taylor 2016), a bestselling, often sensationalistic work of feminist non-fiction, whose success is both dependent upon and further augments its author's celebrity (see also Lilburn et al. 2000). Described by one reviewer as the 'best book of the women's movement' (Lehmann-Haupt 1971), *The Female Eunuch*, though relatively neglected by scholars (Taylor et al. 2016), has never been out of print and has been translated into multiple languages. As Simone Murray notes, Greer's publisher invested considerable time and money to guarantee the book's success, and its campaign then represented 'the most extensive feminist book promotion ever undertaken' (2004, p. 197). Given Greer's centrality in ensuring that her feminism reached as wide an audience as possible, her promotional schedules were gruelling, as archival material reveals (1971).

The Female Eunuch (1970) is a deeply engaging polemic, filled with personal anecdotes, informed by extensive scholarship[1], and brimming with persuasive evidence of women's historical and ongoing subordination. The book – if not embraced by movement activists – rapidly became an international bestseller and transformed its author into a feminist superstar. The 'eunuch' metaphor on which Greer's argument centres is not just about sexuality (though its reclamation is a key aspect) but about how women's lives, and subjectivities, have been stymied, with certain ways of being and embodying womanhood detrimentally privileged over others. She calls for a radical reorganisation of society and urges women to eschew marriage, exercise their sexual agency, become critical consumers, and form alternative communal living arrangements (Greer 1970). Greer's initial addressees, as she routinely stated, were those who had not otherwise been reached by women's liberationists: '"It's a book which is quite useless to women already involved in the movement"' (Lehrmann 1972). I engage further with the book's arguments in Chapter 5, which analyses readers' responses to an extract published in *McCall's* magazine.

While women's liberationists criticised *The Female Eunuch* for failing to be a viable manifesto, or blueprint for feminist action, Sara Ahmed suggests that books can be 'heard' as 'manifestos, as calls to action; as calls to arms' when they 'show how a life can be rewritten' (2017, p. 256). She continues that 'a manifesto is an outstretched hand. And if a manifesto is a political action, it depends on how it is received by others' (2017, p. 256). If we follow Ahmed's definition, Greer's readers certainly appear to have 'heard' her blockbuster as a manifesto. With her groundbreaking polemic, she was able to reach those who felt alienated by women's liberation; for those 'outside the organised women's movement, Greer was a beacon' (Arrow 2019, p. 45; see also Wallace 1997; Sheehan 2016). These reader letters are not just about becoming or feeling close to Greer, they are about articulating a newfound politicised worldview for which they give her and her writing (or other forms of cultural production) credit. In her blockbuster, Greer (1970), in the spirit of feminist consciousness-raising, urges individual women to re-view themselves and their personal circumstances – and these letters make clear that they have obliged, in some cases decades after their initial consumption.

Since much of the fan mail examined here emerged following the consumption of *The Female Eunuch* as well as Greer's later blockbusters, it is necessary to reflect further on the role of popular writing as a form of consciousness-raising ('CR'). In early 1970s CR sessions, particularly in Anglo-American contexts, women 'began to discover that many of their problems were not solely their own' (Samer 2023, p. 148). They found that other women were similarly experiencing discrimination, assault, domestic violence, misogyny and sexism, and 'these shared experiences would come to serve as the basis for demanding social change' (Samer 2023, p. 148). In addition, various forms of 'discursive activism' (Young 1997) – from mimeographed newsletters to novels such as Erica Jong's *Fear of Flying* (1973) – successfully brought diverse women to second-wave feminism (Whelehan 2005). As Jaime Harker and Cecilia Konchar Farr remark, 'books became a provocation to conversation about readers' own lives and experiences' (2016, p. 4). They continue: 'What united them [second wave writers] was a firm belief that books could be revolutionary, that language could remake the world, and that writing mattered in a profound way' (2016, p. 1). This is clearly a position Greer held, too.

In reader letters responding to the feminist health movement manual *Our Bodies, Ourselves* (1970), like those following *The Female Eunuch*, 'reading was often described as a revelatory experience – as a "click" that drew woman out of isolation and into a widespread dialogue' (Kline 2005, p. 90; see also Wu 2016). For women unable to become involved in locally organised

48 Germaine Greer, Celebrity Feminism and the Archive

women's liberation groups and their CR processes, articulating the personal to the political, books like *The Feminine Mystique* (Friedan 1963) and *The Female Eunuch* were crucial. Such widely available books 'enabled readers to experience consciousness-raising at their own kitchen tables' (Kline 2005, p. 90). Reading then became writing, as consumers sought to enter into a dialogue with these transformative celebrity authors, with varying results. As Glanville (2017) notes of the archive's General Correspondence series, 'the publication of *The Female Eunuch* would give birth to a shadow work that would document the inner lives and experiences of women and men from across generations'; it is to such 'shadow work' that this chapter turns.[2]

'Do not think I am a groupie': Self-reflexivity and Greer fandom

In her article on Australian singer Helen Reddy, famous for her 1972 second-wave anthem, 'I am woman', historian Michelle Arrow underscores the scholarly value of fan mail to celebrity feminists, observing that it provides 'tangible evidence of feminism's impact, especially as it was translated and communicated through mass media and popular culture' (2007, p. 223). These letters, offering insights into the 'personal transformation'[s] of many women, extend our understandings of feminist history beyond just those actively involved in the women's movement (Arrow 2007, p. 223). Moreover, in many respects, the writing of these letters themselves can be constituted a feminist act, in the sense of women coming to voice: 'Writing the fan letter is a testing ground for an independent, reflective self' (Grasso 2013, p. 33). Putting this new self down on paper, or bringing her into being while doing so, is a vital feminist gesture.

Evidencing the extraordinary/ordinary paradox constitutive of celebrity itself (Dyer 1979), these letters show Greer to be at once exceptional *and* a regular woman just like readers (Grasso 2013). Greer as a woman intellectual is positioned as extraordinary, yet her 'truths' are seen to emerge not from her intellectual labour but from gendered experiences to which readers relate. As a highly visible celebrity author, she embodies a different way of doing femininity, a viable way of being in the world which in turn opens up this possibility for her readers. Greer is the woman she exhorts them to become: the opposite of a female eunuch. In terms of the sense of a close personal connection, and the 'presumed intimacy' (Rojek 2015) upon which celebrity relies, readers seemed to feel that they knew what Greer was 'really like' because she had directly told them, in her non-fiction and in her various celebrity performances (Coffin 2020). That is, there was no distinguishing between a public and a private Greer – she was seen to just be 'herself' (Bennett 2010), an assumption we also see television viewers making. As Lynne Pearce suggests (2004), women authors of non-fiction are subject to a form of gendered 'bio-mythological' framing, where readers conflate the narrative voice with that of the author – and, of course, celebrity culture itself encourages and indeed relies upon this conflation (Taylor 2016). Those engaged in Greer fandom routinely enact this slippage.

As Angela Firkus argues, 'celebrity is a status negotiated between someone famous and her fans' (2021, p. 1) – this is no less true of the celebrity feminist. These fan letters represent an important space for such negotiations. Fandom is commonly defined as the 'regular, emotionally involved consumption of a given popular narrative or text' (Sandvoss 2005, p. 8). In addition, it is often presumed to entail a publicly performed collective identity, and the production of artistic fan texts or, especially more recently, digital remediation processes (Jenkins 2006), thereby excluding seemingly sporadic and isolated acts such as fan mail. Sharon Marcus, however, writes: 'Authorship and the production of autonomous artworks [should not] be the measure of what makes fandom matter. Most fans who craft their own artifacts favor genres such as scrapbooks and fan mail, which foster proximity, familiarity, and interdependence' (2019, p. 91). Fan studies theorist Matt Hills also argues that 'fan practices are carried out, sometimes within participatory forums and sometimes in highly individualized and non-communal ways, *without the validating support of fan discourses*' (2018, p. 491, original emphasis). Nevertheless, while this fan mail may appear 'highly individualized', these Greer fans do invoke an imagined feminist community to which they contribute and which gives them succour.

Many letter writers proudly and eagerly pronounce themselves Greer fans. However, they simultaneously deride certain forms of fan behaviour. In this way, we see them persistently attempting to distinguish themselves from other kinds of fans, explicitly positioning themselves against obsessive 'fanatics'. Correspondents, therefore, appear to have internalised the deeply gendered critiques that fan studies has long worked to dispel. Joli Jenson establishes that in early studies of fandom '[t]he fan is consistently characterized (referencing the term's origins) as a potential fanatic. This means that fandom is seen as excessive, bordering on deranged, behavior' (1992, p. 9). This 'fan-as-pathology' (Jenson 1992) notion, reinscribed across many letters, is especially problematic given the ways in which the excesses of fandom have been historically gendered feminine (Gray 2003) and denigrated on these grounds. In particular, fans are often criticised for displaying excessive affect, perceived to be misguidedly invested in 'the objects of their fannish affection' (Garg 2022, p. 16).

Greer fans discursively construct the act of penning a fan letter as aberrant, fearing that their idol will dismiss them as 'irrational'. For example, in 1975, a woman from the Victorian outer suburb of Frankston, seeking to forestall such judgement, writes:

When I sit down to write this I feel a bit ridiculous because I've never written this kind of letter in my life. But anyway that doesn't matter. What I wanted to say to you is this – do you realise what a magnificent, gallant

50 Germaine Greer, Celebrity Feminism and the Archive

thing you are doing, and do you know that the women you address understand and hold you in great affection?

(M.B., 11 December, 2014.0042.00126)

As in this instance, they write to reassure her of the esteem in which she is held. Like others, the following correspondent hopes Greer does not misinterpret her actions as those of a 'groupie' (a label, however, that Greer herself proudly adopted [1969a]). Emphasising that such behaviour is remarkably out of character, a Vancouver woman remarks:

Do not think I am a groupie who follows famous names and people and who writes fan letters all the time. The last time I wrote a fan letter was when I was 10 years old, that was addressed to Elvis Presley.

(D.C., 18 August 1971, 2014.0042.00195)

For this woman, fan mail is implicitly a juvenile preoccupation. Nevertheless, like many correspondents, she overtly takes up a 'fan' subject position while exhibiting an awareness of the devalued status of the fan, seeking to distance herself from it by remarking that this is atypical behaviour. One man even explicitly notes that, until now, he has not written fan letters 'because I've always associated the word "fan" with "fanatics"' (P.P., 20 April 1993, Ontario, 2014.0042.00693).

Making similar efforts to differentiate herself from a teen 'fan girl', this Essex woman materially incorporates Greer into her domestic life:

I have never written to a celebrity before and find it difficult to express how I feel about you without sounding like an adolescent with a crush on a pop star. Let me tell you what form this idolatry takes. Photographs of you in the press and magazines are put on a pinboard in the downstairs loo. My friends phone me when you're on the radio or T.V. so that I don't miss it.

(S.G., 23 March 1989, 2014.0042.00342)

This correspondent is clearly deeply invested in traditional fan practices despite her pointed disclaimer. One writer suggests that she performs this 'unusual' gesture of sending a fan letter, at least in part, to counter the hate mail she presumes Greer is receiving:

This book [*The Whole Woman*] may – as The Female Eunuch – did in its day – bring in the lost women from the four winds. I am impelled to this unusual course of writing a fan letter partly because of the strength of my feeling of solidarity and affection, and relief that you are there; and partly because I am afraid that you must get your share of anti-fan mail.

(B.B., 26 February 1998, London, 2014.0042.00081)

'You are the twentieth century messiah!' **51**

This correspondent rationalises her choice to pen such a supportive epistle because of the fear that Greer may unfairly be subject to much harsher appraisals, a presumption we see across the letters. In this respect, to drown out such odious voices, it is worth taking this epistolary 'risk' as a fan.

Many, such as this Southport man, make clear that it is gratitude that motivates them to take such an uncharacteristic step as sending fan mail: 'I have never before written to an author, TV authority, newspaper or whatever...my real purpose is not to praise but to thank. Thank you for your book, for educating me and for communicating to me' (B.J., 2 June 1972, 2014.0042.00440). As elsewhere, this writer underscores Greer's role as a popular pedagogue, and the articulation of gratitude seems to temper his ambivalence about engaging in seemingly undesirable fan-like behaviours. A woman from Melbourne also sent Greer an effusive fan letter: 'I offer you my continual thanks and gratitude for all you have done in the world, that we are lucky enough to have you publicly available'. She concludes, self-reflexively: 'To sign this letter "an adoring fan" sounds trite and silly, but, that is the truth of it, I am, in fact your adoring fan' (S.A., 1990, 2014.0042.00030). This correspondent, like others, mobilises the gendered characterisation of fandom as superficial and asinine but embraces the fan identity regardless (as we also see in the *Dick Cavett* letters).

Readers suggest that they felt 'compelled' to contact Greer, given how she has transformed their understandings of themselves and the social worlds they inhabit (J.E., 7 February 1972, Ontario, 2014.0042.00247). That is, it is something *extraordinary* about Greer and her feminist writing that has moved them deviate from their normal practice and communicate their ardour; one writes, 'I've never thought of writing a letter to an author before – but your book, your thoughts!' (G.C., undated, Long Beach, 2014.0042.00170). As Ken Plummer notes, 'every letter speaks not just of the writer's world, but also of the writer's perceptions of the recipient' (2001, p. 54). Fans often appear awe-struck, as if they may be approaching a Hollywood star, tentative as they attempt to articulate their admiration and gratitude. These correspondents fear that they are taking liberties by approaching Greer so directly and via such an intimate mode of communication. This sense of unease in performing such communicative gestures is also common in fan letters to other women authors, artists, and actors (Grasso 2013; Coffin 2020; Stead 2021). Women, and they are predominantly women, feel the need to explain themselves, outlining what motivated them to boldly approach the celebrities they admire. Even when writing to a woman author or a high-profile feminist, women ironically apologise for their voice (Daugherty 2006, p. 6). These often autobiographical letters to Greer, therefore, bear similarities to those received by other women celebrities at different points in time.

52 Germaine Greer, Celebrity Feminism and the Archive

'A case history of my personal life': Readerly recognition and identification

Fan mail is, of course, an important form of life writing. In Sidonie Smith and Julia Watson's (2010) framing, Greer can be conceptualised as a 'coaxer' of this kind of epistolary life writing, with her own book eliciting these kinds of personalised responses – particularly given its own autobiographical vignettes (Evans 1999, p. 67; Pearce 2004, p. 31). Overwhelmingly, second-wave texts such as *The Female Eunuch* produce 'a thrill of recognition in their (huge) female readership' (Riley 2015, p. 387). Letter writers commonly tell Greer they see themselves, their lives, or their own philosophies mirrored in her bestselling writing: 'Some of 'The Female Eunuch' – large chunks of it – could almost have been a case history of my personal life' (R., no other details, 2014.0042.00746). Similarly, a woman from Los Angeles notes, 'My story is all over your book, a thousand times over' (B.T., 4 September 1973, 2014.0042.00902).

While Rita Felski's (2008) work on reading and recognition centres on literature (as in fictional texts), it is apposite to feminist blockbusters too. Felski argues that, although 'recognition' has been viewed suspiciously within literary theory, it needs to be taken seriously when considering the work that literary texts do in the world. In feminist terms, moments of 'recognition', as in recognising oneself anew, have been the basis of a transformative politics:

> Something that may have been sensed in a vague, diffuse, or semi-conscious way now takes on a distinct shape, is amplified, heightened, or made newly visible. In a mobile interplay of exteriority and interiority, something that exists outside of me inspires a revised or altered sense of who I am.
>
> (Felski 2008, p. 25)

A shift in cognition is narrated in a number of these epistolary texts, precipitated by Greer's writing along with her celebrity persona: 'One learns how to be oneself by taking one's cue from others who are doing the same' (Felski 2008, p. 26) – for these correspondents, Greer is seen to be that 'other'.

Greer and her writing, therefore, induce complex emotional responses from readers. In her work on feminist periodicals, Barbara Green sees feminist work on affect and emotions, such as Sara Ahmed's, as useful given that they 'direct our attention to the ways in which particular emotional states or moods are experienced as shared ones, communicated in such a way that individuals see themselves as stitched into larger groupings' (2016, p. 364). If fandom involves 'shared affective states' (Hannell 2023, p. 69), then those that unite these geographically dispersed readers are hope and anger – anger not in terms of the cultural object, as those discussed in Hannell's study, but

'You are the twentieth century messiah!' **53**

in terms of the injustices that Greer's book has exposed. A woman from the Isle of White puts it this way, 'I feel inspired, depressed, reassured and angered all at the same time' (A.O., April 1999, 2014.0042.00657). Readers tell Greer that they recognise themselves in her portrayal of women as (or as nearly) 'eunuchs', and this is the source of that anger:

> Your book liberated me to an overwhelming degree. You helped me see the feminine image for the arbitrary falsity it is…Your book first brought me a fierce anger and sense of terror that I had almost become a female eunuch – was almost a castrated human being.
> (L.S., 29 August 1971, Maryland, 2014.0042.00813)

In the 1970s in particular, the self-representational possibilities of letters were central 'in helping the women to find meaning out of the turbulent emotional and political struggles they felt themselves caught up in' (Hughes 2014, p. 897). Correspondents relate to the blockbuster author a life story that is tellable in part because part of Greer's revaluing of women and their experiences (Coffin 2020, p. 91). In a deeply confessional letter, an Ohio woman tells Greer that after reading *Eunuch*, 'Somehow I feel relieved. Now I know specifically why I've been so dissatisfied'. As in this letter, what Friedan referred to as 'the problem with no name' (1963) is mapped by Greer's readers. Women were discontented in their gendered prisons but had no vocabulary for naming it – until consuming *The Female Eunuch* (Lake 2016). Discussing her experiences as a wife and mother and particularly how life changes once women have children, one woman confesses: 'I was dying slowly, very painfully'. She tells Greer of her new mode of being and the response it has garnered:

> I have the broken the circle of routine you write about. I go, do, wear what I want and when I want. I have no routines at all. But others do look upon me with disdain…BUT, I cannot live without freedom.
> (C.M., 23 March 1971, 2014.0042.00526)

Greer helped such women see that their discontentment was political and certainly not anomalous. For this woman, living a feminist life is not without its risks (Ahmed 2017) and is an especially brave but worthwhile choice in the early 1970s.

Readers persistently tell Greer that she has 'verbalised' their own thoughts and feelings in ways they had not previously heard publicly articulated (K.K., 8 September 1971, California, 2014.0042.00470, G.P., 15 August 1971, 2014.0042.00670, H.L., 17 February 1972, Sydney, 2014.0042.00517). For many women, who are unable or unsure about exercising it, Greer is effectively *their* voice: 'You are the articulate voice of many women and you have

54 Germaine Greer, Celebrity Feminism and the Archive

the audience to make yourself heard' (T.A., 22 December 2002, Lincoln, 2014.0042.00003). From bedrooms, kitchens, and studies, readers relate their very personal reading experiences. For example, a Luton woman writes: 'I sat up all night reading your book, "The Female Eunuch" – the most worth while thing I've done in years. You express so simply all that I have felt, and still feel, but have been unable to express' (K.E.R., 4 August 1972, 2014.0042.00728). Greer therefore expresses and cements readers' extant feminist convictions; these women felt they lacked the resources to articulate their discontentment with their gendered roles, but the famous author provides them much-needed clarity (A.B., 1972, 2014.0042.00072, N.B., 24 January 1972, Victoria, 2014.0044.00197): 'So many of the things you write about have been in the back of my mind for some time but it felt very difficult to put those thoughts into some coherent expression' (C.Mc., 2 November 1970, 2014.0042.00548). For this woman, as for many others, her own insights are reaffirmed by Greer's analysis. Women feel that these kinds of everyday epistemologies, which have emerged from their personal experiences, are legitimised by Greer as a feminist authority. Across the letters, readers consistently voice their indebtedness to Greer for such apparent validation.

In terms of the book's pedagogical value, letter writers also credit Greer with teaching them, about themselves, other women, men, or feminism itself. While some readers feel the book confirms their own previously held sentiments, this Californian reader finds the book revelatory as well as educational: 'Thank you for writing your book. It was the most educating book I've ever read. What it helped me to learn was about myself, and in the most personal and direct way. I am grateful for your help' (G.C., undated, Long Beach, 2014.0042.00170). For others, also relating an epistemological shift, reading the book is a useful corrective to press coverage of the book's provocative author (television offers this kind of re-presentation too, as the next chapter shows). For example, a Melbourne woman (J.S., 28 May 1972) writes:

> My sincere thanks for your book "The Female Eunuch". I opened your book with utmost scepticism and feel deeply ashamed that my attitude to you was determined by the popular press. Now I have more of an idea of what "women's lib" is about.
>
> (2014.0042.00834)

Having had a distorted perception of feminism, this reader finds that the act of consuming Greer's book has been illuminating – a trope that dominates the archived correspondence.

'Shaft of daylight': Feminist illuminations

As Felski argues in relation to fictional texts, feminist 'narratives of self-discovery' commonly invoke these sudden, enlightening moments or events

'You are the twentieth century messiah!' **55**

(1989, p. 143). Along these lines, many correspondents characterise the book as illuminating, or as 'flicking a switch' – comments that invoke the transformative 'click' moment common to second-wave CR sessions (Hogeland 1998). Indeed, in Greer's (1969b) initial handwritten summary of the book, she makes this impetus clear: 'I believe that the most important factor in overcoming female castration is the beginning of awareness, otherwise I should not bother with a book at all'. For many correspondents, these moments of self-discovery are crucial to fostering an emergent feminist subjectivity (Coffin 2020). In an intensely personal letter, a woman from Petersham in New South Wales (NSW) tells Greer she had recently left her husband: 'I felt like a complete failure as a wife and mother and was starting to wonder if perhaps I was abnormal. Reading your book was like a ray of sunshine amidst the dark confusion surrounding me' (T.H., 24 January 1972, 2014.0042.00368). As this letter indicates, the expectations of idealised wifely and maternal roles left several letter writers feeling inadequate, unable – or unwilling – to dutifully fulfil them. Greer de-personalised, or rather politicised, this discontentment, precipitating epiphanies that fundamentally altered how they perceived the world and their position therein.

For many *Female Eunuch* readers, then, the book and its celebrity author make it possible for them to see themselves and their personal circumstances, and futures, *otherwise* – a goal about which the book and Greer herself were explicit: 'No writer can hope for anything more than to give people something to think about and to increase the possibilities which people can see open to them' (to M.L., 14 June 1972, Toorak, 2014.0042.00508). Being able to see the world anew is crucial to a viable feminist politics (Ahmed 2004): '"The Female Eunuch" is the book which had the greatest influence of [sic] me. I looked with different eyes on all that was happening to me and began to fight back' (B.B., 19 December 1991, Victoria, 2014.0042.00120). Although feminists heavily criticised the book for its failure to provide implementable solutions to improve women's lives, reader letters suggest that this was not necessarily the case:

> Your book arrived on my scene at a pretty crucial moment; and I thought you might like to know that it has helped me in a thoroughly practical way to examine and judge my situation, motives and prospects more dispassionately than I've ever been able to manage in the past. As a result, one female woman is turning, and the relief is incredible.
>
> (W.M., 19 September 1971, Sussex, 2014.0042.00525)

As these letters confirm, 'Greer wrenched from her very guts a book that shook women into a new way of seeing their situation' (Wallace 1997, p. 352).

In telling Greer about the book's often startling impact, readers give some insights into its wider cultural reverberations. For example, in 1972, a woman from Randwick in NSW writes: 'Pow! That's the impact you've had on me,

56 Germaine Greer, Celebrity Feminism and the Archive

or rather your book…The best way to describe it is to compare myself to an electrical circuit and to tell you that you've thrown the switch' (T.W., 19 March 1972, 2014.0042.01015). The kind of affective jolt evoked here is clearly part of *feeling* differently in order to *know* differently, as Clare Hemmings (2012) describes it, and it is these 'different feelings' that Greer and her celebrity feminism stimulate. Paraphrasing Elspeth Probyn's work on 'feminist reflexivity' (1993), Hemmings notes:

> that reflection on the lack of fit between our own sense of being and the world's judgements upon us constitutes a kind of feminist reflexivity, a *negotiation of the difference* between whom one feels oneself to be and the conditions of possibility for a liveable life.
>
> (2012, p. 148, original emphasis)

As Hemmings further remarks, 'Dissonance *has to* arise if a feminist politics is to emerge' (2012, p. 158, original emphasis) – for many, Greer's book helped either to create or to validate the sense of 'affective dissonance' that is vital to feminism as a transformative vision.

Readers like the one above make clear how their desire for an alternative mode of being and living has been pathologised, with many referring to feeling or being positioned as 'mad' or 'abnormal':

> You make me feel that I can and must keep looking for the kinds of relationships I need and that I'm not mad not to compromise…You brought me hope and comfort which is why I wanted to write to you.
>
> (J.Mc., 9 November 1971, Cambridge, 2014.0042.00548)

This woman comes to a new kind of self-acceptance as well as a new sense of hope (to which I shortly return). Greer helps these readers realise that it is not them but culturally sanctioned femininity that is at fault. Their femininities have been illegible, until they are inscribed in Greer's text – and publicly embodied by Greer herself. As they tell her, Greer validates their alternative subjectivity: they feel they can now *be*, without shame. On 20 October 1971, with some anxiety about approaching the famous author, a Massachusetts woman wrote:

> This is my fifth attempt at a letter to you since I finished reading The Female Eunuch tonight…What I want to say is thank you – your book is the first to dispel the illusions I had about marriage being the panacea for all my woe, insecurities or whatever – to dispel them, to show an alternate way of life, and to give me strength to follow it.
>
> (S., Leominister, 2014.0044.00166)

'You are the twentieth century messiah!' **57**

These letters represent vehicles through which private feelings become public (Cvetovich 2003), even if in terms of an individual addressee. After reading Greer's blockbuster, these writers feel reassured – and relieved – that they are on the right path.

For these correspondents, Greer provides the feminist interpretive framework for re-reading their gendered experiences (Hogeland 1998): 'Your book *The Female Eunuch* astounded and excited me…I am deeply grateful for some of the light you have shed on the problems of my own marriage, and the encouragement you have offered simply by your example' (R.F.B., 8 November 1971, New York, 2014.0044.00168). Such letters offer significant insights into 'the emotional world within and the social and political world without' (Hughes 2014, p. 878). Overwhelmingly, the realisation that their views are shared by other women is a great relief (J.H., 26 February 1975, Kent, 2014.0042.00406); an English expatriate living in Malaysia thanks Greer for helping her realise that she is 'not as alone and odd' as she had thought (J.C., 17 March 1972, Johore, 2014.0042.00137). Greer's text ameliorates their sense of isolation, normalising thoughts and opinions they had thought were aberrant:

> It has been like a shaft of daylight into the confusion of my private thoughts and feelings…How amazing to realize that I am not a freak, and that other women have experienced the same things – especially the lack of confidence in oneself.
>
> (P.R., 20 December 1970, Norfolk, 2014.0042.00732)

Part of a community of readers, and implicitly other feminists, this woman now perceives herself as acting within a feminist sisterhood – which Greer and her book have effectively brought into being. Fandom is a way in which people may do important feminist identity work as well as seek belonging (Hannell 2023), which is certainly the case with these Greer fans. This fan mail is a feminist act; letter writers effectively write new feminist selves into being through narrating their connection to Greer, her books, and implicitly other women readers.

As the letters cited thus far indicate, fans imagine themselves socially connected both to Greer and to a community with shared values/feminisms experiencing the same awakenings (Ciba 2020, p. 115; see also Hannell 2023). Aiding in this sense of an imagined community, Greer writes to reassure correspondents that they are not alone in their struggles. To a Canadian woman who suggests she feels 'alone in her head' (L.O., undated), Greer sympathetically replies: 'There are really many women who feel as you do, according to my mail bag, at least' (13 June 1972, 2014.0042.00648). In her study of soap opera fan mail in the 1980s, Leah Steuer (2019) argues, 'these letters suggest the existence of a social network; the writers gesture to the unseen presence of

58 Germaine Greer, Celebrity Feminism and the Archive

other fans writing letters…the isolated letter writer is also in a fandom and knows it'. Such comments are also apposite to the Greer fan mail, and it is this sense of belonging that they appear to most value. In 1991, for instance, imagining herself to be part of an extensive community of women similarly effected by Greer's epiphanic writing, a woman from Victoria writes: 'Here is another of the many thousands of women who are grateful to you for changing and informing their lives' (B.B., 19 December, Elwood, 2014.0042.00120). As Felski observes, 'Reading may offer a solace and relief not to be found elsewhere, confirming that I am not entirely alone, that there are others who think or feel like me' (2008, p. 33). Women who write to Greer emphasise how central this kind of affirmation has been to their very survival: 'Your book has given me the strength to go on' (M.W., 19 August 1971, Lancashire, 2014.0042.01013).

'I feel reborn': Feminist hope and renewal

As is common in second-wave feminist correspondence, Greer's readers appear 'thrilled by their new sense of selfhood' (Jolly 2008, p. 79). To give some sense of the new – or rather more 'authentic' – self that emerges following the consumption of Greer's book/s, the trope of rebirth recurs throughout the archived correspondence. Of the impact of *The Female Eunuch* on her, one woman self-reflexively writes: 'I don't mean to be trite, but it's rather like being reborn!' (K.B., 15 June 1971, 2014.0044.00168). To signal its transformative effect, many express the sense that their very lives began after reading Greer's book. Almost ten years after its publication, a 33-year-old woman from London writes:

> I don't want to gush but never in my life has anything I've read had such a good effect on me, you made me feel as if your book was written for me, I feel reborn. So many of my feelings and views over the years endorsed and explained.
>
> (J.S., 9 January 1979, 2014.0042.00817)

This trope of becoming feminist as a process of 'rebirth' was a common way of characterising coming to feminism in the 1970s if not beyond (Hope 1999, p. 275). In this respect, there is a temporal demarcation, with periods along women's life courses divided into before and after *The Female Eunuch*: 'For such women, the practice of reading the book becomes 'a "turning point", a defining moment, signalling their metamorphosis, or feminist juncture in their lives' (McGrath 1999, p. 178).

For many women, therefore, Greer provides them with some desperately needed hope: 'Reading your book made me feel hopeful. It made me feel that even if I was banging my head against a wall I wasn't doing it for nothing' (J.Mc., 9 November 1971, Cambridge, 2014.0042.00548). Similarly, another reader describes *The Female Eunuch* as 'hope and fire' (A.A., 16 February

'You are the twentieth century messiah!' **59**

1972, London, 2014.0044.00196). As something of which they had been bereft, finding hope in and through the text and its celebrity author, correspondents are able to envision a different future. In this way, hope serves a crucial political function: 'To express hope for another kind of world, one that is unimaginable at present, is a political action' (Ahmed 2004, p. 186). As Ahmed further notes, 'hope is what allows us to feel that what angers us is not inevitable, even if transformation can sometimes feel impossible' (2004, p. 184). For these correspondents, Greer aids them to envisage this "not yet" and provides the encouragement to seek its actualisation. A woman from Washington writes, 'Each time I picked up the book it was like taking some sort of vitamin or tonic for my soul, for my integrity as a woman' (D.B., 1971, 2014.0044.00168). As a form of 'tonic', the book refreshes and revitalises women who have been depleted in their years as unappreciated wives and mothers. In this respect, Greer and her books are often framed as significant forms of comfort during difficult times in women's lives; a Manitoba woman writes that *The Change* 'helped me get through a couple of nasty years' (L.C., 18 April 1997, 2014.0042.00171).

While Greer's books bring readers much solace in their difficult personal circumstances, Greer herself is often celebrated for her courage in embodying a new form of feminine subjectivity: 'We love you, you brave lady!' (D.G., 2 April 1972, Hobart, 2014.0042.00343). That Greer is a role model worthy of emulation features throughout the letters; readers aspire to become more like the feisty feminist. Thanking her for all her books, as well as her 1970s journalism, a Mansfield woman makes this explicit: 'Germaine, you are my hero, my role model, my spiritual guide and my respected elder sister' (T.T., 2 February 1999, 2014.0042.00889). Drawing upon intertextual knowledge of Greer's public persona, another asserts: 'Your whole life is awe inspiring, and it changes others' lives; I would personally like to thank you for changing mine' (A.L., 27 July 2001, Glasgow, 2014.0042.00485). In media commentary as well as in these letters, Greer is seen as 'the epitome of the liberated woman' (Murray 2004, p. 198). As an inspirational figure, Greer moves women to action across her career. With *The Change*, Greer is seen as the embodiment of what is possible for the ageing woman: 'I guess that at fifty-one, struggling still to reach that more detached place you seem to have touched, I'm reassured and refreshed by your experience, your book and your example' (I.Mc., 24 October 1993, Sheffield, 2014.0042.00551).

Readers tell Greer of the feminist forms of 'everyday resistance' in which she has inspired them to engage, the kinds of micropolitical actions through which they have enacted their own 'vernacular feminism' (Lusty 2017, p. 219). When she was a 28-year-old teacher (30 June 1971, 2014.0042.00308), famous Australian author Helen Garner – whose own later feminist blockbuster, *The First Stone* (1995), precipitated an unprecedented feminist media event (Taylor 2008) – says she effectively channels Greer to help deal with bad behaviour from male teaching staff:

60 Germaine Greer, Celebrity Feminism and the Archive

whenever I feel that awful feminine deference eroding my urge to argue back, I call to mind your picture on the back of The Female Eunuch. [A]nd I think, 'F---, SHE wouldn't stand here silent, and neither will I'. And I don't (as cited in McColl 2017).

As these letters make clear, Greer herself functioned as 'an example to women of what it meant to live a feminist life' (Arrow and Arrow 2011, p. 12) – and this is precisely how they addressed her. For many readers, Greer herself is seen as the opposite of the eunuch interrogated in her first blockbuster and, later, the empowered post-menopausal woman she urged readers to become through *The Change*. In this respect, despite her celebrity status, she represents what is possible for women (McGrath 1999).

'Spreading the word': Familial and religious tropes and metaphors

Perhaps unsurprisingly, given the persistence of such metaphors in feminist writing (Henry 2004; Taylor 2008), and indicative of the intimacy they feel that they share with Greer, writers commonly position her in familial roles. Referring to Greer as an 'intellectual and spiritual mother', an English woman remarks: 'You were a major catalyst in my personal development…Everything began with your book and took off from there. I want to thank and let you know that I consider myself one of your daughters' (A.C., undated, Lewes, 2014.0042.00145). An Australian writer expresses gratitude to Greer (who has herself remained childfree) for her '"mothering" of women, especially myself' (J.S., 21 June 1992, Charleville, 2014.0042.00807). Others express the joy of sisterhood, a key second-wave trope for describing the solidarity between women: 'I felt like I was talking to a person, a person who cared and understood. You have a sister in me' (G.C., undated, Long Beach, 2014.0042.00170).

Many speak in terms of 'converting' others to Greer's particular brand of feminism, after themselves experiencing such a conversion. In evangelical rhetoric, readers commit to 'spreading the word', giving others the benefit of the feminist wisdom Greer has imparted to them. The 'disciple' trope is common in these letters and aligns with the persistent positioning of Greer's books as feminist 'bibles':

I have just finished reading your book, 'The Female Eunuch'…I find it impossible to continue believing ignorance is bliss. Thank for you for supplying the push that I needed. You've got yourself a disciple, whether you like it or not, and I'm going to do my best to find you a few more.

(A.W., undated, Liverpool, 2014.0042.01009)

This sense of evangelising is also evident from this Californian woman, 'I'm spreading the word – I celebrate your book!' (G.P., 15 August 1971,

'You are the twentieth century messiah!' **61**

2014.0042.00670). This compulsion to 'spread the word' after reading *The Female Eunuch* recurs, even from within religious circles. For example, a nun from Maitland in NSW tells Greer (S.L.D., 20 December 1971, 2014.0042.00206):

> On behalf of many members of this community of Dominican sisters, I want to write and thank you for <u>The Female Eunuch</u>...Believe me, you have won us to the revolution – your words of advice have been taken to heart, and we, as educators, as an order devoted to Truth, will study, and spread your ideas.

(The top of the letter reads, in Greer's handwriting, 'Spoke to her.') Here, feminism becomes a kind of proselytising, with the 'disciples' Greer's book has produced taking pedagogical action in the world, recruiting others to make similar attachments to feminism.

While fan investments are implicit in many of these epistles, idolatry is explicit in this letter from a Christchurch woman (whose words feature in this chapter's title): 'You are the twentieth century women's messiah! I love you. PS I don't know how you have done what you have done' (J., April 1974, 2014.0042.00440). By positioning her as a messianic figure, of whom she is in awe, this letter writer gives a clear sense of Greer as a transformational, exceptional woman worthy of audience devotion and fannish intensities. For this writer, Greer may be unaware of the immense impact she has had on women's lives; thus, she feels compelled to inform her and encourage her to continue her valiant efforts. Another tells her: 'My husband refers to your book as my Bible, and is very rude about it, I hope that your knew [sic] book will be in print soon and I shall have two Bibles to confound him with' (Anon., undated, 2014.0042.00027). As texts comparable to the 'bible', Greer's bestsellers are seen as guidebooks, despite the careful attention she pays to ensuring that women do not substitute one form of authority (men's, patriarchy's) for another (hers, feminism's).

Greer's third feminist blockbuster, *The Change* (1991), which can be described as what Kelly O'Donnell (2019) dubs 'popular health feminism', was also framed in biblical terms. After so describing the book, one reader suggests that it helped change the course of her medical treatment: 'I was wandering around W.H. Smith when I saw you book and bought it, threw away the horrible pills and now carrying on with my life as I know it should be and looking towards the future' (V.H., 13 January 1994, Hertfordshire, 2014.0042.00408). This letter indicates that Greer was having a real impact on women's lives and, importantly here, their bodies. As in this instance, Greer's critique of the patriarchal medical establishment deeply resonated with readers who were disillusioned by the medicalisation of menopause. Overwhelmingly, Greer's persuasive feminist reframing of this transitional phase in women's lives is seen as a welcome change to the dominant public

62 Germaine Greer, Celebrity Feminism and the Archive

narratives of loss. The book is consistently viewed as vital to women's efforts to make sense of the menopause outside these limited discursive frames, even years after its publication: 'Your book "The Change" was a "bible" that offered me such wisdom as I endured the menopause. It encouraged my own inclinations to see my maturity as a welcome stepping aside from youthful pressures' (E.B., 27 April 2000, Brunswick, 2014.0042.00123). Many women agreed with Greer's claim that menopause ushers in a new phase of empowerment, one in which they are no longer subject to the male gaze or pressured to conform to restrictive gender roles. Moreover, with *The Change*, Greer had validated women's own knowledges about their embodied experiences of the menopause, for which they are enormously grateful. Nevertheless, she resists their attempts to position her as an authority.

'Women's liberation is what you make it': Greer challenges prescriptivism

To varying degrees, correspondents implored the famous feminist for advice or assistance – whether a book recommendation, a nearby CR group, how to escape a stagnate marriage, overcome depression, or manage menopausal symptoms. In her recent study of letters to Beauvoir, Coffin (2020) reveals that, for readers, the famous existential philosopher functions as a kind of 'agony aunt'. She argues that Beauvoir's celebrity, including photographs and profiles in popular newspapers and magazines, rendered her 'approachable'; she was so present, in her writings but also in other forms of mass culture, that correspondents felt – as fans of celebrities always do, if fame has worked (Dyer 1979) – that they 'really knew' her.[3] To Greer, one Californian woman even makes this explicit: 'Your open and honest style made me feel that I have come to know you as a person' (G.P., 15 August 1971, 2014.0042.00670). Like Beauvoir's, Greer's star image circulated widely with profiles in *Life*, *Vogue*, *Rolling Stone*, *Playboy*, and the *Australian Women's Weekly*, creating the sense of accessibility that would lead fans to approach her in this way (Grasso 2013, p. 27). In this respect, Greer's public persona becomes a crucial form of paratext for those who consume her writing (Genette 1997).

Sharing intimate details of their lives was something that Greer's letter writers also did in spades, but unlike Beauvoir she resisted their attempts to position her as an authoritative voice who could tell them the path they should take. In Greer's case, fans often seek her guidance, predominantly in terms of what they should do to become active in the feminist struggle. These letters make clear that Greer, like Beauvoir, 'had many more resources, discursive and other, than most of those who wrote to her', evidencing a series of author–reader inequalities (Coffin 2020, p. 21). In her replies, which are concentrated around the 1970s and became fewer and briefer as her career progressed (Glanville 2017), Greer refuses to speak on behalf of the women's movement. For instance, in response to a letter seeking her views on prostitution, Greer commences her reply (to J.A., 8 April 1976, 2014.0042.00013):

> Thank you for your long letter, which was addressed to me at least partly because you think that I can make statements on behalf of the Women's Liberation Movement. I cannot. Whatever I think or say about prostitution is what I think, no more but so.
>
> (original emphasis)

These kinds of dialogic exchanges suggest the esteem in which Greer holds her correspondents, as she engages thoughtfully with them on crucial personal and political matters.

Greer, however, resists requests for definitions; in response to a writer seeking more details regarding the 'aims and objectives of women's lib' (J.B., 2 July 1972, South Devon, 2014.0044.00197), she writes that this is 'beyond the scope of one letter to describe' but adds: 'Generally speaking, the aims of feminists can be summed up as all those rights and facilities which will enable women to develop their full potential' (7 August 1972). She concludes by offering whatever she can to help achieve feminist goals:

> Women's liberation is what you make it, even if you simply decide to set up a baby-sitting co-operative. If you feel you need some literature to help discussions get off the ground, don't hesitate to get in touch with me again.

Such letters disrupt assumptions that Greer refused to be involved in any collectivist struggles or activist labour or that she did not offer women any practical help (Goodman 1971).

As in her initial polemic, which was by no means prescriptive, Greer is often reluctant to give advice to readers who seek it through personal correspondence. A woman from London, like those who speak of a fog lifting or switch being flicked, writes to Greer on 16 February 1972 (A.A., 2014.0044.00196): 'I have read The Female Eunuch. It is clarity in my confusion.' Telling Greer she needs her advice on how to 'actively participate', she asks if she can go and see her in Warwick. Greer replies (13 June 1972):

> The first significant act of any woman who wishes to liberate herself is to decide what she must do. We have taken advice our whole lives. It is time at last to stop. I do not wish to replace the omnipotent male in his advisory capacity to the female sex.

This approach is, of course, aligned with the text itself (and Greer's libertarianism), wherein she places the onus back on women to forge their own path towards liberation.

64 Germaine Greer, Celebrity Feminism and the Archive

A 15-year-old school girl (J.B., 29 October 1971, 2014.0044.00168) from Somerset also appeals to Greer for advice:

> On reading your book recently The Female Eunuch I was very impressed and determined to do all sorts of high minded acts and devote my life to my own and others [sic] liberation. Unfortunately that rush of ferment has died down a little and left me puzzled as to how to act...I find that everything is propelling me along the path of conforming.

In response to her comments that she is being influenced by others in her life, including her father, Greer replies, underscoring the need for self-determination (7 June 1972):

> But you must convince yourself and not allow other people to brainwash you or to exploit you by asserting their authority. That by the way, includes me, and that is one reason why I did not give any set of rules in my book.

While the book was criticised on the grounds of its failure to offer a practical manifesto, Greer makes explicit that this was a deliberate part of her own feminist strategy. As part of that approach, she encourages these correspondents not to defer to others but to exercise their agency as women, determining their own life course rather than being manipulated by others – be it their husbands, fathers, or bestselling authors.

Despite such advice (or lack thereof), Greer is encouraging to women who wish to learn from her, even if refusing to adopt the pedagogical role they seek. For example, a woman (S.A., 1972) wrote to Greer to see if she would help her, in the form of 'training', in her expressed goal to 'win things for women'. She continues, 'I could work for you in any capacity I can, and learn from you'. Greer's reply is gracious and encouraging, though she notes 'I really don't feel equipped to train anyone at all...'. Nevertheless, she concludes: 'Don't despair and please don't give up. Your sister, Germaine Greer' (14 May 1972, 2014.0042.00032). While reluctant to become a figure of authority in women's lives, Greer did offer practical support for struggling readers. Noting she is reading *The Female Eunuch*, a Hertfordshire woman (M.H., 3 November 1973, 2014.0042.00391) writes of her misery in her marriage, wherein her husband gives her little money, let alone any form of emotional support (including for her studies). Greer's secretary sends her a list of organisations and support services, while Greer replies personally to offer support and to encourage her to keep in touch (11 December 1973): 'You ought not to struggle on alone, whatever happens'. In offering very practical support and guidance, Greer was filling a gap, upon which scholars have remarked. As Agatha Beins notes, 'the *existence* of feminism in the 1970s could be taken for granted, but the *locations* of feminism could not. Women knew that *spaces* for feminism existed but could not find the *places* where it materialized' (2017, p. 42, original emphasis). In this instance, while uncomfortable with being idolised, Greer acted as a willing conduit to these spaces, therefore suggesting a very tangible impact on women's lives. This kind of networking, in and through letters, 'was crucial to [the women's movement's] sustenance' (Jolly 2008, p. 4).

'My credo': The ongoing cultural reverberations of *The Female Eunuch*

Rather than simply being confined to the book's initial publication in the early 1970s, *The Female Eunuch* continues to reverberate through the decades, not least because of Greer's ongoing media visibility and her later blockbusters. That is, the letters reveal the enduring impact of the book and its author. For many, while their Greer fandom may have commenced with *The Female Eunuch*, it extends across their lives. As one Canadian man put it, 'It all started of course with "The Female Eunuch" and continues to the present day' (P.P., April 1993, Ontario, 2014.0042.00693). The letters also offer insights into the reading process itself, and especially the act of re-reading, as many readers return, again and again, to *The Female Eunuch*. Indeed, as Henry Jenkins argues, re-reading is central to and evidence of fan pleasure (1992, p. 69). A man from Oxford tells her, invoking the book's joyfulness, as many do,

> I returned to The Female Eunuch and found it to be a joyous, personal and nurturing manifesto for *now*. I loved its gentleness, rejection of various kinds of shame, and courage – and I felt that it gave me much-needed courage to take action.
> (C.B., 19 April 1996, 2014.0042.00075, original emphasis)

For a number of letter writers, the book has made such a lasting impression that they are motivated to contact Greer years after their initial consumption. Readers are keen to ensure that Greer knows the extent of her blockbuster's impact over time, as in this instance: 'I read "The Female Eunuch" several years ago and it deeply affected me and my attitude to myself and to life' (V.B., 24 October 1979, 2014.0042.00072). Similarly, a woman from Bangor in Northern Ireland (G., 17 March 1999, 2014.0042.00317) writes: 'I read *The Female Eunuch* thirteen years ago while at university and embraced it as my credo'. As for other correspondents, Greer's book is seen to have deeply informed their lifelong personal beliefs.

For many readers of *The Whole Woman* (1999), Greer's 'sequel' to her first blockbuster, wherein she contested narratives of feminist progress and

66 Germaine Greer, Celebrity Feminism and the Archive

implored readers 'to get angry again', it is clear they are reading the book intertextually, which its extensive marketing campaign encouraged.[4] After reading the follow-up, a Hampshire woman writes:

> The Female Eunuch changed myself and my female friends for the better when we were lucky enough to be given it as an A level set text. You say it's time to get angry again, but I wouldn't understand <u>why</u> I was angry if it wasn't for the Female Eunuch.
>
> (T.Y.T., 15 June 1999, 2014.004200892, original emphasis)

Likewise, a Bristol woman, writing to Greer in appreciation for *The Change*, took the opportunity to reflect upon the impact of her earlier work:

> I need to tell you of the profound influence the Female Eunuch had on me in the early 70's as I sat in my neat and respectable suburban home in Melbourne playing Mother and wife. It left me with a sense that someone out there understood the dilemma and disappointment I felt with my life and why I experienced so much guilt for having these feelings.
>
> (6 October 1992, 2014.0042.00805)

Twenty years on, this correspondent gratefully recounts the transformative effect of *The Female Eunuch*.

Many position Greer's blockbusters as part of an overarching feminist project, achieving the same ends despite their different focus, contexts, and arguments. A woman from Sydney's Double Bay (9 January 1992) observes: 'I am reading The Change and love it. It is as full of "Aha" responses as *The Female Eunuch*' (K.P.P., 2014.042.00700). Here, the CR 'click' moment is also attributed to Greer's refiguration of menopause, enabling an ontological and epistemological shift regarding this hitherto largely invisible period in women's lives. Likewise, a Mansfield woman outlines Greer's formative role at various stages of her life:

> *The Female Eunuch* affirmed my suspicions about patriarchy when I was an earnest and budding feminist during the 1970s...as I grow towards another change in my life cycle [referencing *The Change*], it is the words of Germaine Greer that shape and inform my development.
>
> (T.T., 2 February 1999, 2014.0042.00889)

This correspondent concludes, 'You have provided signposts along the way for me and for many thousands of other women. We thank you'. Here, as throughout Greer's archived correspondence, the writer locates herself in a much wider community of grateful women that Greer impacted across their lives.

'You are the twentieth century messiah!' **67**

In addition to those who have been lifelong fans or followers of Greer, the iconic feminist's later books lead readers to her first blockbuster – much like the television appearances analysed in the following chapter. For example, in 2001, a 16-year-old girl from Glasgow writes to praise Greer for both *The Whole Woman* and *The Female Eunuch* (A.L., 27 July, 2014.0042.00485):

> As soon as I read the words "it's time to get angry again", I knew I was right. Your book showed me that my strong feelings were not surplus to requirements, and I could begin to prove to myself my own convictions could be trusted. Two or three months later, I bought "The Female Eunuch". Again I was surprised to find that what I was thinking was what you were writing.

Despite the temporal distance and the generational disparities, this correspondent sees herself as one of Greer's addressees – in the past and in the present. Greer's words, as well as her own example, are seen as life-changing. As many of these letters indicate, Greer's position as an 'enlightener' by no means ended with *The Female Eunuch* but continued through her subsequent blockbusters (along with her journalism and television, as following chapters demonstrate).

Conclusion

The General Correspondence series in the Greer archive is one of the largest contained therein, and Greer's curatorial practice of alphabetising these letters encourages researchers to engage with a much larger sample than perhaps would otherwise have been the case. Her desire of foregrounding 'ordinary' correspondents through her self-reflexive archival processes has, at least in this instance, succeeded. As my analysis has established, a wide spectrum of the community wrote to express their love, gratitude, and admiration for this often controversial figure. Their motivations for doing so vary; sometimes they seek something from Greer (advice or, more materially, an autographed picture), but in most cases they merely wish her to know that she had changed their lives. However, Greer has publicly responded to such claims a number of times, underscoring that it was not her but the women themselves who were responsible for such transformations.[5] Nevertheless, her various modes of cultural production but especially her blockbusters, alongside her public feminist persona, do appear to have helped precipitate some kind of cognitive shift akin to 'consciousness-raising' in audiences, which itself often does lead to feminist action – be it leaving a stale marriage or volunteering in a women's organisation.

Through such acts of epistolary self-construction, as I have argued, women appear to write themselves into being in new ways. The overwhelming sentiment in these letters is that Greer has managed to capture and publicly

68 Germaine Greer, Celebrity Feminism and the Archive

articulate the way women were feeling and that she has given them some much needed hope, and they write with deep affection for her. The kind of 'feminist reflexivity' that Greer inspires reveals the crucial role that such figures play in precipitating both personal and structural change. Moreover, they express gratitude to Greer for raising not just their consciousness but those of other women – they identify themselves as part of a collective project, even if not active women's liberationists. For her part, Greer appreciates these correspondents and their affective labour, commonly replying that they cannot imagine how much such letters mean to her.[6]

Many of these writers seek to define themselves in opposition to a certain image of the 'fan', all the while engaging in behaviours entirely consistent with fandom. These letters also suggest that fans of celebrity feminists share many characteristics with other forms of fan communities, even if participation in such communities is only imagined. Their overtly political nature perhaps differentiates them from other forms of fandom in significant ways. *Fans of feminists are feminist fans*, an important distinction that requires further scholarly attention. Forging intimate connections with Greer, these letter writers share what she and the feminism she has come to represent have meant to them and how she has informed their ways of being in the world. In the next chapter, I focus on how Greer has sought to use television to widely prosecute her feminist vision across her career, with viewer letters suggesting that she has been largely successful.

Notes

1 Index cards for the book have been digitised and reveal the depth of this scholarship.
2 While the overwhelming majority of letters analysed here are from this series, the Early Years series (2014.0044) has two folders of letters from 1971, upon which I also draw here.
3 As Richard Dyer argues in *Heavenly Bodies*, 'the whole media construction of stars encourages us to think in terms of "really"' (1986, p. 52).
4 The archive contains much campaign material relating to the promotion of *The Whole Woman* (2014.0052.0040).
5 For example, on the ABC documentary *Brilliant Creatures* (2014), she remarks of *The Female Eunuch* readers: 'I always say: I didn't change your life, you changed your life, and if I was any help in that process I am grateful and touched, but I didn't change your life.'
6 This reply, in response to a letter about *The Change*, is typical: 'You cannot imagine what it means to get a letter like yours after writing a book like mine. I don't care what reviewers say, but I do care what women think, and whether I am any help to them. Thank you so much' (to P.C., 30 September 1991, Cambridgeshire, 2014.0042.00171).

References

Ahmed, S. (2004) *The Cultural Politics of Emotion*, Edinburgh: Edinburgh University Press.

'You are the twentieth century messiah!' **69**

Ahmed, S. (2017) *Living a Feminist Life*, Durham: Duke University Press.

Arrow, M. (2007) 'IT HAS BECOME MY PERSONAL ANTHEM: 'I Am Woman', Popular Culture and 1970s Feminism', *Australian Feminist Studies*, vol. 22, no. 53: 213–230.

Arrow, M. (2019) *The Seventies: The Personal, the Political and The Making of Modern Australia*, Sydney: New South Press.

Arrow, M. and Arrow, J. (2011) '"The high priestess of women's lib": Germaine Greer and the Australian Women's Liberation Movement', *Teaching History*, vol. 45, no. 2: 11–13.

Beins, A. (2017) *Liberation in Print: Feminist Periodicals and Social Movement Identity*, Atlanta: University of Georgia Press.

Bennett, J. (2010) *Television Personalities: Stardom and the Small Screen*, London: Routledge.

Borges, M.J. (2020) 'Narratives of the Self', in K. Barclay, S. Crozier-de Rosa, and P.N. Stearns (eds.), *Sources for the History of Emotions: A Guide*, London: Routledge, pp. 99–113.

Ciba, D. (2020) 'Williams's Queer Fan Mail and Collective Memory', *The Tennessee Williams Annual Review*, vol. 19: 109–135.

Coffin, J. (2020) *Sex, Love, and Letters: Writing Simone de Beauvoir*, New York: Cornell University Press.

Cvetovich, A. (2003) *An Archive of Feelings: Trauma, Sexuality, and Lesbian Public Cultures*, Durham: Duke University Press.

Daugherty, B.R. (2006) '"You see you kind of belong to us, and what you do matters enormously": Letters from Readers to Virginia Woolf', *Woolf Studies Annual*, vol. 12: 1–12.

Dyer, R. (1979) *Stars*, London: Routledge.

Dyer, R. (1986) *Heavenly Bodies: Film Stars and Society*, London: Routledge.

Evans, M. (1999) *Missing Persons: The Impossibility of Auto/biography*, London: Psychology Press.

Felski, R. (1989) *Beyond Feminist Aesthetics: Feminist Literature and Social Change*, Cambridge, MA: Harvard University Press.

Felski, R. (2008) *Uses of Literature*, London: Wiley Blackwell.

Firkus, A. (2021) *America's Early Women Celebrities: The Famous and Scorned from Martha Washington to Silent Film Star Mary Fuller*, London: McFarland.

Friedan, B. (1963) *The Feminine Mystique*, New York: W.W. Norton.

Garg, D. (2022) 'Diversifying Fan Methodologies and Inquiries', in C. Lam, J. Raphael, R. Middlemost and J. Balanzategui (eds.), *Fame and Fandom: Functioning On and Offline*, University of Iowa Press, pp. 13–29.

Garner, H. (1995) *The First Stone: Sex Questions about Sex and Power*, Sydney: Picador.

Genette, J. (1997) *Paratexts: Thresholds of Interpretation*, Cambridge: Cambridge University Press.

Germaine Greer Archive, General Correspondence, 2014.0042, University of Melbourne.

Glanville, L. (2017) 'Friday Essay: Reading Germaine Greer's Mail', *The Conversation*, 24 March, available from: https://theconversation.com/friday-essay-reading-germaine-greers-mail-74693

Goodman, E. (1971) 'Greer on Lib: Talk, No Tactics', *The Boston Globe*, Early Years, Germaine Greer Archive, 2014.0044.00171, University of Melbourne.

Grasso, L.M. (2013) '"You are no stranger to me" Georgia O'Keeffe's Fan Mail', *Reception: Texts, Readers, Audiences, History*, vol. 5 no. 1: 24–40.

Green, B. (2016) 'The Feel of the Feminist Network: Votes for Women after *The Suffragette*', *Women: A Cultural Review*, vol. 27, no. 4: 359–377.

Greer, G. (1969a) 'The Universal Tonguebath: A Groupie's Vision', *Oz*, 19 March: 30–33.

Greer, G. (1969b) '*The Female Eunuch* Editorial', Germaine Greer Archive, University of Melbourne, accessed via: http://hdl.handle.net/11343/42289

Greer, G. (1970) *The Female Eunuch*, London: Paladin.

Greer, G. (1991) *The Change*, London: Hamish Hamilton.

Greer, G. (1999) *The Whole Woman*, London: Doubleday.

Hannell, B. (2023) *Feminist Fandom: Media Fandom, Digital Feminisms, and Tumblr*, London: Bloomsbury Academic.

Harker, J. and Konchar Farr, C. (2016) 'Introduction', in J. Harker and C. Konchar Farr (eds.), *This Book Is an Action: Feminist Print Culture and Activist Aesthetics*, Chicago: University of Illinois Press, pp. 1–22.

Hemmings, C. (2012) 'Affective Solidarity: Feminist Reflexivity and Political Transformation', *Feminist Theory*, vol. 13, no. 2: 147–161.

Henry, A. (2004) *Not My Mother's Sister: Generational Conflict and Third Wave Feminism*, Bloomington: Indiana University Press.

Hills, M. (2018) 'Implicit Fandom in the Fields of Theatre, Art, and Literature: Studying "Fans" Beyond Fan Discourses', in P. Booth (ed.), *Companion to Media Fandom and Fan Studies*, London: Wiley, pp. 477–494.

Hogeland, L. (1998) *Feminism and Its Fictions: Consciousness-raising Novel and the Women's Liberation Movement*, University of Pennsylvania Press.

Hope, D.S. (1999) 'Love, Work, and Activism', *Women's Studies Quarterly*, vol. 27, no. 3/4: 275–278.

Hughes, C. (2014) 'Left Activism, Succour and Selfhood: The Epistolary Friendship of Two Revolutionary Mothers in 1970s Britain', *Women's History Review*, vol. 23, no. 6: 874–902.

Jenkins, H. (1992) *Textual Poachers: Television Fans and Participatory Culture*, New York: Routledge.

Jenkins, H. (2006) *Convergence Culture: Where Old and New Media Collide*, New York: New York University Press.

Jenson, J. (1992) 'Fandom as Pathology: The Consequences of Characterization', in L. Lewis (ed.), *The Adoring Audience: Fan Culture and Popular Media*, New York: Routledge, pp. 9–29.

Jolly, M. (2008) *In Love and Struggle: Letters in Contemporary Feminism*, New York: Columbia University Press.

Jong, E. (1973) *Fear of Flying*, New York: Holt, Rinehart and Winston.

Kline, W. (2005) '"Please Include This in Your Book": Readers Respond to *Our Bodies, Ourselves*', *Bulletin of the History of Medicine*, vol. 79, no. 1: 81–110.

Lake, M. (2016) '"Revolution for the hell of it": The Transatlantic Genesis and Serial Provocations of *The Female Eunuch*', *Australian Feminist Studies*, vol. 31, no. 87: 7–21.

Lehmann-Haupt, C. (1971) 'The Best Feminist Book So Far', *New York Times*, 20 April, Germaine Greer Archive, Early Years, 2014.0044.00171, University of Melbourne.

Lehrmann, N. (1972) 'Germaine Greer: A Candid Conversation with the Ballsy Author of "The Female Eunuch"', *Playboy*, January: 61–82.

Le Masurier, M. (2009) 'Desiring the (Popular Feminist) Reader: Letters to *Cleo* During the Second Wave', *Media International Australia*, vol. 131: 106–116.

Lilburn, S., Magarey, S., and Sheridan, S. (2000) 'Celebrity Feminism as Synthesis: Germaine Greer, *The Female Eunuch* and the Australian Print Media', *Continuum*, vol. 14, no. 3: 335–348.

Lusty, N. (2017) 'Riot Grrrl Manifestos and Radical Vernacular Feminism', *Australian Feminist Studies*, vol. 32, no. 93: 219–239.

Marcus, S. (2019) *The Drama of Celebrity*, Princeton, NJ: Princeton University.

McColl, G. (2017) 'International Women's Day 2017: Secrets revealed in Germaine Greer's archives', *The Age*, 24 February, accessed via: https://www.theage.com.au/national/victoria/international-womens-day-2017-secrets-revealed-in-germaine-greers-archives-20170224-gukbyv.html

McGrath, A. (1999) '*The Female Eunuch* in the Suburbs: Reflections on Adolescence, Autobiography, and History-Writing', *Journal of Popular Culture*, vol. 33, no. 1: 177–190.

Murray, S. (2004) *Mixed Media: Feminism and Publishing Politics*, London: Pluto.

O'Donnell, K. (2019) 'Our Doctors, Ourselves: Barbara Seaman and Popular Health Feminism in the 1970s', *Bulletin of the History of Medicine*, vol. 93, no. 4: 550–576.

Pearce, L. (2004) *The Rhetoric of Feminism: Readings in Contemporary Cultural Theory and the Popular Press*, London: Routledge.

Plummer, K. (2001) *Documents of Life 2: An Invitation to A Critical Humanism*, London: Sage.

Probyn, E. (1993) *Sexing the Self: Gendered Positions in Cultural Studies*, London: Routledge.

Riley, C. (2015) 'The Intersections between Early Feminist Polemic and Publishing: How Books Changed Lives in the Second Wave', *Women: A Cultural Review*, vol. 26, no. 4: 384–401.

Rojek, C. (2015) *Presuming Intimacy: Parasocial Interaction in Media Society and Celebrity Culture*, London: Polity.

Rowlands, S. and Henderson, M. (1996) 'Damned Bores and Slick Sisters: The Selling of Blockbuster Feminism in Australia', *Australian Feminist Studies*, vol. 11, no. 23: 9–16.

Samer, J. (2023) *Lesbian Potentiality and Feminist Media in the 1970s*, Durham: Duke University Press.

Sandvoss, C. (2005) *Fans: The Mirror of Consumption*, Malden: Polity Press.

Sheehan, R.J. (2016) '"If we had more like her we would no longer be the unheard majority": Germaine Greer's Reception in the United States', *Australian Feminist Studies*, vol. 31, no. 87: 62–77.

Smith, S. and Watson, J. (2010) *Reading Autobiography: A Guide for Interpreting Life Narratives*, Minneapolis: University of Minnesota Press.

Stead, L. (2021) *Reframing Vivien Leigh: Stardom, Gender, and the Archive*, Oxford: Oxford University Press.

Steuer, L. (2019) 'Structural Affects of Soap Opera Fan Correspondence, 1970s–80s', *Transformative Works*, no. 30, accessed via: https://journal.transformativeworks.org/index.php/twc/article/download/1735/2209?inline=1

Taylor, A. (2008) *Mediating Australian Feminism*, Oxford: Peter Lang.

Taylor, A. (2016) *Celebrity and the Feminist Blockbuster*, Basingstoke: Palgrave Macmillan.

Taylor, A., Dever, M., and Adkins, L. (2016) 'Greer Now: Editorial', *Australian Feminist Studies*, vol. 31, no. 87: 1–6.

The Female Eunuch US book tour schedules (1970), Germaine Greer Archive, Correspondence with Publishers, 2014.0052.00073, University of Melbourne.

Wallace, C. (1997) *Greer: Untamed Shrew*, Sydney: Macmillan.

Whelehan, I. (2005) *The Feminist Bestseller: From Sex and the Single Girl to Sex and the City*, London: Palgrave Macmillan.

Wu, Y. (2016) 'Closely, Consciously Reading Feminism', in J. Harker and C. Konchar Farr (eds.), *This Book Is an Action: Feminist Print Culture and Activist Aesthetics*, Chicago: University of Illinois Press, pp. 88–110.

Young, S. (1997) *Changing the Wor(l)d: Discourse, Politics, and the Feminist Movement*, New York: Routledge.

3

'THE BEST THING TO HAPPEN TO NIGHT-TIME TELEVISION'

Consuming the Televisual Greer

Introduction

Television has always been crucial to Greer's cultural visibility, to maintaining and extending her celebrity capital, and to reaching large audiences who perhaps may not have otherwise engaged with (her) feminism. For many, such as this grateful woman from Stockport, it was television that brought the iconoclastic Greer into her life: 'I do believe television is an opiate, but how would I have known of your existence, otherwise?' (R.A., 21 May 1973, 2014.0042.00038). Greer has, I argue, long functioned as a *feminist television personality*, a mode of celebrity feminism which remains un-theorised, perhaps due to its relative rareness. As forms characterised by immediacy, talk and reality television are crucial to creating the sense of intimacy, accessibility, and – that slippery notion upon which celebrity relies – 'authenticity'. The 'televisual personality' needs to be considered as a specific form of fame, with its own internal logics and variegations (Bennett 2010), but Greer is a unique case in that television is only *one* of the modes via which she has constructed and maintained her public visibility.

Most importantly, as I argue, Greer's television work represents a crucial form of little acknowledged on-screen celebrity feminist activism across decades. Television is not merely a site for the promotion of Greer's other feminist work, as Frances Bonner (2002) argues, it is the very *site* of that work (Brady 2021). That is, like the other forms examined here, Greer's television performances constitute important forms of feminist labour that enable her to reach diverse audiences. Television is not merely where feminism is represented, then, it is where the activist work of celebrity feminism itself is done.

DOI: 10.4324/9781315179841-4

74 Germaine Greer, Celebrity Feminism and the Archive

Moreover, Greer's televisual persona across genres differs little from that found in other modes of cultural production, and, as their letters illuminate, viewers (to different degrees) bring to bear their intertextual knowledge of the celebrity 'Greer' to their television consumption.

This chapter foregrounds Greer's feminist interventions in this area, analysing the impact of her work as the guest host of late-night US talk program *The Dick Cavett Show* (1971) and of the BBC's feminist 'salon' *The Last Word* (1994), and concludes with the response to her controversial role as a housemate on Britain's *Celebrity Big Brother* (2005).[1] In all these appearances, Greer cultivates a public self that resonates widely with audiences, within specific generic limits, and most viewers write as Greer fans (even if, as was the case with *The Last Word*, they have feminist suggestions for improvement). Produced at very different historical moments, the extensive viewer letters prompted by Greer's television appearances are shaped by the cultural milieus out of which they emerge, in which the kinds of conversations around gender, sexuality, and feminism that were being publicly staged were markedly different. Historical television audience research is, of course, challenging (Bourdon 2015), and while these letters are by no means an unmediated reflection of the consumption process, they evidence an active viewership that uses the epistolary form to critically reflect upon what they expect from television, and indeed from feminism/feminists, at particular cultural moments.

In the mid-twentieth century, television 'rapidly became a medium for celebrities from other fields to showcase or promote their labour', particularly through talk or variety shows (Lee 2020, p. 85). In fact, as Katja Lee makes clear, 'the failure to cultivate a telegenic personality could hamper the development or maintenance of celebrity' (2020, p. 85). This is something of which Greer appeared to be acutely aware. While the relationship between television personality and celebrity is contested (Langer 1981; Tolson 2015), for James Bennett, the former refers 'to presenters of television programming, whose fame has developed a high degree of intertextuality and longevity that is strongly connected to their work in, and on, television' (2010, p. 19) – such a definition encompasses figures such as Greer, whose attention capital is now inseparable from her work on the small screen, even if not originating there. In Bennett's understanding, which firmly pushes back against the idea that no skill or labour is exercised by personalities who appear 'just as they are', Greer can be classified as a 'vocationally skilled performer', who 'appears on television as a result of, or is validated by, a skill that they hold as a professional within their chosen field' (2008, p. 36). That is, she has not become famous because she is a television presenter and performer but, for the most part, has become a television performer because she is famous (with her 'achieved' celebrity [Rojek 2001] predominantly emanating from her first feminist blockbuster). This reframing of Greer as a television personality who resonated with audiences is made possible by the archive, notwithstanding its absences.

'Archival silences' and Greer on the small screen

When *The Female Eunuch* was first published in 1970, Greer 'became one of the first true feminist stars of the television age' (Dux 2010, p. 9; see also Wallace 1997), though she had previously featured on British television screens in the late 1960s comedy skit show, *Nice Times* (an unaired skit from which, the 'Milk outtake', is one of the archive's few digitised items [Buchanan 2017]). Television ensured that Greer had an exceptionally widespread cultural reach. Of the impact of such a form, Ann McGrath remarks that, whether in the form of interviews or documentaries, 'even in book-free households, people had seen Greer on television' (1999, p. 178). Given that her willingness to appear so regularly on various television programs was remarkable for feminists (perhaps matched only by Gloria Steinem), Greer used an interview with the *New York Post* to justify her approach:

> As far as I'm concerned, I only go through all these flaming hoops because somewhere out there – beyond the TV cameras and the bright lights and the interviewer's head – there's a woman encased in all those shells and you have to make a big noise to be heard.
>
> (Dudar 1971)

And make a 'big noise' she certainly did. For many, a televisual encounter acted as a conduit to her books and, as Sheehan (2016, p. 70) notes, a corrective to more limited print media discursive constructions and sensationalist coverage of Greer as a celebrity.

Greer's preference for television over other media platforms recurs throughout the archive. For example, invoking television's immediacy and its presumption of veracity (Schaefer 2020, p. 178), she replies to a fan who has praised her appearances that television is 'infinitely preferable to print, which invariably falsifies and tends to drag on for hours' (to M., 21 September 1991, 2014.0042.00052). Indeed, Greer's archive is filled with correspondence relating to her refusal to undertake print media interviews because of such perceived distortion.[2] Whether on sitcoms where she plays herself, comic quiz shows, or morning television programs, Greer's ongoing relationship with television has become increasingly complex as both television and feminism themselves have developed (Taylor 2014). She has always been in great demand from television producers; indeed, the archive contains many letters under the heading 'TV refusals'.[3] In 2004, Greer was even invited to participate in the celebrity dance competition *Strictly Come Dancing* (C.O., 20 August 2005, London, 2014.0042.00825).

76 Germaine Greer, Celebrity Feminism and the Archive

The one she accepted, perhaps most surprisingly, was *Celebrity Big Brother*, discussed later in this chapter.

The 2017.0002 series in the Greer archive – Television 1968-c.2012 – includes print records relating to Greer's myriad television appearances as a host, interviewee, interviewer or performer, and would-be documentary-maker. Greer actively sought to complete the record of her television work, undermining assertions that she merely 'kept' the archive as opposed to *constituting* it (Glanville 2018). The archival record – especially in the case of television – can often be incomplete and this was certainly the case with the Greer archive.[4] The absence of some of the programs she attempted to obtain, what Glanville refers to as the archive's 'silences', is a reminder that despite Greer's effort to shape, and indeed create, the archive, she was confronted by institutional limitations (such as lack of adequate archival practices at the broadcaster level) that compromised these efforts.

Given the historical rarity of recording and preserving television programs unless they were deemed to be of international significance (Moseley and Wheatley 2008, p. 154), it is not surprising that Greer and her assistants hit such roadblocks. This is compounded by the fact that television addressed to women, due to its perceived lack of cultural value, was 'even less likely to have been recorded and preserved than other forms or genres' (Moseley and Wheatley 2008, p. 155). The question of 'why so little women's television remains in our archives?' is one with which feminist media historians have been attempting to grapple, and therefore 'archiving remains a feminist issue' (Collie et al. 2013, pp. 114–115) – as this book underscores. Greer's project to complete the archive, then, is, if at times unsuccessful, a vital feminist one that raises urgent questions about media history and women's (in)visibility. While Greer was unable to source copies of her *Dick Cavett* appearances, these efforts, in other respects, were rewarded, and recordings of two of the programs analysed here, *The Last Word* and *Celebrity Big Brother*, do feature in the archive.

Feminist hosting: Greer and *The Dick Cavett Show*

On 14 June and 15 June 1971, Greer was the special guest host for two consecutive episodes of *The Dick Cavett Show* in the US, on abortion and rape respectively. Dick Cavett hosted the celebrity talk show from 1968 to 1975 (ABC), interviewing guests such as Hollywood actors, athletes, politicians, and musicians, while Greer herself featured as an interviewee, both before and after her own guest host episodes. This is perhaps unsurprising as early 1970s 'television was compelled to take notice' of the burgeoning women's movement (Clarke 2024, p. 7), and Greer was its charismatic if unofficial representative. As Daniel McClure argues, *The Dick Cavett Show* exemplified the ways in which talk television during this period incorporated 'anti-establishment discourse[s]' from the Black Power and Women's Liberation movements, crucially providing 'an outlet for more radical or marginalized

'The best thing to happen to night-time television' **77**

voices in society' (2012, p. 27). For Greer, television talk shows were not only integral to *The Female Eunuch*'s publicity campaign (she appeared on *David Susskind*, *Johnny Carson*, and *David Frost* to promote the book) but vital to her efforts to reach new audiences, functioning as a 'rare chance to run a feminist conversation on her own terms' (Sheehan 2016, p. 67). Later in her career, Greer writes to a television producer, 'I like to use TV as a medium, provided I've got a measure of control; the best situation for me is the live interview which I can turn to my own purpose' (to J.M., 26 November 1984, 2017.0002.00052). These *Cavett* letters, the most ever received following a guest host's appearance, indicate that she did indeed turn this form to her feminist 'purpose'.

Women in the television industries during the 1970s were only 'given secondary, subordinate, or supportive roles' (Lee 2020, p. 86), with feminists facing even more intense hostility in news and current affairs programs (Dow 2014). In such a context, having a woman appear repeatedly as a guest host is noteworthy. But to have a feminist – let alone a feminist with Greer's reputation and frank and uninhibited voice – do so on confronting topics is even more exceptional. Moreover, the archived pitch for the 'unmade' *Germaine Greer Show* references her *Cavett* episodes to establish why and how Greer's own talk show would appeal to American viewers. As it notes, 'We're operating from the assumption that <u>she</u> is interesting to the audience, and so her own ideas must always be part of the program' (2014.0044.00166, original emphasis), suggesting that she is 'far too opinionated' for any other approach; this was seen as an exciting feature that would distinguish the series from others in the genre. Similarly, indicative of this style of what Bonner calls (2011) 'presenter-led' television, when Greer was seeking funding for her documentary series, *The Story of Human Reproduction*, the centrality of her public persona to the project's viability was also strategically foregrounded (Taylor 2022).

In this section, focusing on viewer response to Greer's *Cavett* episodes at the peak of feminism's second wave, I demonstrate that her television work – including hosting – complicates dominant critical narratives about television's inherent hostility towards women's liberation (Kay 2015, p. 65). As Bonnie Dow argues in *Watching Women's Liberation*, feminist critics have seen mainstream media as 'function[ing] primarily as feminism's enemy and not its ally in the early period' (2014, p. 4). Such assumptions have led to a failure to recognise how women's liberationists used television to reach those beyond the movement, with some success (Kay 2015, p. 69). More specifically, there has been little exploration of

> how feminism provided an important discursive context for *talk* programming: it helped to delineate and force new topics for discussion in existing television talk formats; to rework existing modes of reportage and commentary; and, occasionally, to create the space and the possibility for entirely new series.
>
> (Kay 2015, p. 69, original emphasis)

78 Germaine Greer, Celebrity Feminism and the Archive

In this regard, Greer's television underscores the feminist capacities of this form, especially in terms of consciousness-raising and affectively coaxing audiences to feminist attachments (Ahmed 2004). It is, as Kay reminds us, archival materials that enable us to contest these prevailing understandings of an invariably antagonistic relationship between feminism and television during the 1970s (2015, p. 74) – and indeed beyond.

One of the largest caches of audience mail in the archive relates to Greer's performances on *The Dick Cavett Show* (1971b). In addition to the 400-odd letters that are preserved together in two bulky folders in the Early Years series (2014.0042.00164 and 2014.0042.00165), all written within a few days of the programs airing, the General Correspondence series contains nearly 100 individual letters, illustrating its impact upon viewers across America. In the letters sent to the network, as in those sent directly to Greer, 'Themes of gratitude and relief run through the letters; gratitude for Greer's willingness to do what she was doing in public and relief that she had a platform to do it' (Sheehan 2016, p. 63). Though previously examined in detail by Sheehan (in an article on which I draw throughout), such letters are worthy of some further consideration here, particularly given that the televisual 'Greer', and the feminism she embodied on the small screen, patently appealed to some viewers in ways that her other mass-mediated versions did not – once again showing the importance of Greer's cross-media feminism. While the archive does not appear to include replies from the star host to *Cavett* viewers, Greer writes from Italy to her literary agent (D.C., undated, though presumably 1971), suggesting that she participated in off-screen dialogues with them: 'You will be pleased to know that I have answered 111 letters in connection with the Cavett show, which only leaves a few hundred more' (Cortona, 2014.0042.00181).

These *Cavett* episodes, as briefly mentioned, represent one of the archive's significant absences. While I am therefore unable to offer a detailed textual analysis of Greer's persona as *Cavett* host, or the kinds of feminist dialogues and debates she may have initiated on screen, there are myriad traces of these performances throughout the archive. In Jason Jacobs's terms, when original audio-visual texts are lost, existing in archives only as 'shadows' (scripts, memos, producer notes, and audience responses), we become reliant upon these 'ghost texts' as our primary material (2000, p. 14). Although there is nothing to indicate precisely how the guest hosting came about, the Early Years Series features running orders and producer notes for Greer's *Cavett* episodes, along with details of guests and the questions that Greer may be asking them (1971a, 2014.0044.00161). From these documents, guests appeared to have been located along the political spectrum, representative of opposing views on these fraught subjects. In an article on hosting *The Last Word*, Greer (1994) suggests that she had shaped the dialogue on the *Cavett* shows through her choice of participants:

'The best thing to happen to night-time television' **79**

> I said I wanted to talk to non-celebrities and they let me. We, that is I, a midwife, a policeman, a baseball player, a raped woman, a district attorney, a social worker and 20 or so other people with some experience of the issues, talked about rape, about sex as sport, and about abortion.

In addition to choosing the two topics for discussion, Greer, it appears, played an active role in crafting the conversations that so deeply resonated with viewers. Furthermore, at 90 minutes long, the late-night talk show episodes allowed issues to be discussed with more complexity and depth than other television formats (Sheehan 2016, p. 67), which viewers found incredibly valuable.

Television texts are polysemic and thereby viewer responses are no means homogeneous (as audience research from within cultural studies, such as Ien Ang's *Watching Dallas* [1982] and David Morley's *The Nationwide Audience* [1980], has long proven). Nevertheless, as Sheehan observes, about 80% of the *Cavett* letters from both women and men are supportive of Greer, her hosting abilities, and her feminism. For Greer, as for some other movement activists, the relationship between the women's movement and the media was a *dialogic* one (Barker-Plummer 1995), something that her work on these conversational television shows literalises. Furthermore, as Kay argues, 'the gender politics of the domestic space historically imagined by broadcasters as a microcosm of a "national family" structured around heteropatriarchal norms – provided a discursive reception context in which feminist talk was a *hostile invader*' (2020, p. 114, emphasis added). Given this domestic 'invasion', the overwhelmingly supportive nature of these letters becomes even more remarkable.

Across the viewer letters, praise for Greer's hosting was lavish, with the shows even characterised as 'so fantastic that they deny description' (17 June, Montana). Greer herself, as in this chapter's title, is seen to be 'the best thing to happen to night-time television' (B.M., 16 June, Madison). For these viewers, evening television is not simply a space of light entertainment but one that can (and should) reflect upon the pressing social and political issues of the day; they see the Greer episodes as exemplary in this regard – because of their feminist host: '[Greer] is just what T.V. and society needs' (M.T., 14 June, New York). In this respect, commonly remarking on the unusually high calibre of the episodes, viewers make explicit their assumptions about what constitutes 'good' or 'quality' television in this particular genre, using their correspondence to ensure that producers know what (and whom) they value and why: 'The program was brilliant, compelling, erudite, entertaining, educational, informative, questioning...Hooray for Germaine Greer!' (C.G., 16 June, New York). The shows, although not airing on a government-funded broadcaster, were widely praised for being 'a real public service' (D.B., 21 June, New York; O.I.N., Arlington).

In particular, Greer's episodes were seen to offer something rare and much needed on American screens: 'Tonight you have brought television back from the wasteland' (R.B., 16 June). Applauding the network and the show's

80 Germaine Greer, Celebrity Feminism and the Archive

producers for their sound and 'courageous' (D.G., 16 June; L.H., 16 June) choice of Greer as guest host – with some even suggesting that she should permanently replace Cavett or at least feature regularly on the show – viewers urge them to provide more of the kinds of thoughtful conversations not generally permissible on late-night talk television: 'Terrific! – the stimulating discussion between Greer and her panel of June 14. Thank you – and let's have more controversial subjects discussed reasonably openly as was abortion (and others)' (J.C.). While talk show hosts may otherwise be valued for impartiality, Greer was repeatedly commended for 'not hide[ing] her own point of view, but in letting it be shown in her direct questions to the guest and in her unruffled forthright replies to their questions' (B.M., Ohio).[5]

As the above quotation indicates, many viewers were supportive of Greer's approach and skills as an interviewer; a 21-year-old woman writes that she 'appreciated this evening's hostess with her directness and probing for information from her guests' (J.C., 15 June). Characterised as 'far superior to most male talk show hosts' (J.O, 17 June, Ohio), Greer was celebrated for asking questions in an 'artful way' (A.S., 16 June, New Jersey), with the celebrity host facilitating refreshingly 'frank' discussions (D.S., 16 June, Colorado). In this way, viewers relate the sense of having watched a conversation unfold in front of them: 'The equation of temporal immediacy with physical presence, on which TV's promise of "being there" depends, renders on- and off-screen worlds continuous' (Schaefer 2020, p. 180). Aligning with television culture's logic of immediacy, this 'impression of frank and unstaged communication is pivotal' to the talk show format and to securing audience investment (Schaefer 2020, p. 178); the presenter is, of course, central to these processes (Bonner 2015).

Reflecting upon the apparent 'lack of artifice' fostered by television's 'claims to immediacy' (Schaefer 2020, p. 180), these viewers were also grateful that Greer had not exploited the topics but handled them with the gravity they deserved: 'I felt that I was part of the discussion in that it seemed so honest and not staged for entertainment' (B.B.S., 25 June, New York). The majority complimented Greer for being well informed and for bringing crucial if 'difficult' (M.M., 15 June) topics to light, bravely tackling issues that had been largely overlooked in such forums. Women who had been raped or who had had abortions even wrote to commend the sensitivity of her approach (Sheehan 2016, p. 68). One viewer describes the episode on rape as 'shockingly enlightening', adding 'Ms Greer led a brilliant discussion of the much neglected topic of rape' (L.W., 24 June, Kansas). In this vein, many celebrate Greer for carefully posing questions that needed to be asked, and in the process they make clear their ideas about what talk television should do as well as the kind of performance they value from presenters.

'Now I know what Women's Lib is about': Screening (celebrity) feminism

As with Greer's bestselling writing, many viewers credit the programs, or more specifically their celebrity host, with fundamentally transforming their understandings of women's liberation. Clearly invoking the pedagogical function of the medium (Giroux 2000), as is common, one viewer refers to the *Cavett* appearance as a '"teach-in" that was 'pure gold' (C.L., 16 June, Oklahoma), while another confesses: 'This woman has changed my entire viewpoint on women's lib' (J.B.S, 15 June). Similarly, a New York woman (R.D., 14 June) asserts that Greer has made her 'rethink and reevaluate' her beliefs, and a man from California remarks (W.A., 16 June): 'You have greatly affected my views on the subject of women's liberation...Female freedom has a new meaning to me'. One even explicitly uses the language of 'consciousness-raising' to describe the impact of the two shows on 'thousands of women' (S.E.P., 15 June, New York). Despite her outsider status therein, viewers commonly see Greer as a valuable asset for the American women's movement (Sheehan 2016, p. 71), with one feminist calling her 'our most articulate spokeswoman' (B.P., 15 June, Ohio). As in Chapter 2, these correspondents are not just fans of Greer but fans of her feminism, with many explicitly identifying in these terms and likewise describing their fan letters as uncharacteristic and as driven by Greer's exceptionality (M.P.C., 14 June; E.S., 15 June, Philadelphia). In such letters, Greer herself is seen as a role model, with both men and women explicitly identifying her as their 'heroine' (R.Mc., 15 June, D., 15 June), mirroring the kind of idolatry we have seen in other forms of fan mail.

While some viewers emphasise that these television shows were their first encounters with Greer (Sheehan 2016, p. 67) – 'We had never even heard of Miss Greer and had to call our TV station to find out her name because we were so taken with her' (S.N., 17 June, Colorado) – others offered an intertextual reading, suggesting that this on-screen 'Greer' exists in tension with those consumed through other forms of celebrity media coverage. In this respect, many claim that Greer's performances have made them rethink their opinions of her, which had been based on sensationalistic profiles such as that offered in *Life* (Sheehan 2016, p. 64). The televisual Greer, therefore, appeared to win supporters in ways that other media forms could not. For example, a viewer from Maryland claims: 'On the basis of *Life*'s coverage, I felt no desire to read your book; on the basis of last night's show, I can't wait to get my hands on it...You have much to teach us' (J.C.B., 16 June, Rockville).

The seemingly 'more real' televisual Greer leads these viewers to seek out Greer-the-author, and thereby her appearances function as a promotional tool through which she more literally sells her feminism. A woman from New York, directly addressing Greer following her *Cavett* appearances, notes, 'I'm leaving now to buy The Female Eunuch' (E.P.S., 15 June, Albany). There are many such letters in which viewers proudly suggest that they will now, often

82 Germaine Greer, Celebrity Feminism and the Archive

with a sense of urgency, purchase Greer's book. In turn, Greer's televisual performances will function as important epitexts (Genette 1997) in these audience members' subsequent readings of *The Female Eunuch*, suggesting that these different layers of Greer's celebrity are difficult to separate. If these audience letters are anything to go by, then Greer's television performances seem to act as a kind of 'gateway feminism' for viewers (Hobson 2017), many of whom suggest that access to this seemingly less unmediated and more directly accessible 'Greer' has made them rethink their position about consuming her writing and about feminism itself.

Celebrity and the 'real' Greer

While 'authenticity' has more recently been seen as highly prized in sustaining influencer fame, it has always been essential currency for all celebrities, including the television personality (Tolson 2010; see also Dyer 1986). Television's 'regime of liveness', as Bennett puts it (2010, p. 129–30), and the spontaneity it signals (despite the rehearsals and producer interventions) creates the sense of intimacy lauded by these viewers; for a Virginia woman, these consecutive appearances intensify this connection: 'Just after having watched you both nights I feel very close to you' (J.D., McLean). According to a Chapel Hill man, Greer is a 'thoroughly human person facing and probing controversial issues with insight and feeling' (D.M.S., 15 June). Television gave access not to the disembodied authorial voice with which some may have been familiar through her books and journalistic writing but to an embodied 'Greer' in various guises (Lewis 2001).

For many of her correspondents, then, her televisual appearances offer the sense of a kind of privileged access to the 'back-stage' Greer (Goffman 1959). As Richard Schickel argues of television,

> It is the primary force in the breaking down of the barriers that formerly existed between the well-known and the unknown. This…has something to do with the way it brings famous folk into our living room in psychically manageable size.
>
> (1985, pp. 9–10)

Letter writers often suggest that television permits a more 'authentic' Greer to shine through in ways precluded by other forms of media. For example, a man from Baltimore, another who revises his opinion following her television appearances, writes directly to Greer:

> I've never seen anyone as quick and eloquent as you have been on the Dick Cavett Show. I must confess that I once thought you were a fraud…but I was amazed at your invulnerable wit and humane good sense the many times you were on television.
>
> (M.M., 29 July 1972, 2014.0042.00572)

For this viewer, the *Cavett* performances were not isolated incidents but indicative of Greer's wider, engaging televisual persona.

Viewers frequently compliment Greer on being 'real', with a number capitalising the adjective: 'I think she is outstanding as a hostess on a talk show – please give us more of her – she knows how to get down to brass tacks – nothing pseudo: she's REAL!' (S.C.B., date illegible, Delaware). The talk show format gave viewers the impression that they had access to this kind of authentic 'Greer' and the intimacy it implies. Amongst many who hoped that Greer would be given her own show, one viewer writes: 'Your shows are FOR REAL. CAVETT IS LAME...PS I just started your book and that too is for real' (P.C., 15 June). As is common, the audience 'sees through the publicity-generated artificial self to the real, deserving, special self' (Gamson 1994, p. 149; see also Dyer 1986). Even though Greer's televisual persona is no less constructed than in other forms, television as a form adds another layer to the seemingly accessible self (Langer 1981). In the intimate close-ups commonly offered in these television texts, as Sean Redmond observes, 'The screen dissolves or melts away in the unfolding moment and one comes into direct contact with the star or celebrity' (2006, p. 38).

The presumption of 'authenticity' and the intimacy it seems to foster are highly valued by these audiences – as we have seen more recently with consumers of women's vlogs (Berryman and Kavka 2017; Henderson and Taylor 2020) – and they appear to make them more sympathetic to Greer's feminism. Critical narratives about feminism's containment and 'superficial appeasement' by those in the television industries, especially during feminism's second wave, continue to prevail (Clarke 2024, p. 8); Greer's work on this show, and viewers' responses to it, very clearly disrupts such assumptions. We must be cautious about claiming that these voices are representative of the wider American public, but as Sheehan observes, 'these viewers tell us how extraordinary it was to see a woman such as Germaine Greer on American television screens in 1971, and how much seeing her meant to them' (2016, p. 74). Greer took up the role of television host again in the mid-1990s, a markedly different time for women and feminism itself than when the *Cavett* shows aired.

A feminist salon? The BBC's *Last Word* (1994)

In the mid-1990s, Greer hosted the BBC Two series, *The Last Word*, about which very little has been known – until now. In addition to containing copies of these episodes, the Greer archive includes various written records (press coverage, correspondence with the BBC, and audience letters) relating to the series which make it especially rich for analysis. As with the *Cavett* material, all the documentation relating to the series is atypically kept together, representing a significant signpost for researchers (Glanville 2018, p. 47). In terms of its genesis, the Assistant Head of Music and Arts at the BBC wrote to Greer on 1 February 1993, asking her about being involved in a 'late night talk

84 Germaine Greer, Celebrity Feminism and the Archive

show' that would have 'the atmosphere of a salon' (K.M., 2017.002.00131). I will return to the idea of the 'salon', and how it might relate to feminism, shortly. He continues, stressing Greer's centrality to the show's perceived viability: 'It would take its tone and style very much from the character of its host and we felt that there was no one who would better host it than you!' As with her other shows, Greer's charisma, wit, and intellect, along with her celebrity capital, are invoked as guarantees of its future success. In this respect, her televisual image, like those of other such personalities, 'can be understood as a key commodity in the economics of television broadcasting' (Bennett 2010, p. 99). The show's apparent feminist ethos was also central to its marketing. An article in the *Times* (Barnard 1994) cites producer Janet Lee, who suggests that it is '"the first time the freedom of conversation that women enjoy when there are no men about has been brought to television"', while the BBC controller, Michael Jackson, reassured prospective viewers that it will take a '"more sophisticated approach"' than competing talk shows (Culf 1994).

The series, like much that Greer has been involved in, received extensive media attention ahead of its screen debut. 'Celebrity', as Phillip Drake reminds us, 'attracts audiences and offsets the risks and costs inherent in cultural production in a crowded attention economy' (2018, p. 271). Pre-publicity considerably relies upon Greer's star power, illustrating her centrality to the show's branding (as it had been to her blockbusters and other forms of writing). For example, an Australian journalist from the *Herald Sun* (17 October 1994) remarked: 'Oprah Winfrey she won't be, but Australian feminist, author and academic Germaine Greer will have her say from next week when she presents a new chat show in Britain'. As this comment implies, the period when Greer was hosting these shows was what Janice Peck (2008) has dubbed the 'Age of Oprah'. That is, the most successful television talk show host was the African-American icon Oprah Winfrey, confirming the viability of women leaders in this space and the power of engaged female audiences in their celebrification. Although there are, of course, many important differences between Greer and Winfrey, the latter's enormous success would have undoubtedly made a program that foregrounded women's voices, such as *The Last Word*, seem more viable to network executives.

Indicative of her immense attention capital, Greer (1994) herself was even given the opportunity to publish a full-page article in the *Telegraph* promoting the show before it aired. In this respect, the boundaries of Greer's media work blur, as we also see with Greer's pre- and post-*Celebrity Big Brother* appearance reflections in newspaper pieces. The article begins 'I have never wanted to be a talk show host', although the archive – especially through *The Germaine Greer Show* pitch (2014.0044.00166; Taylor 2022) – calls this into question. Greer positions herself as an unlikely candidate for such a televisual role, given – she says – that a good host is supposed to pretend they have no opinions:

'The best thing to happen to night-time television' **85**

As I'm not prepared to live that way, I am clearly going to be very bad or at least very a different kind of talk-show host, fat, 55, dishevelled and opinionated...the truth is it is hardly a talk-show at all.

Though questioning the show's generic positioning, Greer suggests that its purpose is to amplify women's voices (the kind of women, however, was something with which viewers took issue): 'So the idea behind my talk show is to find out what clever women are thinking, what worries them and what suggestions they have for better management of affairs or a clearer response to them'. She also seeks to downplay her role, characterising herself as a 'guide' rather than a 'leader': 'My role, I reckon, is to guide the conversation rather than to it run it...One of the tenets of feminism is that all valid testimony is first-person testimony'. Here Greer seeks to position the series as explicitly feminist in nature, providing a space for and legitimising women's alternative knowledges.

Greer's role as *The Last Word*'s presenter, then, cannot be overstated. As Bonner remarks in her work on 'ordinary television', presenters

are the people who are there to greet us at the beginning of a programme, to smooth us through transitions during it and to bid farewell to us at the end. They provide an important reason for watching a programme, or for refusing to do so.

(2002, pp. 66–67)

Each episode of *The Last Word* commences with Greer's short authoritative monologue, functioning to establish the tone and scope of the subsequent discussion. The use of direct address to the audience, in terms of speech and in a look to camera, is a core way in which a sense of intimacy is established between viewer, presenter, and the show they are seen to represent: 'Of those on screen, only the presenter can properly talk directly to viewers to bind them in' (Bonner 2002, p. 68). Greer began each of the six episodes with an introduction to the topic at hand. For example, in the 'Sex Wars' episode, aired on 25 September, Greer commences: 'Men, bless 'em, if you don't need a man to keep you, what do you need them for?' (2014.0041.00045). She adds, seemingly buying into the 'crisis of masculinity' discourse that became common in the 1990s, 'men are confused, angry, frightened, even more trouble than they were before'. Nevertheless, unsurprisingly, Greer refuses to allow feminism to be marked as the culprit: 'Feminism has been blamed for increasing men's insecurities, but the male ego was always fragile...Has the hostility now got out of hand? Are heterosexual women hooked on a self-destruction game?' In each episode, following her monologue, Greer introduces her all-woman panel of guests.

Across the series, the guests are all prominent white British women journalists and commentators, ranging from their 20s to 50s, and only the final episode ('The Men defend their sex', 26 November 1994) featured three men. The panel for the first episode – consisting of Janet Street Porter, Suzanne Moore, Caitlin Moran, Anne Leslie (these four appear regularly), and Christina Ordone – reflects upon shifting, or recalcitrant, understandings of masculinity and how heterosexual women (as they seemingly all are) must negotiate this increasingly fraught terrain. In most cases, the participants' epistemic authority is grounded in their personal gendered experiences, an important feminist gesture (Grant 1993). The set features a fireplace, bookshelves, and cosy antique armchairs, and participants routinely consume glasses of wine and cigarettes (to which viewers negatively responded), creating the sense of a casual get-together of girlfriends on which audiences effectively eavesdrop. The series does not appear to be filmed in front of a live studio, making it seem much more managed than perhaps others of this genre.

Confirming that Greer's '"on-air personality"' is 'a crucial aspect of the programme's televisual identity' (Langer 1981, p. 360), she makes a summarising statement at the end of each program – suggesting that it is *she* who has the last word. All episodes follow this format, with varying results, as the audience response indicates. Other topics covered across the series are 'Infidelity' (22 October 1994), 'Who should have children?' (28 October 1994), 'Work' (5 November 1994), 'Schools' (12 November 1994), 'Ageing' (19 November 1994), and 'The Men defend their sex' (26 November 1994). Produced during postfeminism's ascendancy, this kind of talk show with such a high-profile feminist figure as host is especially noteworthy. In the final episode, Greer outlines the purpose of the series: 'What we've been trying to do is to civilise the talk show, and looking for consensus. We're also interested in giving an insight into how women think when they are not obliged to think like men' (2014.0041.00052). For Greer, the show's centring of women's voices, via this seemingly informal conversational format, produces the kind of fruitful dialogue largely unavailable elsewhere on British television screens. Greer and her participants converse and, to varying degrees, intellectually spar over the pressing gender issues of day.

The audience's last word: Viewers and intersectional feminism

In *The Structural Transformation of the Public Sphere* (1962), Jurgen Habermas reflected upon the salons and coffee houses that were in operation during the eighteenth and nineteenth centuries, including in France and Britain. These salons – forms of literary public spheres – were spaces for intellectual debate and exchange, marked by 'the public use of reason by private individuals' (Habermas 1962, p. 53). While women were traditionally excluded from them, feminist historians have established that alternative, women-only, and often overtly feminist salons concurrently developed. As Deborah Heller (1998) remarks, first-wave feminists, such as Britain's Bluestockings, attempted to create environments where women could

'The best thing to happen to night-time television' **87**

congregate to enter in the kinds of intellectual debates from which they were more publicly excluded.

The framing of *The Last Word* as a 'salon' by the show's creators is remarkable in this context, especially given that those who were excluded from it used the letter form to contest the privileges of those within. While 'ideals of inclusion, freedom, and equality of participation' informed the salon (Heller 1998, p. 72), such ideals required much work to achieve, including in their feminist iterations. Heller (1998, p. 70) argues that 'the Bluestocking salonnières made adjustments to the "scene of conversation" in order to accommodate differences among a diversity of participants'; viewers of *The Last Word* found this diversity overwhelmingly lacking. For many viewers, as we will see, Greer and those who were participating in this televisual 'salon' not only were unrepresentative but did not seem to recognise the exclusionary nature of their intimate (feminist) 'chats'. While Greer's feminism here appears to have missed the mark, its creators were heartened by the media attention. Following its debut, the BBC wrote excitedly to Greer, 'We have never had so much coverage for a late-night talk show!' (K.E., 26 October 1994, London, 2017.0002.000136). However, much of this press – as the archive reveals – was critical of the series, its celebrity host, and its all-woman panel of TV regulars (Berkman 1994; Feay 1994; 'Greer Window', 1994; Massingbed 1994; Moie 1994).

In addition to this coverage, the series prompted considerable viewer correspondence to the BBC (kept together in a folder in the Television Series [1994, 2017.0022.00134], though there are also others in the General Correspondence series sent directly to Greer). As producers had predicted, Greer is roundly seen to be the show's key drawcard: 'I don't watch much T.V. but do go out of my way to catch your "appearances", because, whatever the subject, the perspective and emphasis, will be different and valid...Please continue to assist the progress of enlightenment and meaningful debate' (D.H., 30 October 1994, Essex). For this writer, the series is consistent with Greer's other work in the mediasphere and her insights are what render the show so valuable, upon which pre-publicity had also sought to capitalise. Calling the programme 'splendid', and like the readers analysed in the previous chapter, a woman viewer from Cambridge concludes: 'I hope it doesn't sound mawkish to say that, as a person, you are a positive inspiration and have given me energy and courage to get through some difficult times' (T.C., 29 November 1994). For many viewers, then, it is Greer who makes consumption of the series so worthwhile and rewarding. One woman, identifying herself as Greer's age, sees the life experience of the famous feminist and her participants as one of the show's greatest virtues: 'It makes a change from having some twenty year old who really has relatively little experience of life' (V.A., 1 November 1994, London).

Critics have emphasised the therapeutic value of talk shows – Jane Shattuc (1997) reads them in terms of the Freudian 'talking cure' – but for *Last Word* viewers, this element compromised the shows:

88 Germaine Greer, Celebrity Feminism and the Archive

Tonight's programme was more like a therapy session than a discussion. This is particularly regrettable as it provides fodder for the men who are longing to pour scorn on all-women discussions...I've admired your determination to take a back seat in discussion, but isn't it time you came forward to keep Ann Leslie in check?

(B.H., 29 November 1994, London)

This letter suggests that the role Greer had imagined in pre-publicity, of merely guiding the discussion rather than seeking to dominate it, was how the series played out. Her apparent passivity, however, was seen to have a detrimental effect on the show, especially when the other women's contributions were seen as trite or ill informed. Moreover, the above viewer fears that these limitations will be used by those predisposed to dismiss women's television. The unevenness in terms of the contributions and Greer's apparent failure to effectively moderate features across the correspondence. In this regard, a man from London writes: 'Unfortunately, as with all such programmes, one or two tended to dominate the conversation' (S.P., 20 November 1994, 2014.0042. 00703). For such viewers, Greer was expected to adopt more of an active moderator role, as she had in *The Dick Cavett Show*.

Some viewers felt that the program failed in its remit to offer engaging dialogue and debate for thoughtful audiences, with the apparent consensus amongst the homogeneous panel rendering the show nearly unwatchable:

I am writing to say how disappointed I am with your Sat. evening programme...it came across like a female lunch party of the chattering classes in suburbia...The general air of smugness, self-centred, self-conscious "we've made it" was nauseating. There was no debate, you all appeared to agree with each other on everything.

(P.F., 7 November 1994, Doncaster)

From this viewer's perspective, the women chosen to participate were those who had most benefitted from gains of the second wave, and thereby the series reinscribed its elision of the voices of marginalised women (Thompson 2002). Because its host was such a renowned feminist, viewers had anticipated the elevation of such voices. The panel's overwhelming privilege saw the program inflected with a limited worldview, they complained. In relation to the 'Ageing' program, one correspondent (E.M., 20 November 1994) chided the participants for failing to sufficiently acknowledge those caring for ageing parents. She concludes, 'Yours guests seemed to me to be a lot of over-indulged, self-centred, spoilt women with few responsibilities who were incapable of overviewing the subject'. Greer appeared to agree, responding that the episode had 'many problems' as the subject was 'so poorly defined' (4 December 1994) – by whom is left unstated.

'The best thing to happen to night-time television' **89**

As the above suggests, while fans of Greer and sympathetic to the show's aims, many viewers offered a critique of what we would now routinely call the series' lack of intersectionality (Crenshaw 1989), underscoring the privilege of the participants and problematising the assumption that they are representative of British women. While the concept of intersectionality has recently gained popular currency, and scholarly critiques of popular feminism's whiteness have become more pronounced (Phipps 2020), these letters make clear that audiences have been deploying this kind of critique for much longer than is often presumed. Moreover, although digital media is often credited with bringing to the fore a more inclusive feminism that attends to gender in relation to other modalities of difference, these viewers indicate that this understanding has long informed 'vernacular feminisms' (Lusty 2017). Few of the *Cavett* viewers explicitly specified their racial or class background, but these writers see the elision of their experiences and the lack of inclusivity on *The Last Word* as grounds for significant criticism. For example, though finding some value in a series like this, a woman of colour criticises the program's whiteness, and middle-class bias, while wondering about its addressees:

> Congratulations on your new programme...As a Black working class woman, I was frustrated to only hear the views of white middle class women who neither represented or recognised any who were from different backgrounds...I must admit I do not know who "The Last Word" is targeted at.
> (S.M., 24 October 1994, London)

This view, that the series represents only one specific type of woman, thereby excluding many others, recurs across the correspondence.

Similarly, a self-described Greer 'admirer' from Cardiff – who sees Greer's hosting role as evidence of her greater 'power' within the media – gently scolds the well-known feminist for *The Last Word*'s failure to be representative of a diverse cross-section of the community:

> It would be a good idea to include Black/Scottish/Welsh/Irish/Working class/Disabled women on future shows...We are strong, we are intelligent, but we need a forum to express ourselves. I know many suitable women and would be honoured to put you in touch with them.
> (L.M., 23 October 1994, Cardiff; see also M.W., 26 October 1994, Birmingham)

Identifying herself as part of a group of marginalised women, this viewer appeals to Greer to use the power she does hold to give such women voice. In an overtly participatory gesture, audience members like this often volunteered to help rectify the show's limited feminism. For instance, a Cornwall woman (R.T., 31 October 1994) writes to suggest that Greer include an '"ordinary" member of the public', such as herself, on the panel, as does another woman who is a stand-up comedian and single mother (D.D., 5 November 1994, London). Such failures, in terms of representation, are largely seen to be Greer's; viewers expect more from the famous feminist.

These writers are by no means anti-feminist, but they are critical of what is passing for feminism – and the women who are authorised to speak on its behalf – in such popular spaces. Writing about the 'Infidelity' show, another woman (J.B., 23 October 1994, Manchester) complains, 'why were the panelists all white, middle class, gainfully employed, able bodied and apparently heterosexual? I don't say this to be politically correct, but because the views represented reflect those of a tiny minority of women in Britain'. Here, the seemingly homogeneous participants served to limit the kinds of debate and dialogue that were possible. These letters evidence audiences with a high degree of critical media literacy and reflexivity, especially in terms of underscoring the privilege of those who are given the opportunity to speak on behalf of women. Such letters thereby demonstrate how viewer positionality informs their televisual experiences and intellectual and affective responses in important ways. The series therefore did produce some generative commentary about the kinds of feminisms (and feminists) that audiences wanted to see foregrounded on television; in this respect, through their letters they perform a kind of media activism, lobbying for a more intersectional feminism. There is no material relating to the commissioning of a second series in the archive,[6] but these more critical letters perhaps give some sense of why it ran for only one season. The final television series analysed here suggests that Greer has continued to maintain her public visibility into the twenty-first century through different formats and genres, about which commentators and viewers have had conflicting views.

Greer takes on reality television: *Celebrity Big Brother*

Greer's television appearances, as I have remarked, have been myriad and diverse, especially in the UK in the 1990s and 2000s. As new genres and formats have emerged, Greer has opted in and used what may seem unlikely vehicles to publicly perform her feminism in ways that might appeal to new and larger audiences (Taylor 2014). In 2005, Greer made what many have seen as an unusual decision to feature as a contestant on Britain's *Celebrity Big Brother* (Channel 4). Her choice, however, appears entirely consistent with her lifelong feminist media strategy. But after less than a week, she left due to the humiliating tasks in which she had to participate as a housemate, and which she – in her many post-exit interview and opinion pieces – characterised as 'bullying'. Although not a talk show like the others discussed here, the series and its response are nonetheless important in terms of Greer's celebrity and fandom. Audience letters suggest that Greer's participation was valuable on a number of fronts, not least in rendering her feminism accessible to those who may not otherwise have encountered her (much like some of the *Cavett* viewers). Rather than being filed together, dozens of letters, either to producers or directly to Greer, are dispersed across the alphabetised General Correspondence series. Greer preserved not just fan letters about her *Celebrity Big Brother* appearance directly addressed to her but those forwarded to her by the television studio.

As with *The Last Word*, and indicative of Greer's enduring attention capital, her decision to appear on the show garnered extensive media coverage in the British press (although it also featured in Australian and American newspapers), much of which appeared at best confounded and at worst contemptuous of the ageing feminist and her ongoing efforts to remain publicly visible. For example, a *Daily Mail* journalist asked,

> WHAT possessed Germaine Greer to offer herself up for abuse on *Celebrity Big Brother*? She is disgracing herself, betraying millions of devoted feminist groupies, failing the university students who take her very seriously indeed, and contaminating her reputation as a sharp intellectual and inimitable critic.
>
> (Alibhai-Brown 2005)

Similarly, in a later, deeply ageist assessment, Australian playwright Louis Nowra (2010, p. 40) suggested that Greer's 'pathetic' participation on a 'cheap, often-degrading reality show' evidences a kind of publicity hunger that is believed to be particularly undesirable for older women (see York forthcoming). Even Greer's most recent biographer judgementally labelled it 'the most embarrassing mistake of her public life' (Kleinhenz 2018, p. 353). Monica Dux sums up this tendency to characterise Greer's reality television participation as a sullying of her legacy: her 'appearance on *Celebrity Big Brother* is cited as a problematic postscript to her greatness' (2010, p. 13).

For such commentators, Greer's decision to appear on the show is seen as an instance of 'downward celebrity migration', a phrase used to signal a 'celebrity's move from one field to a less "legitimate" field' and 'the risks that it may entail for their status' (Oliva 2020, p. 19). Given that she is a writer and an intellectual, many commentators identify a tension between the ostensible low culture of reality television and Greer's high cultural capital. In this respect, Greer is widely perceived to have compromised herself and done herself (and implicitly her feminism) a disservice by participating in the yet devalued realm of popular culture. Perhaps in response to these kinds of criticisms, Greer made explicit her motivation after leaving the house. In 'Why I said yes to Big Brother's shilling' (Greer 2005a), she noted that it was to finance her rainforest regeneration project in southeast Queensland: 'So why did I put myself through this entirely avoidable ordeal? My reason is the rainforest'. Her appearance fee was reportedly GBP£40,000 (Gibson 2005).

92 Germaine Greer, Celebrity Feminism and the Archive

The enormously popular British reality show, a spin-off of the original *Big Brother* series, ran for 22 seasons (2000–2023). In contrast to the 'DIY' or 'ordinary' celebrities produced in/through reality television (Turner 2004), in this version it is extant celebrity that secures a spot in the house, with participants in possession of varying degrees of celebrity capital; like other 'power resources', as Olivier Driessens remarks, 'celebrity is distributed unequally' (2012, p. 643). For flailing celebrities, reality television programs commanding vast audiences such as *Celebrity Big Brother* are seen to offer 'the prospect of renewed fame' (Deller 2016, p. 382). In 2005, nearly five decades into her public career, this was arguably a new kind of audience for Greer, which is perhaps what made the form seem attractive. In this vein, Paul Bleakley underscores the generative aspects of reality television for fading stars, conceptualising it as a vehicle through which celebrities can access larger audiences than they might otherwise be able to reach:

> Despite its reputation for attracting D-list talent in lieu of "real celebrities", *Celebrity Big Brother* has consistently proven to be popular with British audiences and serves as a vehicle for prominent people to communicate their identity directly to a broader audience than they would normally command.
>
> (2016, p. 421)

Given the latter, which aligns with Greer's broader approach to media engagement, her decision to participate in this seemingly unlikely form makes more sense. When it comes to celebrity maintenance or renewal, Ruth Deller argues,

> there are many for whom reality television has been a failure…Sometimes these failures can be as important as the successes, for they remind us – and the celebrities – that only certain characters, willing to perform correctly according to genre rules… are allowed to succeed.
>
> (2016, p. 384)

Greer, as we shall see, was unwilling to work within such generic constraints and responded accordingly; she may not have 'succeeded' as a reality television celebrity, but she did appear to nevertheless resonate with audiences while drawing attention to the genre's limitations.

During this iteration of *Celebrity Big Brother* (2005), the house is organised like a faux monarchy, wherein Greer is a peasant assigned the gendered role of cook. Across the six days she is in the house, Greer and her housemates are subject to various humiliating, often vomit-inducing trials set by Big Brother. She sardonically asks one of the other contestants, 'do you think big brother will pipe some gas in here to put us out of our misery?' Perhaps not surprisingly, it does not take long for Greer to refuse to undertake the allocated tasks and attempt to initiate a revolt: 'I think it's time we overthrow Big Brother...this is revolution' (2005, 2014.0041.00280). Greer is, in Ahmed's terms, a 'willful [feminist] subject'; 'willfulness is a diagnosis of the failure to comply with those whose authority is given' (2014, p. 1). The ultimate 'feminist killjoy' (Ahmed 2014), Greer simply refused, as she has throughout her life, to be disciplined and withdraws.

While the panoptical premise of the show, as with much reality television (Weber 2009), could have been expected to ring feminist alarm bells, Greer's ultimate defiance of its disciplinary regime was perhaps to be expected. Her decision to leave the house early featured in much media coverage, especially in the UK (though even the *New York Times* covered her premature departure [Lyall 2005]), and she also wrote her own *Sunday Times* opinion piece, 'Filth!' (2005a), to justify her decision.[7] In this and in her *Telegraph* (2005b) article, Greer locates her experiences within a wider culture of bullying:

> Big Brother is bullying in all its forms writ large. It is the politics of the playground projected back to people for entertainment, and its gives children in particular and people in general absolutely the wrong idea about what is acceptable behaviour.

Greer's appearance, however, had perhaps unexpected feminist consequences, leading some viewers to her other modes of feminist cultural production, such as her blockbusters – as the *Cavett* appearances had more than three decades earlier. In this vein, after watching *Celebrity Big Brother*, a woman makes clear she had 'discovered' the renowned feminist only through this popular form: 'It wasn't until my husband looked you up on the computer that I learnt about the books you have written, so I am now about to call at the local library' (M.T., 13 January 2005, Manchester, 2014.0042.00889). This viewer also notes that, while she found Greer's discursive constitution in the news to be off-putting, her presence on the small screen disrupted these pre-conceived assumptions and encouraged a reassessment of her and her feminism – once again echoing some of the *Cavett* letters. This helps further the argument, made in the previous section, about the way that television has functioned as a vital form of consciousness-raising, in the second wave but also beyond.

Aside from the viewer cited above, the majority of *Big Brother* correspondents already appear to be fans and use the epistolary form in support of Greer:

> I am a HUGE fan of Germaine Greer – she is an amazing woman and she has been a hero of mine for many years. I was so thrilled when she entered the *Celebrity Big Brother* house, as it was chance to glimpse the

94 Germaine Greer, Celebrity Feminism and the Archive

> "everyday" Germaine…Although I didn't really want to see her go, I completely understood her reasons for leaving the house and I really admired her courage in doing so.
>
> (J.A., 18 January 2005, Kent, 2014.0042.00013)

This promise of a new kind of backstage access to an 'everyday Germaine' was much desired by this fan. Likewise, a self-professed long-time fan is certain that Greer's reality television appearance will expand her audience:

> dear fabulous Germaine, you have been my inspiration and delight for 40 years. You will give a whole new audience a glimpse of your greatness in Big Brother. Your cultural impact is huge & long may you make everyone question their narrowness…I am one of your greatest and long-lasting fans.
>
> (J.W., undated, Wales, 2014.0042.00988)

Similarly convinced that Greer's appearance would expose a greater audience to her feminism, one woman emailed Greer, disappointed that she had departed the *Big Brother* house: 'by standing up and being so public, you were bringing yourself to the notice of hundreds and thousands of ordinary working women who have probably never opened anything more demanding than the *Daily Mail* or the *Mirror* in their lives' (A.B., 12 January 2005, 2014.0042.00107). Here, Greer's decision to participate is framed as a feminist one; the famous feminist was actively resisting patriarchy's bullies, exemplified by the disembodied, disciplinary gaze of 'Big Brother'.

Given that her choice to depart early appeared to garner much criticism, many viewers felt compelled to offer support for the beleaguered Greer and make explicit that this is what drove their correspondence. For example, a woman from London (L.H., 13 January 2005, 2014.0042.00366) reiterates Greer's concern about the effect of shows like *Celebrity Big Brother* on society at large, while another man worried about its impact upon Greer remarks, 'Just a line hoping you have recovered from Big Brother, what can I say' (P.A., 22 February 2005, Hebburn, 2014.0042.00013). One self-identified fan writes to reaffirm Greer's much-criticised choice to exit the house early and, as is common, invokes her intertextual knowledge of her public persona: 'I'm a 22 year old and a big fan of yours. I enjoyed watching you on celeb big brother but I think you did the right thing and in true Germaine style' (L.B., 26 April 2005, Norfolk, 2014.0042.00071). In response, Greer confesses (26 January 2005): 'I would have preferred to stay and fight but I couldn't see any way of doing it at the time. So forgive me'. That Greer feels the need to apologise to her fans is telling, as if she has let them down through her early exit. Similarly, a woman notes that she herself was 'bullied' on a reality television show and, in the affectionate tone of an intimate friend, reassures Greer that she 'did the right thing' in leaving the *Big Brother* house (J.D., 19 January 2005, London),

'The best thing to happen to night-time television' **95**

to which Greer replies: 'Thank you for your letter. It still doesn't feel like the right thing, so I need the reassurance' (undated, 2014.0042.00210). Greer appears to gain succour from her supportive fan base, who overwhelmingly endorse her (feminist) decision to depart the house.

Greer had earlier in her career expressed a preference for television as it seemingly enabled more potential to exercise control than other media forms, but her *Big Brother* experience somewhat undermines such a claim. An embodied, ageing feminist subject necessarily challenges the kinds of hyper-femininities we have come to associate with reality television (Wood 2017), so perhaps Greer's early departure was inevitable. Her decision to depart – much like her decision to simply refuse to give interviews to print journalists – is further indicative of her career-long attempt to push back against media positionings with which she disagreed or found offensive. In exiting early, Greer exercised the only form of agency she could: she withdrew her celebrity labour as she has done at various points – such as pulling articles in protest of unwelcome editorial interventions (Buchanan 2018) – without fear of the political or material repercussions, a position that many viewers found admirable.

Conclusion

Greer has clearly been a charismatic and often provocative television performer, so no wonder Dick Cavett's production company, Daphne Productions, was interested in pursuing a show with her at the helm. While there is no indication why *The Germaine Greer Show* never came to pass – perhaps this was one step too far for a yet conservative television industry that would tolerate feminism/feminists only up to a point – Greer's experience of attempting to secure funding for her own television documentary series, *The Story of Human Reproduction*, also gives us insights into the obstacles that women faced as television makers, especially in the 1970s and '80s (Taylor 2022). Professionally, as a woman *and* as a feminist seeking to disrupt hegemonic understandings of gender and sexuality, Greer was dually disadvantaged, perhaps explaining the various instances of 'unmade' film and television in her archive (Beeston and Solomon 2023). Despite these setbacks and the missed opportunities in terms of furthering audience engagement with key feminist issues (Sheehan 2016; Buchanan 2018), Greer has nevertheless continued her televisual feminist activism.

Greer's career as a feminist television personality has been long and varied, something that her preservation of written records and active sourcing of audio-visual materials brings into full view. Once again, Greer's archival practices are overtly feminist in nature, as she provides material about a woman's working life in television and its effects which would otherwise have been lost. Her work on-screen has been enormously impactful, as viewer letters examined here demonstrate, with audiences at times themselves

96 Germaine Greer, Celebrity Feminism and the Archive

subsequently pursuing feminist activism, consuming Greer's writing, or just critically reflecting on the debates staged in and through her appearances. The immediacy of the televisual form appeared to promise a more 'real' Greer with whom viewers felt they established a connection, which in turn appeared to lead to more sympathetic responses to her feminism. Greer's television work, whether on- or off-screen, has been crucial to her celebrity feminism and has continued well into the 2000s. There is therefore much more to be said about Greer as a television worker and performer, especially given the extent of the archive's audio-visual series.

Here, I have aimed to illustrate the importance of television to Greer's celebrity feminism; an embodied, seemingly more 'authentic' Greer entered loungerooms, studies, and kitchens, a larger-than-life figure seeking to challenge previously uncontested assumptions about sex, gender, intimacy, rape, abortion, motherhood, and feminism itself, and viewer letters suggest that at times she may have succeeded. They write to thank her and praise her hosting skills (*The Dick Cavett Show*); they write when they are disappointed in her (*The Last Word*); and they write in gestures of support to combat public criticism (*Celebrity Big Brother*). While these responses, given the differences in style of program and cultural and historical contexts, are diverse, viewers all use the epistolary form to reflect on what they expect from television and its celebrities – including when it comes to feminism. Television, however, was not the only form of media through which Greer sought to ensure that her feminist voice was widely heard. Even before the publication of her first blockbuster, Greer's media work extended into the realm of print media journalism. As the next chapter demonstrates, her journalistic writing prompted varied public responses from readers, largely in the form of unpublished letters to the editor which are preserved in the archive.

Notes

1 Australian television appears a noteworthy omission here. Nevertheless, the archive does contain information about a four-part documentary series for commercial network 10, which appears to have been made but is not contained in the archive (Glanville 2018), as well as much material relating to *The Story of Human Reproduction*, which was initially funded by the Australian government but appeared to be caught up in Prime Minister Whitlam's dismissal in 1975 (Taylor 2022).

2 An email from Greer's assistant to the publisher of *Shakespeare's Wife* (2008), Allen and Unwin, asserts: 'Professor Greer NEVER does print interviews, mostly because it is too difficult struggling to give intelligent answers to stupid questions, but also because they are time-consuming and usually directed by editor bias. Professor Greer will do any radio and TV' (2 August 2007, 2014.0052.00153).

3 See, for example, 2017.0002.00089, 'TV refusals 1990', which, despite the title, contains refusals dating back to the early 1970s.

4 The 'Control Record' (2018.0054) makes clear that Greer made a concerted effort to locate copies of her television appearances to include in the archive.

'The best thing to happen to night-time television' **97**

5 One of the less-than-impressed viewers, however, lodged a complaint with the Federal Communications Commission, protesting the 'completely biased' host (J.L.R., 16 June 1971).
6 In reply to a correspondent, Greer suggests that she hoped there would be another series but was unsure (26 November, 2017.0002.00134).
7 As Buchanan observes, there was a 'bidding war' between the *Mail on Sunday* and the *Sunday Times* for this 4,000-word piece (2018, p. 24), with the latter winning out.

References

Ahmed, S. (2004) *The Cultural Politics of Emotion*, Edinburgh: Edinburgh University Press.

Ahmed, S. (2014) *Willful Subjects*, Durham: Duke University Press.

Alibhai-Brown, Y. (2005) 'Germaine Greer Quits Big Brother', *Daily Mail*, 11 January, accessed via https://www.dailymail.co.uk/tvshowbiz/article-333715/Germaine-Greer-quits-Big-Brother.html

Ang, I. (1982) *Watching Dallas: Soap Opera and the Melodramatic Imagination*, London: Routledge.

Barker-Plummer, B. (1995) 'News as a Political Resource: Media Strategies and Political Identity in the U. S. Women's Movement, 1966–1975', *Critical Studies in Mass Communication*, vol. 12. no. 3: 306–324.

Barnard, P. (1994) 'Fairer, Brighter and Moving Ahead', *The Times*, 22 October, Germaine Greer Archive, General Correspondence, 2014.0042.00261, University of Melbourne.

Beeston, A. and Solomon, S. (2023) *Incomplete: The Feminist Possibilities of the Unfinished Film*, Los Angeles: University of California Press.

Bennett, J. (2008) 'The Television Personality System: Televisual Stardom Revisited After Film Theory', *Screen*, vol. 49, no. 1: 32–50.

Bennett, J. (2010) *Television Personalities: Stardom and The Small Screen*, London: Routledge.

Berkman, M. (1994) 'Cushions at the Ready', *Daily Mail*, 7 November, Germaine Greer Archive, General Correspondence, 2014.0042.00261, University of Melbourne.

Berryman, R., & Kavka, M. (2017) '"I Guess A Lot of People See Me as a Big Sister or a Friend": The Role of Intimacy in the Celebrification of Beauty Vloggers', *Journal of Gender Studies*, vol. 26, no. 3: 307–320.

Bleakley, P. (2016) '"Love me or hate me – I don't care": Katie Hopkins, *Celebrity Big Brother* and the Destruction of a Negative Image', *Continuum*, vol. 30, no. 4: 419–432.

Bonner, F. (2002) *Ordinary Television: Analyzing Popular TV*, London: Sage.

Bonner, F. (2011) *Personality Presenters: Television's Intermediaries with Viewers*, London: Routledge.

Bourdon, J. (2015) 'Detextualizing: How to Write a History of Audiences', *European Journal of Communication*, vol. 30, no. 1: 7–21.

Brady, A. (2021) 'Clementine Ford, Online Misogyny, and the Labour of Celebrity Feminism', in A. Taylor and J. McIntyre (eds.), *Gender and Australian Celebrity Culture*, London: Routledge, pp. 91–108.

98 Germaine Greer, Celebrity Feminism and the Archive

Buchanan, R. (2017) 'Milk Outtake – Germaine Greer' (26 February 1969), accessed via:https://archives.unimelb.edu.au/explore/feature-images/milk-outtakes-germaine-greer

Buchanan, R. (2018) 'Foreign Correspondence: Journalism in the Germaine Greer Archive', *Archives and Manuscripts*, vol. 46, no. 1: 18–39.

Celebrity Big Brother (2005), Germaine Greer Archive, Audiovisual Recordings Produced and Received by Germaine Greer, 1969–2014, 2014.0041.00280, University of Melbourne.

Clarke, J.S. (2024) *Producing Feminism: Television Work in the Age of Women's Liberation*, Los Angeles: University of California Press.

Collie, H., Irwin, M., Moseley, R., Wheatley, H. and Wood, H. (2013) 'Researching the History of Television for Women in Britain, 1947–1989', *Media History*, vol. 19, no. 1: 107–117.

Crenshaw, K. (1989) 'Demarginalizing the Intersection of Race and Sex: A Black Feminist Critique of Antidiscrimination Doctrine', Feminist Theory and Antiracist Politics', *The University of Chicago Legal Forum*, 140:139–167.

Culf, A. (1994) 'BBC chief denies surfeit of chat as Oprah Winfrey is brought from BSkyB to add to Rantzen, Greer and Street-Porter talk show', *The Guardian*, 28 September, Germaine Greer Archive, General Correspondence, 2014.0042.00261, University of Melbourne.

Deller, R. (2016) 'Star Image, Celebrity Reality Television and the Fame Cycle', *Celebrity Studies*, vol. 7, no. 3: 373–389.

Dick Cavett Show (1971a), Producer's notes, Germaine Greer Archive, Early Years, 2014.0044.00161, University of Melbourne.

Dick Cavett Show (1971b), Viewer Letters, Germaine Greer Archive, Early Years, 2014.0042.00164 and 2014.0042.00165, University of Melbourne.

Dow, B.J. (2014) *Watching Women's Liberation 1970: Feminism's Pivotal Year on the Network News*, Urbana: University of Illinois.

Drake, P. (2018) 'Celebrity, Reputational Capital and the Media Industries', in A. Elliott (ed.) *Routledge Handbook of Celebrity Studies*, London: Routledge, pp. 271–284.

Driessens, O. (2012) 'The Celebritization of Society and Culture: Understanding the Structural Dynamics of Celebrity Culture', *International Journal of Cultural Studies*, vol. 16, no. 6: 641–657.

Dudar, H. (1971) 'Female, but not feminine', *New York Post*, April 10, Germaine Greer Archive, Early Years, 2014.0044.00171, University of Melbourne.

Dyer, R. (1986) *Heavenly Bodies: Film Stars and Society*, London: Routledge.

Dux, M. (2010) 'Temple of *The Female Eunuch*: Germaine Greer 40 years on', *Kill your darlings*, Issue 2: 9–17.

Feay, S. (1994) 'Maven Haven', *Time Out*, 19–26 October, Germaine Greer Archive, General Correspondence, 2014.0042.00261, University of Melbourne.

Gamson, J. (1994) *Claims to Fame: Celebrity in Contemporary America*, Los Angeles: University of California Press.

Genette, J. (1997) *Paratexts: Thresholds of Interpretation*, Cambridge: Cambridge University Press.

Germaine Greer Archive. Correspondence with Publishers, 1970-2014, 2014a.0052, University of Melbourne.

Germaine Greer Archive. General Correspondence, 2014b.0042, University of Melbourne.

Germaine Greer Archive. Early Years, 2014c.0044, University of Melbourne.

Germaine Greer Archive. Television 1968–c.2012, 2017.0002, University of Melbourne.

Gibson, O. (2005) 'Greer walks out of "bullying" Big Brother', *The Guardian*, 12 January, accessed via: https://www.theguardian.com/media/2005/jan/12/bigbrother.broadcasting

Giroux, H. (2000) *Impure Acts: The Practical Politics of Cultural Studies*, New York: Routledge.

Glanville, L. (2018) 'The End of Reckoning – Archival Silences in the Germaine Greer Archive', *Archives and Manuscripts*, vol. 46, no. 1: 45–48.

Goffman, E. (1959) *The Presentation of Self in Everyday Life*, London: Penguin.

Grant, L. (1993) *Fundamental Feminism: Radical Feminist History for the Future*, New York: Routledge.

'Greer Window' (1994), *Sunday Times*, 30 October, Germaine Greer Archive, General Correspondence, 2014.0042.00261, University of Melbourne.

Greer, G. (1994) 'Keeping the mud wrestling to a minimum', *The Telegraph*, 17 October, Germaine Greer Archive, Print Journalism, 2014.0046.00397, University of Melbourne.

Greer, G. (2005a) 'Why I said yes to Big Brother's shilling', *Daily Telegraph*, 12 January.

Greer, G. (2005b) 'Filth!', *Sunday Times*, 16 January, Germaine Greer Archive, Print Journalism, 2014.0046.000984, University of Melbourne.

Habermas, J. (1962/1991) *The Structural Transformation of the Public Sphere*, Cambridge: MIT Press.

Henderson, M. and Taylor, A. (2020) *Postfeminism in Context*, London: Routledge.

Heller, D. (1998) 'Bluestocking Salons and the Public Sphere', *Eighteenth-century Life*, vol. 22, no. 2: 59–82.

Hobson, J. (2017) 'Celebrity Feminism: More than a Gateway', *Signs: Journal of Women in Culture and Society*, vol. 42, no. 4: 999–1007.

Jacobs, J. (2000) *The Intimate Screen: Early British Television Drama*, Oxford: Oxford University Press.

Kay, J.B. (2015) 'Speaking Bitterness: Second-Wave Feminism, Television Talk, and the Case of *No Man's Land* (1973)', *Feminist Media Histories*, vol. 1, no. 2: 64–89.

Kay, J.B. (2020) *Gender, Media and Voice: Communicative Injustice and Public Speech*, London: Palgrave Macmillan.

Kleinhenz, E. (2018) *Germaine: The Life of Germaine Greer*, North Sydney: Knopf.

Langer, J. (1981) 'Television's "Personality System"', *Media, Culture and Society*, vol. 4: 351–365.

Lee, K. (2020) *Limelight: Canadian Women and the Rise of Celebrity Autobiography*, Toronto: Wilfred Laurier University Press.

Lewis, T. (2001) 'Embodied Experts: Robert Hughes, Cultural Studies and the Celebrity Intellectual', *Continuum*, vol. 15, no. 2: 233–247.

Lusty, N. (2017) 'Riot Grrrl Manifestos and Radical Vernacular Feminism', *Australian Feminist Studies*, vol. 32, no. 93: 219–239.

Lyall, S. (2005) 'Germaine Greer's Orwellian Ordeal on "Big Brother"', *New York Times*, 20 January, accessed via: https://www.nytimes.com/2005/01/20/arts/television/germaine-greers-orwellian-ordeal-on-big-brother.html

Massingbed, H. (1994) 'The Last Word', *The Telegraph*, 24 October, Germaine Greer Archive, General Correspondence, 2014.0042.00261, University of Melbourne.

McClure, D.R. (2012) '"Have you understood anything I've said?": *The Dick Cavett Show*, Jimi Hendrix, and the Framing of the Black Counterculture in 1969', *The Sixties*, vol. 5, no. 1: 23–46.

McGrath, A. (1999) '*The Female Eunuch* in the Suburbs: Reflections on Adolescence, Autobiography, and History-Writing', *Journal of Popular Culture*, vol. 33. no. 1: 177–190.

Moie, J. (1994) 'A word too far', *The Guardian*, 11 November, Germaine Greer Archive, Television 1968–c.2012, 2017.002.00133, University of Melbourne.

Morley, D. (1980) *The Nationwide Audience: Structure and Decoding*, London: BFI.

Moseley, R. and Wheatley, H. (2008) 'Is Archiving a Feminist Issue? Historical Research and the Past, Present and Future of Television Studies', *Cinema Journal*, vol. 47, no. 3: 152–158.

Nowra L. (2010) 'The Better self? Germaine Greer and *The Female Eunuch*', *The Monthly*, March: 40–46.

Oliva, M. (2020) 'From the Literary field to Reality TV: The Perils of Downward Celebrity Migration', *European Journal of Cultural Studies*, vol. 23, no. 1: 18–34.

Peck, J. (2008) *Age of Oprah: Cultural Icon for the Neoliberal Era*, New York: Routledge.

Phipps, A. (2020) *Me, Not You: The Trouble with Mainstream Feminism*, Manchester: Manchester University Press.

Redmond, S. (2006) 'Intimate Fame Everywhere', in S. Holmes and S. Redmond eds. *Framing Celebrity: New Directions in Celebrity Culture*, London: Routledge, pp.

Rojek, C. (2001) *Celebrity*, London: Reaktion.

Schaefer, H. (2020) *American Literature and Immediacy: Literary Innovation and the Emergence of Photography, Film, and Television*, Cambridge: Cambridge University Press.

Schickel, R. (1985) *Common Fame: The Culture of Celebrity*, London: Pavilion Books

Shattuc, J. (1997) *The Talking Cure: TV Talk Shows and Women*, London: Routledge.

Sheehan, R.J. (2016) '"If we had more like her we would no longer be the unheard majority": Germaine Greer's Reception in the United States', *Australian Feminist Studies*, vol. 31. no. 87: 62–77.

Taylor, A. (2014) 'Germaine Greer's Adaptable Celebrity: Feminism, Unruliness, and Humour on the British Small Screen', *Feminist Media Studies*, vol. 14, no. 5: 759–774.

Taylor, A. (2022) 'Germaine Greer's *Story of Human Reproduction*, the Dismissal, and Feminist "Unproduction Studies"', unpublished conference paper, Cultural Studies Association of Australasia Conference, 28–30 June, Edith Cowan University.

The Germaine Greer Show Proposal (n.d.), Daphne Productions, Germaine Greer Archive, Early Years, 2014.0044.00166, University of Melbourne.

The Last Word (1994), BBC2, Germaine Greer Archive, Audiovisual Recordings Produced and Received by Germaine Greer, 1969–2014, 2014.0041, University of Melbourne.

The Last Word (1994), Viewer letters, Germaine Greer Archive, Television 1968–c.2012, 2017.0022.00134, University of Melbourne.

Thompson, B. (2002) 'Multiracial Feminism: Recasting the Chronology of Second Wave Feminism', *Feminist Studies*, vol. 28, no. 2: 336–360.

Tolson, A. (2010) 'A New Authenticity? Communicative Practices on YouTube', *Critical Discourse Studies*, vol. 7, no. 4: 277–289.

Tolson, A. (2015) 'The History of Television Celebrity: A Discursive Approach', *Celebrity Studies*, vol. 6, no. 3: 341–354.

Turner, G. (2004) *Understanding Celebrity*, London: Sage.

Wallace, C. (1997) *Germaine Greer: Untamed Shrew*, Sydney: Macmillan.

Weber, B. (2009) *Makeover TV: Selfhood, Citizenship, and Celebrity*, Durham: Duke University Press.

Wood, H. (2017) 'The Politics of Hyperbole on *Geordie Shore*: Class, Gender, Youth and Excess', *European Journal of Cultural Studies*, vol. 20, no. 1: 39–55.

York, L. (forthcoming) 'Unseemly Affects: Gender, Celebrity, and the Policing of Fame Hunger', in J. McIntyre and A. Taylor. (eds), *The Routledge Companion to Gender and Celebrity*, London: Routledge.

4

'GREER HAS DONE IT AGAIN!'

Reader-writers and Feminist Journalism

Introduction

In *The Female Eunuch*, Greer articulated a clear theory of feminist media engagement, heavily criticising women's liberationists who chose a separatist approach. Claiming that women's voices are commonly subordinated to men's in the press simply because women refuse to contribute, she emphasised that they needed to take up their pens: 'It is to be hoped that more and more women decide to influence the media by writing for them, not being written about' (1970a, p. 309). Taking her own advice, Greer traded on the celebrity capital garnered from the success of her first blockbuster to exchange her long history writing for student magazines and the underground press for column space in various mainstream newspapers and magazines. From the early 1970s onwards, Greer, rather than simply being represented in the mainstream media, *became* the media (Buchanan 2018, p. 34). She did this by seeking out and accepting columnist and contributor roles in predominantly British newspapers and magazines as well as some Australian and US publications – including the unlikely *Playboy* – when other feminists pointedly refused such assignments (Sheehan 2019). Through such journalistic labour, via which Greer's voice was amplified over those of other feminists, she actively shaped the kind of feminist debates that were being publicly staged. This chapter continues the project of reframing Greer, analysing her thus far critically overlooked work as a celebrity journalist (as in a celebrity who is a journalist) and political commentator and the varying, at times contradictory, responses it garnered from readers, in the form of letters to the editor.

While Greer took advantage of her post-*Female Eunuch* visibility to become more deeply involved in mainstream journalistic outlets, this should not be

DOI: 10.4324/9781315179841-5

seen as a 'migration' from the literary to the journalistic sphere. 'Field migration' occurs when celebrities leverage the fame resulting from their work in one area to diversify, deploying their celebrity capital to move into another field (Giles 2015; see also Driessens 2012, p. 648). In contrast, Greer has always used magazines and newspapers to develop and circulate her feminist voice, from counter-cultural magazines like *Suck* (of which she was a founding editor) and *Oz* to regular columns in Britain's *Times* and *Guardian*, thus signalling more of a field 'amplification'. In her article on the huge amount of journalistic material contained in the Greer archive, including that relating to her work as a foreign correspondent, Rachel Buchanan (2018, p. 33) convincingly argues that 'Greer's journalism needs to be reassessed and recognised as having equal value to her other types of writing', especially given the number of reader responses which leave no doubt as to its resonance; this chapter contributes to such re-evaluation.

Through her journalism, Greer was able to shift from object to subject, itself a crucial feminist gesture. That is, while she (understandably) found her depiction as a sexy feminist superstar in the press troublesome, through journalism she was able to write herself into being and articulate her feminist positions on key political issues with some degree of autonomy (though not without editorial interference or mediation). In Everette Dennis's (2017, p. 105) terms, Greer could be classified an 'advocacy journalist', a descriptor for those who – increasingly from the early 1970s – used the journalistic form to further activist causes. Remarkably, however, Greer's writing for mainstream newspapers and magazines has been largely critically overlooked.[1] More broadly, most scholarship on second-wave feminist journalism tends to focus on feminist periodicals (Farrell 1998; Sedgwick 2020; Strimpel 2022; Waters 2016), often nostalgically celebrating these woman-only spaces, ostensibly unsullied by patriarchal commodity capitalism. Such criticism fails to recognise that radical voices such as Greer's (and even Gloria Steinem's) were incorporated into the mainstream press *without* being diluted (Taylor 2016). Once again, as with television, this is an example of how Greer as a celebrity complicates or exceeds more pessimistic critical narratives about the feminism–media nexus.

In this chapter, in addition to the pieces themselves, I consider the kinds of debates and dialogues precipitated by select examples of Greer's feminist journalism. The articles I analyse here were produced in distinct publishing outlets, each with very different addressees: 'Seduction is a Four-letter Word' (1973b), published in pornographic men's magazine *Playboy* (resulting in by far the largest cache of letters discussed in this chapter); a pro-abortion piece (1972a), one of Greer's weekly columns in Britain's *Sunday Times*, published as 'Germaine Greer on why the Abortion Act is a calamity'; and 'McGovern, The Big Tease' (1972e), Greer's feminist coverage of the 1972 US Democratic Convention, commissioned by *Harper's* magazine. While all these pieces were coincidentally published in the same 12-month period, they were

104 Germaine Greer, Celebrity Feminism and the Archive

chosen for analysis because they each attracted considerable letters to the editor, which have been preserved together in the archive's General Correspondence series (rather than with the article in the Print Journalism series). This series, as previously mentioned, is usually organised alphabetically, so this represents a deviation from her normal practice, which effectively directs archival researchers to such letters (Glanville 2018, p. 47). Some characterise themselves as Greer fans, some are ambivalent about her feminist interventions into the journalistic sphere, and others still express hostility at her patent challenges to their own ideological frames, indicating – like other chapters – the historical complexity of reader response to Greer and her celebrity feminism.

Readers-writers: 'Citizen critics'?

Letters penned to editors of magazines or newspapers are a material record of the active meaning-making in which media consumers always engage (Hall 1980), moving from 'semiotic productivity' to 'textual productivity' (Fiske 1992). They are a crucial way in which citizens seek to participate in deliberative democracy (Wahl-Jorgensen 2002), staging debate and dialogue with newspaper staff as well as other readers. These letters, of course, are by no means representative. Instead, they include only readers who were 'motivated enough' to write to the newspaper or editor (Farrell 1998, p. 152) to express how they felt about a specific piece and, in these cases, its celebrity author. I should also note that the letters discussed here are those held in the archive, the original handwritten or typed reader letters which were carbon-copied to Greer or which editors and agents forwarded to her. Some were published, some were not; my concern is their place in the Greer archive and how their inclusion allows us to reflect upon her journalism and its impact.

Such letters, as this chapter demonstrates, 'reveal the traces of readers' interactions with a paper [or magazine]', offering insights into how 'periodicals addressed their readers, invited them to try on new identities, and engaged them in the debates of the public sphere' (Green 2012, p. 462). Pre-social media and the participatory opportunities of convergence culture, such a form was one of the only ways that audiences could stage these kinds of interventions; in doing so, they become 'reader-writers' who seek to shape the content of the newspapers or magazines to which they contribute (Farrell 1998; Taylor 2004; Le Masurier 2007; Le Masurier 2009). Importantly, many letters to editors in the archive, in contrast to the fan letters examined in Chapter 2, appear to be written by men (to men), often seeking to challenge Greer's feminist authority. Greer had herself written in *The Female Eunuch*, 'for every woman who writes a letter to the editor there are hundreds who can't manage it' (1970a, p. 309). Women felt, as Greer implies, that their voices were devalued, thus explaining their relative

'Greer has done it again!' **105**

lack of participation in this public forum (perhaps with the exception of women's magazines, which are directly addressed to them [Strimpel 2022; Chapter 5 here]).

The motivations for these kinds of letters are often less explicitly stated than in the more private forms also held in the archive. We can speculate that their authors wrote from a desire to be heard in increasingly charged public conversations about how gender, intimacy, sociality, and sexuality were being refigured. Like viewers, the topics that, according to the archive at least, drove readers to become writers include rape, abortion, and reformist versus revolutionary feminism (or the question of whether, or to what extent, feminists should operate within existing political institutions and structures). These are all political preoccupations of Greer's across decades, and her position on them remains remarkably consistent despite claims to the contrary (Winant 2015).[2] In her journalism, Greer deployed discourses, tropes, and metaphors that were deeply informed by her radical variant of feminism, something which provoked intense responses from some readers and shook others into new ways of seeing.

As 'public acts of interpretation by citizen critics', letters to the editor 'can reveal the very unsettled and polyphonic nature of texts as well as the widely divergent judgements of actual readers' (Eberly 2002, p. 2). Greer's celebrity profoundly shaped these responses. She was not merely a nameless columnist but a high-profile provocateur whose by-line would guarantee an engaged readership, perhaps provoking the kinds of controversy that could increase circulation; as with many viewers, readers often brought to bear their intertextual knowledge of Greer-as-celebrity to their assessments. While their letters were not addressed to her, they spoke *of* a 'Greer' whom they felt they knew (like those discussed in the fan mail chapter), a sense of intimacy or at least knowability fostered by celebrity culture (Dyer 1986; Rojek 2015).

Greer, of course, would never be an 'objective' journalistic voice. While such an idea itself is clearly a fiction, it was arguably Greer's overt feminist 'I' that made her attractive to editors (as to television producers) seeking to provide content on one of the most newsworthy topics of the day. That said, even feminist scholars appear to have taken Greer to task for this patent interestedness. For Carolyn Steedman, Greer wrote pieces one would expect to see in more overtly political spaces rather than mainstream newspapers. Steedman (1986), arguing that Greer's polemicism effectively compromises her as a journalist, makes the criticism that her journalism is

> constructed in the mode of the political pamphlet, and this is one of the reasons why the pieces of journalism from the Seventies make generally unsatisfactory reading: she is too inclined to move away from the good journalist's practice of making narrative sense out of something observed or heard, of just telling the story.

106 Germaine Greer, Celebrity Feminism and the Archive

This claim that she failed to 'just tell the story', however, yearns for an impossible form of objectivity, itself rooted in masculinist assumptions long critiqued by feminists as well as proponents of what would become known as the 'new journalism' (Pauly 2014). As Patrice McDermott (1994, p. 26) emphasises, feminist journalists commonly appropriated rhetorical techniques that had proven successful in the underground press: 'Stressing the importance of subjectivity, politically informed reporting, and the integrity of emotion rather than the mainstream claims to dispassionate, objective authority'. Greer's training in the underground press, as well as her feminism, ensured that her voice was never dispassionate – which arguably gives her celebrity feminist journalism its appeal.

Greer's journalistic labour in the archive

Following the publication of her first bestseller, Greer became increasingly sought after as a journalistic commentator, particularly in the US, where her *Female Eunuch* book tour – described as 'a full-blown marketing event in the tradition of P. T. Barnum' (Scott 2000, p. 24) – helped rocket the book to number one on American bestseller lists by August 1971 (Murray 2004, p. 181). Greer herself remarked on *The Female Eunuch*'s role in her journalistic currency, noting that when it 'began to take off...I too became flavour of the month' (1986, p. xxv). Greer, conceptualising journalism as a key resource for the women's movement (Barker-Plummer 1995), then capitalised on this desire for her voice. While other second-wave feminists saw mainstream media as inevitably heterosexist and unavoidably seeped in patriarchal bias, and to be avoided at all costs (Barker-Plummer 1995; Dow 1996; Mendes 2011), Greer had an alternative approach based on her libertarianism: 'True to her anarchist-libertarian background, Greer regarded a boycott of the mass media as a form of inverse censorship' (Le Masurier 2016, pp. 38–39).

The Print Journalism series in the Greer archive is made up of 24 boxes, featuring 1,270 items from 1959 to 2010 (and though extensive it is by no means exhaustive).[3] Without Greer's 'methodical recordkeeping', many of these pieces and their effects would be lost (Buchanan 2018, p. 20; see also Weber and Buchanan 2019). In addition to pieces that she pitched herself, Greer has been in great demand as a feminist journalist, as illustrated by the archive's copious requests from newspaper and magazine editors. For periods in her life, journalism has been Greer's primary source of income, and this was certainly the case when she retired from her position at Warwick University to focus on her popular writing in 1973 – itself a move that was considered newsworthy (though she did later return to the academy, pursuing careers as an academic and journalist concurrently).[4] Under the finding aid subject heading 'Wages – Journalists', the archive itself contains much evidence of her work as a freelance journalist, including details about pay rates and negotiations with editors (with Greer often scribbling 'No fee, no work' on correspondence), that are not usually made public in such a way (Weber and Buchanan 2019, p. 237).

Although it might be rare to consider Greer in these terms (Nolan 1999), her status as a respected professional journalist was underscored by her invitations to deliver addresses to the Washington and the Canberra Press Clubs, in 1971 and 1972 respectively – she was the first woman to do so at both (Buchanan 2018, p. 24). Greer also edited various magazines, either for extended periods (such as *Suck* and *Oz*) or as a guest editor, including for the Australian magazine *POL* in 1972. For this issue, she unsurprisingly received much criticism; it included articles on her love life and a victim-blaming piece entitled 'How to avoid being a pack rape victim' (Greer 1972d).[5] Later in her career, the archive reveals, she was even approached to guest edit British men's magazine *Loaded* but sagaciously 'decided that the whole proposal is too risky'. As she self-reflexively concludes, 'I don't have any difficulty attracting publicity' (to D.I., Colman Getty PR Consultancy, 20 December 1999, London, 2014.0052.00044).

Replying to a correspondent who worried about the personal cost of her media visibility, Greer outlines what has for decades been her philosophy vis-à-vis media interventions:

> I wrote for the underground press for seven years and no pay. What I am doing now is a hundred times harder and I spend many more hours vomiting. That does not mean it's better necessarily. Nor does it mean I've sold out…Purity is the only significant privilege in a world of universal prostitution and I have renounced it.
>
> (to J.H., 14 September 1971, 2014.0042.00405)

In contrast to other feminists, including those writing more recently about popular feminism and its lamentable commodification (Zielser 2017; Banet-Weiser 2018), Greer rejected the idea that feminism and celebrity culture (and media more broadly) were fundamentally incompatible. Rather, like Jennifer Wicke (1994, p. 334), Greer recognised that 'our [feminism's] mass cultural tag sale took place long'. Despite the discomfort, including physically (i.e., the reference to 'vomiting'), that it causes, Greer, explicitly addressing the oft-repeated claim she has 'sold out' (Dreifus 1971), sees no other option than mainstream media engagement. Greer herself did toy with the idea of starting her own women's magazine, a plan that never came to fruition.[6] Regardless, the magnetic author had no shortage of outlets for her own feminist journalism, including those addressed to men.

Greer and the 'men's press'

Enacting her conviction that men as well as women needed to begin the process of rethinking (hetero)sex and its fraught power dynamics, Greer wrote for what we might call the *men's press*, including *Esquire*, most notably 'My Mailer Problem' (Greer 1971a) and 'What Turns Women On' (Greer 1973a).

108 Germaine Greer, Celebrity Feminism and the Archive

Such relationships, coupled with her apparent reluctance to write for women's movement publications, also buttressed claims from radical feminists that her feminism and her approach to the 'malestream press' were suspect (Spongberg 1993, p. 415). Without doubt, one of the most controversial mainstream publications in which Greer chose to appear and for which she chose to write was *Playboy*. In the early 1970s, Greer was highly sought after by the magazine, including for a ten-page interview in 1972. She anticipated considerable feminist blow-back for her tactical decision to be interviewed which she attempted to manage by telling interviewer Nat Lehrmann that her '"role is simply to preach to the unconverted"'. Underscoring the difference between herself and other feminists, she adds: '"I'm the one who talks to *Playboy*"' (1972, p. 64). Moreover, true to her libertarian roots in the Sydney Push – a sub-cultural group of left-wing intellectuals from the 1940s to 1970s who rejected authoritarianism and conventional morality (Coombs 1996) – Greer herself had co-founded the pornographic magazine *Suck* in 1969 (and in which she herself had posed nude in an unsuccessful attempt to undermine women's objectification[7]). Such a history perhaps suggested that she would be more amenable to requests to write for *Playboy* than other women's liberationists would. She did, nevertheless, reject other approaches from them and used her extended interview to launch a scathing critique of the magazine and its sexual politics.[8]

While it is unclear whether Greer pitched the article or whether the magazine commissioned the piece, in January 1973 *Playboy* published Greer's anti-rape piece, 'Seduction is a Four- Letter Word'.[9] In a response to a reader letter, Greer makes explicit her implied addressee and her purpose in writing the article:

> The piece I wrote in *Playboy* I didn't write for women, I wrote it for men because, although they claim that something like a million women read *Playboy* in the United State alone, it's only the cads who buy it.
> (to M.R., 21 February 1973, New York, 2014.0042.00736)

These 'cads' needed to be 'turned on to' sexual liberation as well. In another letter, she also expresses her disapproval of the article's title, which 'was not my idea and never earned my approval' (to W.H., 28 January 1973, 2014.0042.00406) – an instance of her dissatisfaction with what happened to her copy after it left her hands, examples of which can be found throughout the archive (Buchanan 2018a; Kleinhenz 2019).

For magazines like *Playboy*, Greer's celebrity feminism was seen to be more acceptable than the forms embodied by other feminists, presumably due to her heterosexual desirability as well as her pioneering sex positivity. Such sex positivity was evidenced especially by her prior 'cunt power' writing for *Suck* and *Oz*, including 'The Politics of Female Sexuality' (1970b) and 'Lady love your cunt' (1971b). As Carrie Pitzulo remarks, 'Here was a version of feminism that *Playboy* could happily support' (2011, p. 282). The fact that the young Greer (like Steinem) was conventionally attractive, playful, fashionable, and glamourous is undoubtedly crucial to her celebrification and acceptance by mainstream media, including the men's press (Mosmann 2016; Taylor 2016). Although I do not downplay the limits of this positioning, I argue, contra previous critics (Spongberg 1993; Bradley 2003; Murray 2004), that it did not serve to take the edge off or undermine Greer's radicalism. Quite the contrary, as we will now see.

'Seduction is a four-letter word': Reframing rape

Through her journalism in the early 1970s, Greer engaged with some of the women's liberation movement's key issues, including rape (and abortion, as the next section demonstrates). In *The Female Eunuch*, as Lisa Featherstone argues, Greer refused to position rape as anomalous or exceptional behaviour. Instead, by seeing it as part of an entrenched culturally sanctioned hatred against women, she sought to reposition it as 'ordinary and banal' (Featherstone 2021, p. 79). Greer's article, as Rebecca Sheehan notes, was part of a growing antirape activist movement that 'understood rape as a tool of patriarchy and an act of male dominance' which needed to be exposed (2024, pp. 742–43). In this regard, Greer repeatedly invoked her own rape as a university student in interviews and in her own writing (Sheehan 2024, p. 744). Given the focus on 'speaking out' (Serisier 2018) and validating women's personal experiences during the second wave, including of sexual violence, feminist journalists like Greer used their column space to render visible this abuse as a crucial step in its eradication.

In the *Playboy* piece, Greer foregrounds the shortcomings of the legal system in terms of redressing the harms of sexual assault, underscoring low conviction rates as well as how women are discursively constituted during trials in ways which ensure that their testimonies are discredited. That is, how they come be positioned as 'tainted witnesses' (Gilmore 2017; see also Gilmore 2023) – which continues to this day. As Greer asserts, women's rape testimonies are subject to gendered judgements and often racialised 'economies of believability' (Banet-Weiser and Higgins 2023). To give a sense of the legal system's inadequacies and lack of successful sexual assault prosecutions, she observes: 'A man is very unlucky to be convicted of the crime of rape' and 'an adult woman is called actually upon to prove her innocence in the course of a rape prosecution' (Greer 1973b/1986, p. 155). She also characterises the courtroom experience in terms of re-traumatisation (p. 156).[10] While she argues that structural deficiencies are important, Greer's key preoccupation in the article is to expand what readers think of as rape. That is, the central goal of the piece is to reframe 'seduction' as what she dubs 'petty rape', which she emphasises is no less egregious than 'grand rape' (p. 162). Throughout, Greer seeks to persuade *Playboy* readers that attempting to coerce women into sex *is* rape, a sentiment that would have been remarkable at the time of publication and likely a belief foreign to most of *Playboy*'s readers.

To demonstrate its ubiquity in the US, in her *Playboy* article Greer casts rape as 'a national pastime' (p. 153). She also argues for 'affirmative consent', a principle that has been codified recently in a number of contexts in response to #MeToo: 'Rather than rely on the negative criterion that absence of resistance justifies sexual congress, we must insist that positive desire alone dignifies sexual intercourse and makes it joyful' (p. 155). Here, we see the sex-positive feminism of Greer's earlier writing (Thompson 2016) coupled with an emphasis on consent. As feminist criminologist Tanya Serisier (2020) notes, affirmative consent has only recently begun to receive the kind of cultural legitimacy that eluded it historically. In this respect, Greer's arguments are remarkable for the period in which they were articulated as well as the publication in which they were aired. For Greer, the project of refiguring what we think of as sexual assault has continued well into the twenty-first century, including most recently in *On Rape* (2018), which focuses on what she dubs 'everyday rape' (Bueskens 2020).

In Greer's assessment, it is women's growing feminist consciousness that will allow them to fearlessly call out men's behaviours: 'As women develop more confidence and more self-esteem, and become as supportive towards each other as they have been to men, they also lose their reluctance to denounce men for petty rape' (p. 167). Women's solidarity and sisterhood, too, will provide them with the strength to identify such sexual 'coercion' as assault. She uses italics to enforce her position, directly addressing the (male) reader and using the personal pronoun 'us' to signal that she is speaking for women collectively: '*If you do not like us, cannot listen to our part of the conversation, if we are only meat to you, then leave us alone*' (p. 167, original emphasis). While such anger has more recently been seen to be 'all the rage', especially in the context of #MeToo (Kay 2019), the generative power of women's anger has a much longer history (Lorde 1981), particularly in writing from the second wave, such as Greer's. The article concludes with a warning: 'Women are sick to their souls of being fucked over. Now that sex has become political the petty rapist had better watch his ass; he won't be getting away with it too much longer' (p. 168). As in this quotation, Greer's voice in the piece is uncompromising; it is fierce, unapologetic, and threatening.

With a polemical piece that sought to extend popular understandings of what constitutes sexual assault, Greer successfully brought second-wave feminism to the pages of *Playboy*. For the popular men's magazine, then, this incorporation of feminist content represented a canny form of branding, itself designed to stave off criticisms of its inherent sexism (perhaps an impossible goal given the magazine's focus), while enabling Greer access to a readership that patently needed to be exposed to a feminist reconceptualisation of heterosex (Fraterrigo 2009). As Pitzulo argues,

Greer pointed out that sex was political and public and warned readers that the tide of the sex wars was shifting. The feminist antirape movement was just beginning in 1973, but *Playboy*'s readers were already being educated on the subject by a leading feminist.

(2011, p. 283)

This is a pedagogical role that Greer had been playing in the underground press in the preceding years (Gil-Glazer 2023), a counter-cultural space which she would deliberately eschew in favour of more mainstream, potentially more impactful, venues. Archival material demonstrates that such readerly 'education' was indeed accomplished.

The General Correspondence series includes a lengthy typed summary of unattributed reader mail in response to Greer's article, in the form of an internal magazine memo sent to editor Hugh Hefner and forwarded to Greer (N.L., 21 February 1973, 2014.0042.00688)[11]: 'Readers responded personally and emphatically to Germaine Greer's plea for an honest contemporary sexual ethic in Seduction is a Four-Letter Word.' The summary does not include any reader details, just what were thought to be salient quotes from the letters; it is also not apparent from the archive if any of them subsequently appeared in the magazine. To signal that this readerly outpouring was unique, the memo notes that the magazine received about 400 more letters in January 1973 (when the article was published) than in January 1972.

Many *Playboy* readers expressed intense praise for Greer's article and appreciation for its author's clarity, one describing it as 'the most far-out, up-to-date, straightforward, pull-no-punches article that I have ever had the pleasure of reading and rereading'. The value this reader-writer places on the article is also evident in the reference to 'rereading'. Somewhat ironically, given the magazine they consume and to which they write, readers consider Greer a valuable interlocutor and willingly question the objectification of women: 'It is time to eliminate the fantasies of men when they decide what the wills of women are. It is time to realize that women are whole human beings. Greer's article was a very positive step in this direction'. For others, Greer's feminism, through this particular piece, has reached them in a way no other form had (a claim we commonly see in letters): 'The first written work by or about Germaine Greer to which I have reacted favorably both intellectually and emotionally'. While Greer's feminism had hitherto failed to resonate, this piece marks a welcome exception.

Women readers of Greer's blockbuster saw themselves as the disempowered 'eunuchs' identified therein, but in a similar process of identification, the male *Playboy* reader-writers saw themselves as the often violent oppressors invoked throughout this article:

Unfortunately, I found myself described, rather vividly, more than once. I am determined now to take a woman at her word and to eliminate any

112 Germaine Greer, Celebrity Feminism and the Archive

element of trickery. I can't help feeling that both sexes would be much happier if we all did.

This man emphasises that Greer's writing has effectively transformed his understanding of consent: the article's central aim. After self-identifying as a 'staunch antifeminist' who was reluctant to tackle Greer's piece, another reader-writer also reinterprets his sexual history through the feminist lens it provides:

> it caused me to review my part [sic] sex relationships and I came to the startling conclusion that I have been a petty rapist. I realized that my sexual encounters were not associated with names or faces but merely with bodies painted on the fuselage of my ego. I wish to publicly thank Germaine Greer for shocking me into this difficult realization.

Like others, this reader-writer reassesses his behaviours and treatment of women and even, with shame, explicitly identifies himself as the 'petty rapist' described by Greer. Her article transformed his perception of women, forcing him to realise that he treated them as mere objects for his pleasure (something, of course, encouraged by the pornographic magazine in which the piece appeared).

Some reader-writers take the opportunity to praise not only the author but *Playboy* for opening up a space for such cogent critique. Indicating a familiarity with the famous author and her feminism, this writer – whose words appear in this chapter title – underscores that the brave Greer has successfully challenged fixed gendered assumptions: 'Greer has done it again! She has opened wide yet another closely guarded, heavily locked door of fear, prejudice and hypocrisy. I admire her gutsy ability to tell it like it is in an intelligent manner'. The inclusion of Greer's article also appears to have added value to the *Playboy* brand which, in the context of women's burgeoning freedom and sexual agency, was increasingly starting to appear anachronistic. Congratulating the editors for a serious engagement with women's liberation, a couple writes: 'Thank heavens for your January issue. We were nearly ready to place PLAYBOY in the trash with the rest of the decadence and smut. Seduction is a Four-Letter Word is your saving grace. It deserves to be read'. For these reader-writers, Greer's article has worked to recuperate the near-worthless magazine in the era of women's liberation.

It was not only the magazine's key addressees (i.e., men), but women who wrote to the editor to express their appreciation of, and firm agreement with, Greer's insights. Feeling that Greer reaffirms her own convictions, a woman writes:

> At last someone has publicly proclaimed something I've known for a long time. I remember a man once told me that the difference between rape and

seduction was the skill of the salesman…If the guy can't wait until I want him, then I throw his ass out.

As with the fans discussed in Chapter 2, this woman sees her experiences validated in Greer's article and, like others, emphasises how important it is to raise men's awareness of consent – which she praises Greer for doing in a forum such as this. Another woman suggests that Greer's piece will resonate with all women readers, whether victims of sexual assault or otherwise: 'Greer has expressed at length the sentiments of thousands of women, rape victims or not'. She also alludes to the ongoing trauma of rape, which Greer likewise foregrounds.

Given the topic and the magazine's implied addressees, the summary inevitably features more hostile, misogynistic responses:

With one swoop of her pen, Greer has asked men to give up the last vestiges of their natural instincts. In answer to this, I tell all men to listen to women only with the tops of their penises. This is the only end of the conversation worth hearing.

This reader-writer uses biological essentialism to discredit Greer's discursive reconstruction of 'seduction' while using deeply sexist language to silence Greer and women like her. *Ad feminam* attacks, heavily reliant upon misogynistic tropes, are used to dismiss Greer variously as being 'extremely childish and immature' and 'illogical' and as having 'penis envy'. One makes clear that Greer's 'failure' is speaking publicly at all: 'If I wanted to read the militant ravings of a feminist bitch, I'd buy their magazines. I buy PLAYBOY to look at broads, not to listen to them'. As Chapter 6 explores in more depth, feminists have long been subject to such disciplining by threatened men (Kay 2020). For this correspondent, Greer, as an outspoken woman contesting gendered hierarchies, is misplaced in a magazine whose raison d'être is to objectify women. Another mobilises the kinds of offensive victim-blaming assumptions that Greer uses her article to destabilise: 'Greer reminds me of the many girls who anxiously spread their legs while pleading no'. Despite these more sexist letters, the majority of the *Playboy* letter writers value Greer's work and are thoroughly persuaded by her feminist reframing of consent, thereby demonstrating the transformative power of such popular feminist journalism.

Perhaps owing at least in part to these reader responses, in 1973 *Playboy* chose 'Seduction is a Four-Letter word' as its 'Best Essay of the Year' (A.K., 5 November 1973, Chicago, 2014.0042.00688) – Greer's only award as a professional journalist (Buchanan 2018, p. 24). In response to the letter informing her of the award, Greer replies that it is an 'honour' to be selected but expresses her discomfort with the accolade and its accompanying cash prize (15 November 1973, Cortona). Accordingly, she donates the US$1000 to the Women's Legal

114 Germaine Greer, Celebrity Feminism and the Archive

Defense and Education Fund. While Greer herself refuses an all-expense-paid trip to New York to collect the prize and attend a luncheon in her honour, she worries that the women's organisation may refuse to take the money (for obvious reasons): 'Dear sisters, all money is dirty money. Take it as coming from me, with my love and hope that you can do some good with it' (All Saints Day 1973, 2014.0042.00688). This comment encapsulates Greer's attitude towards commercial publishing, which was at odds with that of some other feminists. It also challenges feminist arguments about Greer's lack of support for activist feminist organisations; for its part, the group gratefully accepted her offer.

Greer in the mainstream press: On abortion

Across her career, Greer has held various regular newspaper columnist appointments, commencing in the early 1970s and continuing into the ensuing decades. As Buchanan notes, Greer's diary reveals that she began her regular, bi-weekly *Sunday Times* column on 1 June 1971, after being invited to do so by editor Harold Evans, 'her first paid gig' as a journalist (2018, p. 18). Greer's column refused the opposition between public and private spheres which, despite feminist challenges (Pauly 2014a), dominated journalistic practice. Greer's focus and her goal for the column are clear; to the editor of the *Times*' 'Look Pages', where her columns would appear, she pronounces 'no cause moves my pen so readily as revolutionary feminism' (to A.H., 13 August 1971, 2014.0042.00869). As with *Playboy*, Greer's inclusion enabled the newspaper to suggest that it was taking the women's movement seriously while capitalising on the controversies she would invariably provoke.

The Female Eunuch was criticised for its lack of attention to reproductive politics (Winant 2015), but to redress this omission and defuse such criticisms, Greer wrote a series of short articles on abortion for the *Sunday Times* in 1972, which elicited intense reactions from the paper's pro-life readers. Moreover, Greer herself was heavily involved in abortion politics, including participating in a March 1972 debate – 'Abortion: Right or Wrong?' – at Sydney's Town Hall. Most controversially, owing to the famous author's apparent media 'overexposure', the ABC axed an episode of *Four Corners* which was to feature the abortion debate (Wallace 1997, p. 256). Sue Wills reports that around 3,000 people were in attendance, with a further 2,000 (of which she was one) 'locked out and overflowing onto the footpath outside' (1981, p. 26).[12] Such was the pull of the international celebrity feminist; Greer was clearly a significant drawcard for the event's organiser, the Abortion Reform Society.[13] As this event indicates, abortion was at the centre of Greer's feminist politics – and her journalism.

Reproductive rights have long been a key battleground for the women's liberation movement, with the US Supreme Court not affirming abortion as a constitutional right until the Roe v Wade decision in 1973 (its recent overturning, of course, makes clear that there is no linear model of feminist progress in this heavily contested area). As Australian historian Erica Rose Millar notes, 'In the mid-1960s through the 1970s, abortion began to be discussed publicly on a scale never before witnessed, and with these public articulations came new, and increasingly stylised, modes of representing abortion' (2018, p. 50). However, as Millar observes, by advocating a woman-centric rather than the dominant foeto-centric position and by opposing the victim-in-need-of-a-saviour model, 'Greer and other liberationists argued instead that abortion should be recognised in law as a rational decision made by psychologically stable women' (2018, p. 61). In order to challenge the stigma around abortion, Greer had publicly discussed her own in numerous forums, an important second-wave tactic deployed by other celebrity feminists such as Beauvoir (Millar 2018, p. 64).

In 1972, Greer was due to file three columns for the *Sunday Times* on abortion. The first piece, 'Abortion i', was published on 7 May (as 'Germaine Greer on why the Abortion Act is a calamity'), while the second ('The Friends of the Foetus') appeared two weeks later on 21 May. The third, however, was 'dropped without explanation' (Greer 1986, p. 117) by the paper; 'Abortion iii: Killing no murder', slated for 4 June, was instead published by feminist magazine *Spare Rib* (Greer 1972c). We can infer that readerly disdain underpinned this editorial decision, suggesting that readers were indeed helping to shape the newspaper's content. Greer's second abortion column begins with reference to the hostile correspondence she received following the initial piece: 'The friends of the foetus are a contentious lot. No sooner had they twigged that my last column was written in favour of abortion than they sprang to their escritoires' (Greer 1972b). Greer also reveals that she has been sent anti-abortion propaganda material, including pictures of aborted foetuses, in response to her article.

Although not included alongside the letters in the archive, the first abortion piece begins by criticising a Catholic anti-abortion protest organised in Liverpool, England. Of the clergy's attempts to intervene in these debates, Greer remarks: 'In most cases of sudden and unwelcome pregnancy, the intrusion of some celibate or senile, reformed reprobate persuading you to have the baby is the last thing you desire' (1972a/1986, p. 111). Greer calls into question the patriarchal authority of anti-abortionists, and her target is the Catholic establishment. Identifying flaws in their logic, she writes: 'The rigorous Catholic position is that there is no real difference between battering a conscious, sentient child piecemeal to death and sucking a lump of jelly with remarkable potential out of the uterus' (p. 112). Such characterisation ('lump of jelly') incensed readers, as we will see.

Emphasising the practical and financial difficulties of procuring an abortion, despite claims to the contrary from anti-abortionists who lament its

116 Germaine Greer, Celebrity Feminism and the Archive

widespread accessibility, Greer demands access to safe and affordable abortion, a key goal for women's liberationists:

> At the moment it is possible to get an abortion, but if abortion is right in principle, it must also be cheap, quick, safe and easy. Those who object to that idea, need not undergo the procedure; it is hardly coincidental that few of them could reasonably expect to.
>
> (p. 112)

She outlines the extremes to which a woman must go to convince medical authorities of her psychological need for an abortion. As Greer argues, the pregnant woman who wishes not to be,

> must behave as if she is incapable of a rational decision, pretending that her sanity is threatened by the birth of a child. If she is highly skilled in the manifestations of hysteria, she might even manage an abortion on the National Health.
>
> (p. 112)

This is a position that Greer reiterated in a radio interview during her Australian book tour; as Millar remarks, Greer 'criticised the staunch paternalism embedded in laws that had medicalised abortion for forcing a woman "to claim that she'd go off her rocker if she had a baby"' (2018, p. 61).

Like the others in this chapter, the unpublished letters to the editor in response to Greer's first abortion piece are filed together in the archive (1972, 2014.0042.00869). For many reader-writers, such as this woman from Edinburgh, Greer is being given too much column space to express her opinions on such a controversial subject: 'Germaine Greer's articles are overemotional, and a disproportionate number of them are concerned with abortion, to which Miss Greer appears to be morbidly attracted' (S.K., 7 May 1972). This writer's critique is also deeply gendered, as she charges Greer with overemotionalism. In such dismissals, 'to be emotional', as Sara Ahmed notes, 'is to have one's judgement affected' (2004, p. 3). Greer's interest in the topic is reframed as pathological rather than stemming from a legitimate feminist interest in women's lives and, most importantly in this instance, their bodies. Similarly, this reader-writer is impatient with Greer and her publicly articulated feminism: 'I think it is about time Germaine Greer widened her horizons on topics and life. I, for one, am heartily sick of the same old charade, week, after week, regarding women's lib and abortion and all that jazz' (V.C., 8 May 1972, Leeds). This woman uses her letter to publicly express wider antifeminist sentiments, as other correspondents in the Greer archive do.

As is to be expected from pro-life readers, abortion in these letters is inflammatorily constructed as 'killing'. Readers took issue particularly with

Greer's characterisation of foetuses: 'It is consoling to think of the aborted foetus as simply "a lump of jelly" in Germaine Greer's words…the stage of development of a human living being cannot possibly affect the morality of killing it' (P.M.F., 10 May 1972). As Linda Gordon notes, this kind of redefinition of the 'fetus [sic] as a pre-born child turns abortion into baby killing' (2002, p. 305), making women's liberationists calls for its greater accessibility seem morally reprehensible. Another likewise challenges this framing, calling into question Greer's status as an authoritative speaker. Seeking to discredit her, she notes that if Greer believes a foetus is nothing more than 'jelly', then 'she knows so little of her subject that it might have been wiser for her to keep quiet. If she knows better, then she is just lying' (S.G.W., 7 May 1972, Birkenhead).

That Greer was endorsing 'murder' was a recurrent presumption from these pro-life letter writers. This is consistent with the dominant way of framing pro-choice positions in the 1970s, with anti-abortion activists commonly replacing placard slogans such as 'the right to choose' with 'the right to kill' (Millar 2018, p. 76). For one man, women who have refused to 'kill' their unborn child have benefitted immeasurably: '[Greer's] whole story is killing & resenting, without a single word to suggest that love for a child is possible and can actually triumph over difficulties' (J.H.S., 7 May 1972). Proudly reclaiming Greer's moniker for the anti-abortionists who had been challenging her, one letter writer identifies herself as speaking on behalf of the 'Catholic Friends of Foetuses'. Albeit conceding that 'Miss Greer does a lot of good work highlighting injustices against women', she concludes that 'her personal hate has pushed her into an extreme stance' (S.G., 7 May 1972). In repositioning Greer's pro-abortion stance as one of personal 'hatred', this woman seeks to locate her support for reproductive rights as extremist.

Anti-abortion rhetoric commonly discursively constitutes the practice as 'a longstanding social problem, one that has arisen from the decline of social morals' (Smith 2014, p. 146), something we see at work in this letter:

> Miss Greer would do well to remember that a woman's power lies not in her readiness to jump into bed with any Tom, Dick or Harry to prove how emancipated they are, but their ability to stay out of bed at all costs.
> (V.C., 8 May 1972, Leeds)

Such identification of abortion with 'sexual permissiveness' (Gordon 2002, p. 297) has been common in conservative attacks on reproductive freedoms. This reader-writer makes the assumption that women's greater sexual agency is a form of moral degradation that must be avoided, including through limiting reproductive freedom. For this woman, questioning the equation of sexual liberation with women's liberation, women's 'power' lies instead in their ability to withhold sex from licentious, uncaring men. Her moral judgement of the

118 Germaine Greer, Celebrity Feminism and the Archive

sexually agentic woman is clear; abstinence is the ultimate exercise of feminine power – an argument Greer, in her book and in her 'cunt power' journalism, was seeking to radically undermine (Le Masurier 2016).

These pro-life writers question a fundamental tenet of women's liberation: women's right to bodily integrity and autonomy. In this foeto-centric rhetoric, abortion is located 'as an issue that distinguishes those who willingly violate human rights (abortion supporters) from those who preserve and protect the rights of innocent citizens at all costs (abortion opponents)' (Smith 2014, p. 142). A key rhetorical strategy for 1970s anti-abortion activists, reluctant to condemn pregnant women as murderers, was to identify an external 'enemy' who could instead be held morally responsible (Smith 2014, p. 143) – in this instance, Greer. Deploying the argument that abortion will lead to euthanasia for society's more vulnerable members, this writer, a Reverend from Bath, positions anti-abortionists as righteous defenders of those who have no voice:

> Was anything so predictable as the parade of half-truths in Miss Greer's article on abortion?... She speaks of the "friends of the foetus": she does not mention the "foes of the foetus"…The sort of coercive blackmail used by the abortionists could so easily be brought to bear upon the old and infirm, who are, so to speak, merely bundles of decaying tissue with no potential whatever – except that of being a nuisance to everyone.
>
> (R.P., 8 May 1972)

This reader-writer contests Greer's truth-claims and identifies her as a danger to unborn children and their purportedly distressed and vulnerable mothers. As a hotly contested issue – as much in the 1970s as in the present (especially in the US) – Greer's position on reproductive freedom in the *Sunday Times* saw the mobilisation of a pro-life 'interpretive community' (Fish 1978) who used the letter to the editor form to attempt to rationalise and promote their anti-feminism and to critique the platform that celebrity had afforded Greer.

'The Big Tease': US (feminist) politics

In October 1972, *Harper's* magazine published Greer's analysis of the Democratic Convention in Miami, under the provocative title, 'McGovern, The Big Tease'. *Harper's* during the 1970s was known for publishing long-form journalism in the style of what would come to be characterised as the 'new journalism'. Greer's fellow celebrity feminist Gloria Steinem is even said to be the 'most celebrated practitioner' of this kind of 'participant observer' style of journalism (Dennis 2017, p. 108).[14] However, women writers, with the exception of Joan Didion, have largely been excluded from studies of the new journalism (Phillips 2019, p. 78). Key elements of the genre, which can clearly be seen to make it appealing to feminists, include 'immersion reporting, the use of a distinctive voice, the potential use of a first-person point of view, and even a personal involvement with the subject matter' (Phillips 2019, p. 80). Greer's *Harper's* piece, if not her other articles, certainly conforms to such a definition. So-called new journalists 'styled themselves as interpreters of large social trends...and magazines like *Esquire*, *Harper's*, and *New York* sought the work of those writers in order to create an identity that would appeal to educated, upscale readers' (Pauly 2014a, p. 592). In line with this emphasis on 'large social trends', movements such as women's liberation could not be ignored. Given Greer's high profile in the US media at this time, as well as the style of writing for which she was known, it is perhaps unsurprising that *Harper's* chose to publish her political commentary.

The cover (2014.0046.00063) of the *Harper's* edition in which 'McGovern, The Big Tease' appears features a naked woman's back, with 'GERMAINE GREER' in red print immediately beneath the mast head, across the woman's spine. As Carmen Winant (2015) remarks, indicative of Greer's superstar status, her 'name appeared much larger than her subject's on the cover'. The provocative quotation from her article appears in blue, making the entire cover an evocation of the American flag: 'Womanlike they do not want to get tough with their man, and so, womanlike, they got screwed'. Hoping to pique readers' interest, such a quotation pits Greer against other women, creating a dramatic sense of disunity within feminist ranks.

Across this long-form piece, Greer recounts her experiences as an observer at the 1972 Democratic Convention in Miami, with a focus on the National Women's Political Caucus. As in her books (Pearce 2004), Greer as the feminist 'I' is thoroughly implicated in the narrative. She expresses a 'fervent desire' to 'see the women distinguish themselves and win some representation in the party platform and some power to implement their own will' (1972e/1986, p. 131). Greer continues, 'after several days of following their activities I found myself in a morass of passionate wishing and utter disappointment' (p. 131). The article's provocative title refers to Presidential Candidate George McGovern's efforts to court the women's movement but ultimate failure to deliver on key issues, particularly abortion. Throughout this article, Greer harshly judges women participants for compromising on abortion, seeing feminist principles engulfed by the convention's wider political machinations: 'We allowed ourselves the luxury of believing that sisterhood is strong, although the events of the day had left me feeling that the mere fact of femaleness does not constitute sisterhood, and sisterhood itself does not confer power' (p. 133). This deployment of 'we' is important here, as Greer firmly positions herself within this 'sisterhood', thus implicating herself in the inadequate political strategising, including a lack of female solidarity, that saw their defeat.

Despite their efforts, Greer perceives the women's caucus to have held little power: 'The miserable fact was that the women's caucus was not a caucus in any meaningful sense; the McGovern machine had already pulled the rug out from under them' (p. 134). Here, however, her pronouns shift and she writes of 'them', suggesting perhaps her ambivalence and outsider status in terms of the US women's movement (upon which many readers seized). Greer contemplates the electoral impact of the decision not to more vigorously secure the convention's commitment to abortion:

> If the "abortion" plank had been adopted as part of the party platform, thousands of people with energy and experience would have campaigned for McGovern in a positive and intense way, just as they had done in the primaries; they might lose, but they would lose honourably.
>
> (pp. 138–39)

For Greer, this failure to meaningfully respond to feminist activism will have dire political consequences for the Left. In this respect, it appears a pre-cursor to the Equal Rights Amendment's (ERA) failed ratification, a cautionary tale regarding feminist reliance on state-based equality measures, as the television series *Mrs America* recently dramatised (Henderson and Taylor 2023).

The Greer archive contains a series of unpublished letters to the editor in response to her extended rumination on the convention's political machinations (1972, 2014.0042.000355). Greer's position, particularly regarding her querying of the efficacy of mainstream political cultures to redress gendered inequities, precipitated debate amongst readers, the majority of whom seemed to dismiss her views as idealistic and immature. Readers, both women and men, widely took issue with Greer's apparent contempt for the women who participated in the convention and how they were positioned as mere pawns in a political game controlled by men. For instance, a New York man complained that Greer's dismissal of forthright feminist figures such as Gloria Steinem, Shirley Chisolm, and Bella Azbug as pawns to be 'led or discarded as [McGovern] wished' was 'as libelous a statement as it is mendacious' (J.J.A., 10 October 1972). Greer's deprivation of the agency of such formidable women is, for this reader-writer, disingenuous.

One Maryland woman, using a patronising tone, also critiques Greer's naïve interpretation of electoral politics, seeing her inability to compromise as a failure to recognise the reality of the political world:

> It is quite true that compromises were made but cannot there by some consideration of the larger issues without accusing the candidate of being a "tease" (What sexual connotations that epithet conjures up.) You perennial innocents will never realize that there is no heaven on earth, we must settle for the best our human imperfections can muster.
>
> (A.T.B., 6 October 1972)

This woman also draws attention to the feminist limits of the 'tease' trope. Another reader-writer sees Greer as attacking democracy itself; juxtaposing democratic nations with totalitarian ones, she contests Greer's romanticised view of political processes:

> She says the girls were "screwed" on the abortion issue by the manipulators at the convention; a peck on the cheek compared to what happens to both sexes at a peoples' party rally in a totalitarian state. But no matter. There is more dignity in giving all to a dictator than in compromising with a democrat.
>
> (K.G., undated, New York)

Of Greer's blockbuster, which she confesses she has not read, this reader-writer suggests that 'the title is descriptive of her personally' and, though herself a woman, disparages its author as 'psychologically all female'.

This woman reader-writer from Ohio also highlights the dangers of leftist tactics, which could see votes funnelled towards the conservatives:

> Germaine Greer's disappointment with McGovern's failure to declare himself on the abortion issue at the Democratic Convention points up a suspect inability by many people-in-causes to see beyond the boundaries of their own movements. Her "Big Tease" article in October's issue will certainly throw some votes [Richard] Nixon's way.
>
> (K.R.G., undated)

Here, Greer's article is seen as potentially damaging the Democratic vote. A reader from Santa Fe similarly accuses Greer of a failure to be pragmatic, a failure which could have dire electoral consequences: 'It is easy to be a "radical". You can sit and denounce people who are basically your friends while they go out and do the dirtywork'. He concludes by urging Greer, whom he tellingly and repeatedly refers to as Ms rather Dr, to become more actively involved in the fight to defeat Nixon rather than judging those who do: 'Get a voter to register, Ms Greer. Give some money to the campaign, Ms Greer. Help America to wake up from this current nightmare, not drag us deeper into it' (J.S., undated).

Many objected to Greer seeking to shape domestic political debate in the US; that is, they use their responses to question her authority to speak, as a woman, as a feminist, and as an Australian. This woman, like other reader-writers, queries why an outsider has been chosen to provide commentary on the upcoming election:

> I am an American citizen living in Canada. Even if I were as brilliant as Germaine Greer and as talented a writer, I would consider it an insult to the people of this country and to myself to interpret their national election for them in one of their leading magazines…Evidentally [sic] the American

people have closed their ears and eyes this election. Ms Greer's article has not helped to open them.

(B.C.M., 6 October 1972)

This reader-writer challenges the cultural legitimacy of Greer's voice, arguing that *Harper's* has misjudged its readers and misguidedly given an 'outsider' feminist a platform to publicly discuss issues about which she knows little.

Such a critique is arguably gendered, as – despite women's liberation – it was rare for women in the early 1970s to be given the opportunity to report on politics and economics (Phillips 2019, p. 83), hence the uneasiness about Greer as a political commentator. Another reader-writer harshly criticises Greer's lack of objectivity, her feminist perspective, and her outsider status. Dismissing the article as 'banal drivel', he notes that it was 'badly misla-belled' and proposes the more apt title, '"The Democratic Convention – from a Fem-Rad-Lib's Vaginal Viewpoint"'. Also arguing that Greer is not qualified to intervene in debates about American politics, he further remarks: 'No one could have expected an objective, perceptive and intelligent appraisal of a complex American political process which has baffled the most erudite of American political journalists by a gad-fly man-hating, one-non-book foreign "journalist"' (J.J.A., 10 October 1972, New York). The placement of 'journalist' in scare quotes clearly questions Greer's credentials and the authority that *Harper's* appears to have granted her. These kinds of personal attacks, perhaps unsurprisingly, tend to characterise letters that take issue with Greer's feminist positions.

In contrast to most of the *Harper's* reader letters contained in the archive, a Philadelphia woman supports Greer's claims about the inadequacies of reformism. This reader-writer appreciates Greer's argument in the piece, exemplifying her more revolutionary feminism, about the inherent flaws in masculinist political cultures:

A resounding cheer for Ms Greer's perceptive observations of the Great Democratic Rip-Off. Her article points out the futility of women seeking freedom in ideas and systems so obscenely male and obviously bankrupt. True freedom for women will not come until we stop demanding those things that amount to nothing but acceptance of male standards and values.

(B.E.T., undated)

Greer had previously criticised reformist feminist groups like NOW (National Organisation for Women), including in *The Female Eunuch*, and her *Harper's* piece reaffirms this position. Women's liberationists, however, were dispirited with Greer's intervention into mainstream political debate, with Steinem telling Greer's biographer that they were '"all quite depressed when we read the piece"' (Wallace 1997, p. 241). In Steinem's rendering, Greer disappointingly "'just really condemned all of us for being in the electoral system at all"' (Wallace 1997, p. 241). Greer's apparent ideological purity in this piece is noteworthy, given her own efforts to convince other feminists that they needed to be more pragmatic when it came to media engagement.

Conclusion

Greer's journalism has been an integral part of her lifelong 'discursive [feminist] activism' (Young 1997) in that, as a celebrity journalist, she exercised an important form of 'cultural leadership' (Kirkby 2013). Of course, journalism has always been vital to social movements, allowing 'radical ideas to spread and readers to build networks and mobilise new political identities' (Kirkby 2013, p. 82). For Greer, the print media was a feminist tool that needed to be more strategically wielded, with varying degrees of success. Greer's work as a feminist creative labourer, including in the journalistic field, is illuminated by archival material, allowing us to see this work as an integral part of her celebrity feminist practice. In the 1970s and beyond, Greer's name (i.e., her attention capital as a celebrity) garnered her spaces in which to speak, while her journalism also amplified this capital and expanded the reach and audience for her feminist commentary. From unlikely venues such as the pornographic magazine *Playboy*, Greer's feminist critique came to resonate with diverse groups of readers.

Not all the reader-writers in this chapter identified with feminism or as feminists; indeed, many sought to distance themselves from Greer's feminist position on issues such as abortion. In other instances, they *did* narrate a process of coming to feminist consciousness, as in the many *Playboy* letters which expressed the authors' feelings of shame and remorse about their past efforts to 'seduce' women. As those considered here have suggested, 'letters to the editor can provide access to the narratives that people used to construct, understand, and analyze social and political phenomena' (Groeneveld 2018, p. 158). Readers used Greer's writing to reflect upon, or in some cases to reinforce, their gendered assumptions, showing how her celebrity feminist journalism was precipitating public conversations and contestations amongst American and British newspaper and magazine readers.

Although the archive reveals that Greer wrote extensively for Australian magazines such as the *Australian Women's Weekly* and *Cleo* and newspapers such as *The Age* in the 1990s and 2000s, the relative absence of Australian journalism in the 1970s can perhaps be explained by Greer's contemptuous attitude at this time towards the press in her former homeland, by which she felt poorly treated (as I discuss further in Chapter 6). There is much more work, therefore, that needs to be done on this vast journalistic archive, as on popular feminist journalism more broadly. Some letter writers in this chapter

124 Germaine Greer, Celebrity Feminism and the Archive

were hostile towards the famous feminist, but in the final two chapters – also focusing on Greer's writing in magazines and newspapers – I turn to those who used letters to the editor and emails to launch even more scathing attacks on Greer and her feminism.

Notes

1 Le Masurier (2016) and Thompson (2016) are two exceptions.
2 In contrast, Jay Daniel Thompson (2016) argues that Greer, especially in terms of sex positivity, has remained consistent on key feminist issues.
3 See 2014.0046 Print Journalism Finding Aid.
4 The 'Press 1973' folder in the Early Years series in the archive contains many reports of this resignation (2014.0044.00211).
5 On 5 June 1972, she tells Indigenous activist Roberta Sykes: 'I have already had one snot-nosed phone call from the Australians carrying on about how disappointed they were that it wasn't more feminist' (2014.0042.00828).
6 See Greer's letters to B.S., London, 8 June 1972 (2014.0042.00808) and A.B., June 1972 (2014.0044.00197).
7 Of the *Suck* photo, she outlines how she was effectively tricked into having it taken as all members of the editorial were going to do so; however, this did not occur and her photo was used without her permission: 'once again, I allowed myself to be cold-bloodedly exploited' (to G.L., 2 February 1972, 2014.0042.00492).
8 Barbara Ellis of *Playboy* writes (26 April 1971) asking whether Greer would participate in a 'serious panel about women's liberation'. Greer replies: 'I am afraid Playboy's record vis-à-vis feminists does not inspire confidence. I am particularly uninterested in being contrasted with other feminists or in being edited by anyone' (2014.0042.00688).
9 The draft copy appears in the archive at 2014.0046.00076; however, I refer here to the printed version in *The Madwoman's Underclothes*.
10 In this article, however, in a deeply unethical gesture, Greer also appropriated the story of black civil rights activist Roberta Sykes, who became pregnant after being raped as a teenager and whose perpetrators were, unusually for the time, convicted (Sheehan 2024). Within the frame of settler colonialism, Sheehan convincingly sees such appropriation as 'theft' (Sheehan 2024, p. 23).
11 I am grateful to Rebecca Sheehan for sharing her transcription of these letters with me.
12 A flyer contained in the archive suggests that the debate was held on 2 March at 7.30 pm for an of admission price of AU$1 and 50c for students (2014.0044.00198).
13 The decision to pull the program featuring the debate, however, did not go unchallenged. Around 60 to 70 people protested at the ABC's Sydney offices on 27 March 1972 (Wills 1981, p. 26). Newspapers featured coupons for readers to complete, with 580 coupons and 180 letters from New South Wales alone sent to the ABC to demand the film's screening (Wills 1981, p. 26).
14 This includes her infamous undercover exposé of Hugh Hefner's Playboy clubs in 'A Bunny's Tale' (Steinem 1963).

References

Ahmed, S. (2004) *The Cultural Politics of Emotion*, London: Routledge.
Banet-Weiser, S. (2018) *Empowered: Popular Feminism and Popular Misogyny*, Durham: Duke University Press.

'Greer has done it again!' **125**

Banet-Weiser, S. and Higgins, K.C. (2023) *Believability: Sexual Violence, Media, and the Politics of Doubt*, London: Wiley.

Barker-Plummer, B. (1995) 'News as a Political Resource: Media Strategies and Political Identity in the U. S. Women's Movement, 1966–1975', *Critical Studies in Mass Communication*, vol. 12, no. 3: 306–324.

Bradley, P. (2003) *Mass Media and the Shaping of American Feminism*, Mississippi: University of Mississippi.

Buchanan, R. (2018) 'Foreign Correspondence: Journalism in the Germaine Greer Archive', *Archives and Manuscripts*, vol. 46, no. 1: 18–39.

Bueskens, P. (2020) 'Germaine Greer's *On Rape* Revisited: Clarifying the Long-standing Relationship Between Rape and Heterosexual Pleasure in Greer's Work', *Hecate*, vol. 45, no. 1–2: 268–288.

Coombs, A. (1996) *Sex and Anarchy: The Life and Death of the Sydney Push*, London: Viking.

Dennis, E. (2017) *Other Voices: The New Journalism in America*, New York: Routledge.

Dow, B.J. (1996) *Prime-time Feminism: Television, Media Culture, and the Women's Movement since 1970*, Philadelphia: University of Pennsylvania Press.

Dreifus, C. (1971) 'The Selling of a Feminist', *Notes From the Third Year: Women's Liberation*: 100–101.

Driessens, O. (2012) 'The Celebritization of Society and Culture: Understanding the Structural Dynamics of Celebrity Culture', *International Journal of Cultural Studies*, vol. 16, no. 6, 641–657.

Dyer, R. (1986) *Heavenly Bodies: Film Stars and Identity*, London: Routledge.

Eberly, R.A. (2002) *Citizen Critics: Literary Public Spheres*, Chicago: University of Illinois Press.

Farrell, A.E. (1998) *Yours in Sisterhood: Ms Magazine and The Making of Popular Feminism*, Chapel Hill: University of North Carolina.

Featherstone, L. (2021) *Sexual Violence in Australia, 1970s–1980s: Rape and Child Sexual Abuse*, London: Palgrave Macmillan.

Fish, S. (1978) *Is There is a Text in this Class?*, Cambridge: Harvard University Press.

Fiske, J. (1992) 'The Cultural Economy of Fandom', in L. Lewis (ed.), *The Adoring Audience*, New York: Routledge.

Fraterrigo, E. (2009) *Playboy and the Making of the Good Life in Modern America*, New York: Oxford University Press.

Germaine Greer Archive. Early Years, 2014.0044, University of Melbourne.

Germaine Greer Archive. General Correspondence, 2014.0042, University of Melbourne.

Germaine Greer Archive. Print Journalism, 2014.0446, University of Melbourne.

Germaine Greer Archive. Major Works, 2014.0045, University of Melbourne.

Giles, D. (2015) '*Field Migration*, Cultural Mobility and Celebrity: The Case of Paul McCartney', *Celebrity Studies*, vol. 6, no. 4: 538–552.

Gil-Glazer, Y. (2023) 'Between Sexism and Sexual Liberation: *Oz* Magazine as Sex Education Agent in Britain in the 1960s–1970s', *Sexuality & Culture*, vol. 27: 211–241.

Gilmore, L. (2017) *Tainted Witness: Why We Doubt What Women Say About Their Lives*, New York: Columbia University Press.

Gilmore, L. (2023) *The #MeToo Effect: What Happens When We Believe Women*, New York: Columbia University Press.

126 Germaine Greer, Celebrity Feminism and the Archive

Glanville, L. (2018) 'The End of Reckoning – Archival Silences in the Germaine Greer Archive', *Archives and Manuscripts*, vol. 46, no. 1: 45–48.

Gordon, L. (2002) *The Moral Property of Women: A History of Birth Control Politics in America*, Chicago: University of Illinois Press.

Green, B. (2012) 'Complaints of Everyday Life: Feminist Periodical Culture and Correspondence Columns in *The Woman Worker*, *Women Folk* and *The Freewoman*', *Modernism/Modernity*, vol. 19, no. 3: 461–485.

Greer, G. (1970a) *The Female Eunuch*, London: Paladin.

Greer, G. (1970b) 'The Politics of Female Sexuality', *Oz*, May, in *The Madwoman's Underclothes: Essays and Occasional Writings, 1968–1985*, London: Picador, pp. 36–40.

Greer, G. (1971a) 'My Mailer Problem', *Esquire*, 1 September, pp. 90–93, continued on p. 214, accessed via: https://classic.esquire.com/issue/19710901

Greer, G. (1971b) 'Lady love your cunt', *Suck*, Germaine Greer Archive, Print Journalism, 2014.0044.00177, University of Melbourne.

Greer, G. (1972a) 'Abortion i', *Sunday Times*, in *The Madwoman's Underclothes: Essays and Occasional Writings, 1968–1985*, London: Picador, pp.111–13.

Greer, G. (1972b) 'Abortion ii', *Sunday Times*, in *The Madwoman's Underclothes: Essays and Occasional Writings, 1968–1985*, London: Picador, pp.114–16.

Greer, G. (1972c) 'Abortion iii: Killing No Murder', *Spare Rib*, Germaine Greer Archive, Print Journalism, 2014.0046.00072, University of Melbourne.

Greer, G. ed. (1972d) *POL Magazine*, vol. 5, no. 4, Germaine Greer Archive, Print Journalism, 2014.0046.00114, University of Melbourne.

Greer, G. (1972e) 'McGovern, The Big Tease', *Harper's*, October, in *The Madwoman's Underclothes: Essays and Occasional Writings, 1968–1985*, London: Picador, pp. 125–46.

Greer, G. (1973a) 'What Turns Women On', *Esquire*, July, accessed via: https://classic.esquire.com/article/1973/07/01/what-turns-women-on

Greer, G. (1973b) 'Seduction is a Four-letter Word', *Playboy*, in *The Madwoman's Underclothes: Essays and Occasional Writings, 1968–1985*, London: Picador, pp. 152–168.

Greer, G. (1986) *The Mad Woman's Underclothes: Essays and Occasional Writings, 1968–1985*, London: Picador.

Greer, G. (2018) *On Rape*, Melbourne: University of Melbourne Press.

Groeneveld, E. (2018) 'Letters to the Editor as "Archives of Feeling": *On Our Backs* Magazine and the Sex Wars', *American Periodical Studies*, vol. 28, no. 2: 53–167.

Hall, S. (1980) 'Encoding/Decoding', in S. Hall, D. Hobson, A. Lowe and P. Willis (eds.), *Culture Media, Language*, London: Hutchison University Library, pp. 128–138.

Harper's Magazine, Letters to the Editor (1972), 'McGovern, The Big Tease', Germaine Greer Archive, General Correspondence, 2014.0042.000355, University of Melbourne.

Henderson, M. and Taylor, A. (2023) 'A Prosthetic Popular Feminism in Postfeminist Times: *Mrs America*'s Cool Feminism and Anti-Feminist Celebrity', *Signs: Journal of Women in Culture and Society*, vol. 48, no. 4: 1015–1039.

Kay, J.B. (2019) 'Introduction: Anger, Media, and Feminism: The Gender Politics of Mediated Rage', *Feminist Media Studies*, vol. 19, no. 4: 591–615.

Kay, J.B. (2020) *Gender, Media and Voice: Communicative Injustice and Public Speech*, London: Palgrave Macmillan.

Kirkby, D. (2013). '"Those Knights of the Pen and Pencil": Women Journalists and Cultural Leadership of the Women's Movement in Australia and the United States'. *Labour History*, vol. 104: 81–100.

Kleinhenz, E. (2019) *Germaine: The Life of Germaine Greer*, North Sydney: Knopf.

Lehrmann, N. (1972) 'Germaine Greer: A Candid Conversation with the Ballsy Author of "The Female Eunuch"', *Playboy*, January: 61–82.

Le Masurier, M. (2007) 'My Other, My Self: *Cleo* Magazine and Feminism in 1970s Australia', *Australian Feminist Studies*, vol. 22, no. 53: 191–211.

Le Masurier, M. (2009) 'Desiring the (Popular Feminist) Reader: Letters to *Cleo* During the Second Wave', *Media International Australia*, vol. 131: 106–116.

Le Masurier, M. (2016) 'Resurrecting Germaine's Theory of Cuntpower', *Australian Feminist Studies*, vol. 31, no. 87: 28–42.

Lorde, A. (1981) 'The Uses of Anger', *Women's Studies Quarterly*, vol. 9, no. 3: 7–10.

McDermott, P. (1994) *Politics and Scholarship: Feminist Academic Journals and the Production of Knowledge*, Chicago: University of Illinois Press.

Mendes, K. (2011) *Feminism in the News*, London: Palgrave Macmillan.

Millar, E. (2018) *Happy Abortions: Our Bodies in the Era of Choice*, London: Zed Books.

Mosmann, P. (2016) 'A Feminist Fashion Icon: Germaine Greer's Paisley Coat', *Australian Feminist Studies*, vol. 31, no. 87: 78–94.

Murray, S. (2004) *Mixed Media: Feminism and Publishing Politics*, London: Pluto.

Nolan, S. (1999) 'Tabloid Women', *Meanjin*, vol. 58, no. 2: 165–177.

Pauly, J.J. (2014), 'The New Journalism and the Struggle for Interpretation', *Journalism*, vol. 15, no. 5: 589–604.

Pearce, L. (2004) *The Rhetoric of Feminism*, London: Routledge.

Phillips, L. (2019) '"Every Year There's a Pretty Girl Who Comes to New York and Pretends to Be a Writer": Gender, the New Journalism, and the Early Careers of Gloria Steinem and Gail Sheehy', *Literary Journalism Studies*, vol. 13, nos. 1 and 2: 276–98.

Pitzulo, C. (2011) *Bachelors and Bunnies: The Sexual Politics of Playboy*, Chicago: University of Chicago Press.

Playboy (1972), Letters to the Editor summary, 'Seduction is a Four-Letter Word', Germaine Greer Archive, General Correspondence, 2014.0042.00688, University of Melbourne.

Rojek, R. (2015) *Presumed Intimacy: Parasocial Interaction in Media Society and Celebrity Culture*, London: Wiley.

Scott, L.M. (2000) 'Market Feminism: The Case for a Paradigm Shift', in Miriam Catterall, Lorna Stevens, and Pauline MacLaren (eds.), *Marketing and Feminism: Current Issues and Research*, London: Routledge, pp. 16–38.

Sedgwick, C. (2020) *Feminist Media: From Second Wave to the Digital Age*, London: Rowman & Littlefield.

Serisier, T. (2018) *Speaking Out: Feminism Rape and Narrative Politics*, London: Palgrave Macmillan

Serisier, T. (2020) 'From Date Rape Jeopardy to (Not) Drinking Tea: Consent Humour, Ridicule and Cultural Change', *Australian Feminist Law Journal*, vol. 46, no. 2: 189–204.

Sheehan, R.J. (2019) 'Intersectional Feminist Friendship: Restoring Colour to the Second-wave through the Letters of Florynce Kennedy and Germaine Greer', *Lilith*, vol. 25: 76–92.

Sheehan, R. (2024) 'Settler Colonialism in Black and White: Roberta Sykes, Germaine Greer, and the Different Embodied Experiences of Womanhood, Rape, and Sovereignty', *Signs: Journal of Women in Culture and Society.*, vol. 49, no. 4: 731–754.

Smith, L.D. (2014) *Righteous Rhetoric: Sex, Speech, and the Politics of Concerned Women for America*, Oxford: Oxford University Press.

Spongberg, M. (1993) '"If she's so great, how come so many pigs dig her?": Germaine Greer and the Malestream Press', *Women's History Review*, vol. 2, no. 3: 407–419.

Steedman, C. (1986) 'Wonderwoman', 4 December, *London Review of Books*, vol. 8, no. 21, accessed via: https://www.lrb.co.uk/the-paper/v08/n21/carolyn-steedman/wonderwoman

Steinem, G. (1963) 'A Bunny's Tale-Part I', *Show Magazine*, May: 114.

Strimpel, Z. (2022) '*Spare Rib*, The British Women's Health Movement and the Empowerment of Misery', *Social History of Medicine*, vol. 35, no 1: 217–236.

Sunday Times, Letters to editor, 'Abortion i' (1972), Germaine Greer Archive, General Correspondence, 2014.0042.00869, University of Melbourne.

Taylor, A. (2004) 'Readers Writing *The First Stone* Media Event: Letters to the Editor, Australian Feminisms and Mediated Citizenship', *Journal of Australian Studies*, vol. 83: 75–87.

Taylor, A. (2016) *Celebrity and the Feminist Blockbuster*, Basingstoke: Palgrave Macmillan.

Thompson, J. D. (2016) 'Porn Sucks: The Transformation of Germaine Greer', *M/C Journal: A Journal of Media and Culture*, vol. 19, no. 4, accessed via: https://journal.media-culture.org.au/index.php/mcjournal/article/view/1107

Wahl-Jorgensen, K. (2002) 'The Normative-Economic Justification for Public Discourse: Letters to the Editor as a "Wide Open" Forum', *Journalism & Mass Communication Quarterly*, vol. 79, no. 1: 121–133.

Wallace, C. (1997) *Germaine Greer: Untamed Shrew*, Melbourne: Pan Macmillan.

Waters, M. (2016) '"Yours in Struggle": Bad Feelings and Revolutionary Politics in Spare Rib', *Women: A Cultural Review*, vol. 27, no. 4, 446–465.

Weber, M. and Buchanan, R. (2019) 'Metadata as a Machine for Feeling in Germaine Greer's Archive', *Archives and Manuscripts*, vol. 47, no. 2: 230–241.

Wicke, J. (1994) 'Celebrity Material: Materialist Feminism and the Culture of Celebrity', *South Atlantic Quarterly*, vol. 93, no. 4: 751–778.

Wills, S. (1981) '*The Politics of Sexual Liberation*', unpublished doctoral thesis, University of Sydney.

Winant, C. (2015) 'The Meaningful Disappearance of Germaine Greer: The Contributions and Contradictions of a Feminist Icon', *Cabinet Magazine*, Issue 57, accessed via: http://www.cabinetmagazine.org/issues/57/winant.php

Young, S. (1997) *Changing The Wor(l)d: Discourse, Politics, and the Feminist Movement*, London: Routledge.

Zielser, A. (2017) *We Were Feminists Once: From Riot Grrrl to CoverGirl®, the Buying and Selling of a Political Movement*, New York: PublicAffairs.

5

'MISS GREER IS THE MOST PATHETIC EUNUCH OF ALL'

Anti-fandom and *McCall's* Magazine

Introduction

In March 1971, popular American women's magazine *McCall's* published an extract of *The Female Eunuch*, ahead of the book's publication the following month. While the archive does not offer any insight into how the *McCall's* extract came to be, nor include a copy of the extract itself, it was clearly part of the extensive publicity campaign preceding *The Female Eunuch*'s entry into the American market – we know from an entry in Greer's archived 1971 diary that this was 20 April (2014.0044.00153). Her first book received 'a widely enthusiastic welcome in the U.S.' (Roxon 1971), but not all readers were impressed. Myriad unpublished letters to the *McCall's* editor contained in the Greer archive reveal that the magazine's white, middle-class readers were largely dismissive of Greer's feminist vision. These reader-writers, best conceptualised as 'anti-fans', took both author and editor to task for devaluing them as wives and mothers. Through an analysis of these letters, I argue that their authors contested Greer's burgeoning authority as a second-wave celebrity feminist by pathologising her, invoking essentialist assumptions about femininity, and mobilising discourses of 'choice' which are more commonly seen to be products of a so-called postfeminist representational environment.

Complicating dominant ways of framing the feminist past and the postfeminist present, this chapter – like the others in this book – demonstrates that celebrity feminists like Greer have always elicited complex affective responses from 'ordinary' women or those who may not have been actively involved in the women's movement. Importantly, in terms of American audience responses to Greer, these *McCall's* letters represent a stark contrast to

DOI: 10.4324/9781315179841-6

130 Germaine Greer, Celebrity Feminism and the Archive

those she received after guest-hosting *The Dick Cavett Show* in mid-June of the same year. As her agent notes when she forwards the *Cavett* letters, they are 'a sight more intelligent than those that resulted from McCall's' (D.C., 2 July 1971, London, 2014.0042.00181). Those correspondents, as Chapter 3 has demonstrated, largely effusively celebrated Greer and her 'reasoned' feminist approach to the controversial topics (abortion and rape) covered in each show (Sheehan 2016). Perhaps unlike a diverse, national television audience, readers of *McCall's* expected the magazine to be supportive of their more traditional life choices, something which had been central to its brand. These *McCall's* readers clearly form an 'interpretive community' (Fish 1978) that, based on their proud housewife identity and shared experiences, responds more or less consistently to Greer's book and her star text (and that clearly differs from the readers examined in Chapter 2). As I argue, there appear to be three key, often interrelated, ways in which readers commonly responded to the *McCall's* extract from *The Female Eunuch*: through the expression of readerly disappointment in the magazine's editor, through personal attacks on its author's identity and way of life, and through an impassioned defense of housewives and domesticity. In particular, these reader-writers seek to reframe marriage and motherhood as empowering 'choices' for women – in many respects using Greer's feminist arguments against her.

Reading such responses as performances of anti-fandom, I demonstrate how narratives of choice around traditional gender identities are not a recent postfeminist phenomenon but have been mobilised for decades by women, especially those with class and racial privilege, who refuse to accept feminist attempts to position them as subordinated subjects. Through their anti-fan practices, these women challenge Greer's attempts to deprive housewives of agency, often deploying rhetorical strategies that are at once reliant upon and highly critical of second-wave feminist rhetoric. These letters offer irrefutable evidence that 'women and feminists are different creatures, certainly in the sense that the one is not necessarily the other' (Hemmings 2012, p. 156). Moreover, like the others in *Germaine Greer, Celebrity Feminism and the Archive*, these affective responses from the *McCall's* readers make clear that current, ongoing debates about popular feminism (including its celebrity variants) and its efficacy (Brady 2016; Gill 2016; Banet-Weiser 2018; Lawson 2023), especially in terms of the constituency on whose behalf it claims to speak, have a much longer history than is sometimes acknowledged.

Given they are a form of life writing, and as I underscore throughout this book, we must conceptualise these archived letters, 'not as sites of the truth of a life but as creative self-engagements' (Smith and Watson 2010, p. 203). Writers of letters to the editor construct strategic, publicly performed selves, often for political purposes (Dever et al. 2009), using the form to 'try on' different identities for an imagined public (Green 2012). These housewives strategically mobilise narratives of contentment for a *McCall's* audience which was presumed to share their values and discomfort with women's liberation and its casting of them as victims of patriarchy's representative: their husbands. These women correspondents spoke to (and for) a 'supportive imagined community' (Le Masurier 2009, p. 140), who would be similarly affronted by Greer's dismissive approach to marriage and motherhood. The archive's General Correspondence series contains over three dozen letters (2014.0042.00547) written to the editor of *McCall's* following its publication of an extract from Greer's forthcoming book, which are filed together, in contrast to Greer's more common archival practice of correspondence alphabetisation (Buchanan 2018).

As the previous chapter argued, authors of letters to editors can be seen as 'reader-writers' (Farrell 1998), working to attempt to shape the direction of the newspaper or magazine to which they contribute, acting as very clear evidence of media literacy and critical reflexivity (Taylor 2004; Le Masurier 2009). In her study of *Ms* magazine and popular feminism, Amy Erdman Farrell (1998) argues that letters to the editor functioned as a way in which readers could effectively become co-creators of the magazine. Staging a dialogue with editors enabled them to contest and rework the form of feminism that was being authorised in the magazine's pages. Furthermore, although 'addressed to an editor, a real individual', as Liz Stanley notes, such letters are 'actually addressed to "the public", a collectivity of addressees' (2004, p. 208). Most of these letters did not actually reach this 'collectivity', remaining unpublished in the magazine, but they were written with a broader public in mind. In this way, the *McCall's* letters to the editor sought to shape, if not the magazine itself, then at least its readers' responses to and perceptions of Greer.[1] Such letters also represent a challenge to assumptions that active, and especially highly critical, audiences have largely been brought into being by the affordances of digital media. In this respect, opportunities for 'produsage' created by convergence culture (Jenkins 2006; Bruns 2008) need to be seen to exist on a continuum with these earlier forms of participatory engagement (Thomas 2014; Steuer 2019), whereby audiences actively seek, perhaps less directly than in the current convergent environment, to mould the content of the magazine.

The Female Eunuch and popular feminism in *McCall's*

The *McCall's* extract, as briefly mentioned, was part of the publisher's plan to make Greer's feminist book 'an absolute smash here in the States' (R.S.S., McGraw Hill, to Greer, October 26 1970, New York, 2014.0052.00073). Prepublicity and promotional hype prior to *The Female Eunuch*'s 1971 American publication was extensive (Murray 2004; Scott 2000). As well as the extract published in *McCall's*, this campaign, with the flamboyant Greer at its centre, was staged across various newspapers and magazines, and involved gruelling cross-country book tours, myriad television appearances, including the cinema verité–style documentary *Germaine Greer versus the USA* (1971), and high-profile public events such as the infamous Town Hall debate with Norman Mailer (1971; see Deem 2003). Greer's excerpt in *McCall's* was a crucial part of this multipronged promotional strategy, which itself helped transform her into the celebrity feminist de jour. As Simone Murray puts it, her fame was 'meticulously constructed – with Greer's avid participation – by the machinery of book publicity' (2004, p. 179).

Unusual as they were for a feminist, Greer's promotional efforts, and her own critical reflections on them, were themselves considered newsworthy. However, journalists criticised these strategies, invoking feminist arguments about the antithetical nature of mainstream media outlets and radical feminist ideas. One even queried Greer's decision to allow her writing to appear in *McCall's*:

> The feminist message of Germaine Greer, author of "The Female Eunuch", has been appearing in some unlikely places, such as *Cosmopolitan* and *McCall's* magazines. Why has she allowed parts of her book to appear in these publications, which contain much feminists find offensive?
>
> (Hamilton 1971)

Refusing to accept the opposition between feminism and commercial culture which underpinned this journalist's question, Greer was unapologetic about taking advantage of the resources that were available to her: '"I don't care who pays as long as it's my message. They paid me and used my words so why not take it?"' (Hamilton 1971). This rejection of ideological purity is something we see across these chapters, a position that made her more open to celebrification than other feminists.

Women's magazines, far from needing to be boycotted, were key to Greer's strategy of reaching as wide an audience as possible. In this vein, Greer's initial summary of the book indicated: 'I intend to outrage the editress (male or female) of every women's matazine [sic] in the country' (1969). Whether *McCall's* editors were so 'outraged' is unclear, but its readers most certainly were. The extract, which includes Greer's critique of marriage and domestic drudgery as well as the pressure on women to maintain a stereotypically 'feminine' appearance, shook *McCall's* readers, who took such criticism – especially of their status as wives and mothers – extremely personally. These hostile letters to the *McCall's* editor, which were forwarded to Greer, reveal much about the historical operations of anti-fandom as well as how readers do (or, in this case, do not) affectively invest in popular feminist texts and their celebrity authors.

With her book's serialisation in a prominent women's magazine, Greer was in good company; excerpts of Betty Friedan's *The Feminine Mystique* (1963) had been published in both *McCall's* and *Ladies' Home Journal*, and Simone de Beauvoir's *The Second Sex* (1949) had appeared in American

Vogue in 1947 (Coffin 2020, p. 13). Such extracts were undoubtedly crucial in helping transform their authors into 'blockbuster celebrity feminists' (Taylor 2016), working to create the pre-publicity 'buzz' which is essential to what John Thompson (2010) calls 'big books'. Reaching beyond those already persuaded by the need for a change in the condition of women was a core commitment for these popular feminist writers. The extract's inclusion was also likely part of *McCall's* own efforts – like *Playboy*'s, as we saw in the previous chapter – to engage more deeply with second-wave feminism. In this respect, in a study of how the magazine had changed between 1964 and 1974 in response to women's liberation, Sheila Silver found that

> *McCall's* has extrapolated from "women's lib" those ideas it feels to be "useful" to a reader of a "magazine for suburban women" (a readership which includes a growing number of young women), without betraying a loyal readership that was nurtured on more traditional fare.
>
> (1976, p. 31)

However, in the case of the Greer extract, the 'usefulness' of such ideas was highly contested by readers – which could perhaps have been expected given its audience demographics. Silver's survey of *McCall's* readership across 1974–1975, though a few years after *The Female Eunuch* extract, found that nearly 70% were married; and, indicative of their middle-class status, close to three-quarters owned their homes (with their husbands, of course); and almost 64% were over 35 years old (1976, pp. 13–14). Although Silver did not address race, and as I will further argue, the implied addressees of *McCall's* appear to be white and privileged in their ability to reframe domesticity as liberation. The magazine's popular feminism, such as it was, thereby reinscribed the limitations and biases of second-wave feminism more broadly (Thompson 2002).

Nevertheless, women's magazines, as Megan Le Masurier (2007, 2009) argues, have long been vehicles for the 'translation' of ideas about women's and sexual liberation, making them a crucial form of popular feminism, especially in the early 1970s (see also Farrell 1998). Importantly, Patricia Carbine, who went on to co-found *Ms* magazine with Gloria Steinem in 1972, took over as editor of *McCall's* in early 1971 ('Woman Leaves *Look* to Become Editorial Director of *McCall's*', 1970); therefore, the Greer extract was published under the leadership of a self-professed women's liberationist.[2] Around this time, *McCall's* magazine began to incorporate more editorial content on the women's movement (Dow 2014, p. 113). For example, from January 1971, *McCall's* included a new monthly section, 'Right Now: A Monthly Newsletter for Women', which explicitly engaged with women's liberation and its key issues (Dow 2014, p. 113), while celebrity feminist Friedan wrote a regular column for the magazine, 'Betty Friedan's Notebook', between 1971 and 1974

134 Germaine Greer, Celebrity Feminism and the Archive

(Taylor 2016, p. 100). The inclusion of Greer's writing was clearly part of the magazine's wider strategy to engage more with feminist ideas.

Given that the extract comes to metonymically stand in for *The Female Eunuch* as a whole, the sections chosen for inclusion in *McCall's* are important. The five-page extract includes sections from 'Stereotype', taken from the chapter 'SOUL', and parts of the book's concluding chapter, entitled 'REVOLUTION'. The section on 'Stereotype' offers a critique of commodity capitalism and women's role in both advertising and consumption – especially of beauty products, via which women are reduced to an object of the male gaze (Greer 1971, p. 92). Greer also criticises women's magazines themselves, for their role in exhorting women to adhere to the 'stereotype of the Eternal Feminine', noting: 'young women study the latest forms of the stereotype in magazines, where the models stare out from advertisements for fabulous real estate, furs, and jewels' (Greer 1971, p. 92). From Greer's perspective, in an innovative position for the time, consumer culture (including via women's magazines) places unrealistic expectations on women and requires them to adhere to a specific way of embodying femininity. To be free, she argues, women must refuse this kind of commodified womanhood.

The second part of the extract encompasses *The Female Eunuch*'s critique of the social organisation of Western society, particularly marriage: 'If women are to effect a significant amelioration in their condition it seems obvious that they must refuse to marry' (Greer 1971, p. 145). For Greer, the institution of marriage must be subverted if women are to be truly liberated. She also underscores the sheer monotony of domesticity, or what she calls the 'ideology of the routine' (Greer 1971, p. 146). Motherhood, especially, is seen as a key site in the oppression of women:

> The plight of mothers is more desperate than that of other women, and the more numerous the children the more helpless the situation seems to be. And yet women with children do break free, with or without their offspring…Most women, because of the assumptions that they have formed about the importance of their role as bearers and socializers of children, would shrink at the notion of leaving husband and children, but this is precisely the case in which brutally clear rethinking must be undertaken.
>
> (Greer 1971, p. 145)

This suggestion, that women should contemplate leaving their family home, and especially their children, incensed the wives and mothers who regularly read *McCall's*. Perhaps to encourage this fiery response, the extract is editorialised in this way: 'An outspoken young critic from England assails the fakery of femininity and offers some radical proposals for women's self-realization' (*McCall's* 1971, p. 92).

'Miss Greer is the most pathetic eunuch of all' **135**

With *McCall's* predominantly home-making audience, it is unsurprising that this part of the book, urging women to reimagine their lives *otherwise* (i.e., beyond marriage and motherhood), provoked the ire of its readers. This was not, however, the first time that *McCall's* readers had felt badly portrayed by a blockbuster celebrity feminist author and the magazine that brought her critique to them. In February 1963, when *McCall's* published 'The Fraud of Femininity', an excerpt from Betty Friedan's *The Feminine Mystique* (1963), readers responded in a similar fashion. As Eva Moskowitz (2001, p. 176) notes, 'readers reject[ed] Friedan's argument about the myth of domestic bliss, insisting that their own perfectly happy and contented lives were proof that the "myth" was real'. This earlier example suggests that *McCall's* readers, when it came to popular feminist books and their celebrity authors and indeed to the magazine itself, had a long history of using the letter to the editor form in this way.

Only three of these letters in response to the Greer extract made it into the pages of *McCall's*; unlike the overwhelming majority of reader responses, the first of these was positive, while the remaining two were more representative of the letters as a whole ('Letters to the editor', *McCall's*, May 1971, p. 10). Mary Parker, perhaps not from *McCall's* target audience, remarks that the piece made 'more sense about Women's Liberation than anything I have read' and made her realise that 'McCALL's readers and I, even though I am one of those hairy/hippie students, have much in common. Right on, sisters'. The inclusion of Parker's letter, one of very few supportive responses, was arguably a strategic editorial choice, especially given her attempts to bridge the gap between feminists and *McCall's* readers. In contrast, a letter from a husband and wife suggests that Greer suffers from excessive 'self-indulgence' and 'blindly lashes out at family, marriage, and customs'; it concludes that 'the companionship and growth of love is missing from her life' (Ann and Warren Himmelberger). Finally, another reader directly challenges Greer's characterisation of domesticity as slavery (a characterisation which, while prevalent during the second wave, is deeply problematic given the US's history [Stevenson 2019]): 'If freedom means giving up the close loving relationship of mother and child or the love of a devoted husband, give me slavery any time!' (Roberta Finsilver). Such negative public responses to Greer's popular feminist writing, and indeed Greer herself, represent instances of anti-fandom.

Anti-fandom and affective (dis)investments

As Lawrence Grossberg (1992) emphasises and as the Introduction canvassed, 'affective investment' is vital to the work of media and popular culture, including fan – and anti-fan – practices. Historically within cultural studies, anti-fans have not received the same kinds of critical attention as

136 Germaine Greer, Celebrity Feminism and the Archive

fans, while Chapter 2 emphasised that neither form has been considered in relation to celebrity feminists. These epistolary texts, as I argue here, are most fruitfully conceptualised as forms of what Jonathan Gray (2003) describes as 'anti-fandom'. As Gray contends, the study of anti-fan activity can suggest as much about the affective engagements of consumers as fans:

> Fan studies have taken us to one end of a spectrum of involvement with a text, but we should also look at the other end to those individuals spinning around a text in its electron cloud, variously bothered, insulted or otherwise assaulted by its presence.
>
> (2003, p. 70)

McCall's readers were indeed 'assaulted by [*The Female Eunuch's*] presence' and especially its presence in their beloved magazine. As Gray further posits, 'studying the anti-fan could also provide further insight into the nature of affective involvement, for many of us care as deeply (if not more so) about those texts that we dislike as we do about those that we like' (2003, p. 73) – including bestselling feminist texts and their celebrity authors.

More recently, in response to such calls for greater critical attention to anti-fans, studies have been conducted on the kinds of anti-fandom produced in the wake of much-derided publications such as teen vampire series *Twilight* (Pinkowitz 2011) and its fan fiction spinoff, *Fifty Shades of Grey* (Harman and Jones 2013), or *My Little Pony* (Jones 2015), the children's series that has been appropriated by queer communities. Commonly, 'instead of seeing themselves in the text', anti-fans 'find elements within the text that they react against and oppose' (Harman and Jones 2013, p. 955). The *McCall's* readers analysed here *do* see themselves in this extract, but they resent and challenge Greer's characterisation of them as oppressed wives and mothers, and they use the letters to the editor forum to 'react against and oppose' this portrayal. While much of the recent scholarly work mapping anti-fan labour, unsurprisingly, turns to digital media and its affordances, such as memes, online fiction, vlogs and blogs, or websites devoted to the object of disdain (Click 2019), letters to the editor are a historically significant form through which negative affective responses to popular cultural forms have been articulated.

The *McCall's* letter writers, as I establish here, are indeed Greer anti-fans. Whereas fandom is commonly seen to be performed collectively, through various types of extended sub-cultural activity (Hills 2002), anti-fandom is perhaps more often ephemeral and individualised. However, I argue that being affectively motivated to publicly critique a specific figure or text, even if only in one instance, constitutes a significant act of anti-fandom (much as the letters in Chapter 2 were identified as an important type of fandom). Indeed, as Gray makes clear, this 'fleeting' anti-fandom may be representative of much broader cultural anxieties: 'Fleeting anti-fandom is likely indicative of a larger anti-fandom or concern, in which the momentarily disliked object serves largely and perhaps only as an instance of something grander that is disliked' (2019, p. 39). Moreover, although it is impossible to know, these writers may in fact have continued to be anti-fans of Greer and her blockbuster, or of *McCall's*, over the proceeding decades.

Criticising *McCall's* and its editor

As Elizabeth Groeneveld argues, letters to the editor make clear that reading magazines 'is about far more than simply consuming information or entertainment: it is a personal and intimate activity closely tied to individual and collective identity formation' (2018, p. 165). In this instance, the identities that are formed have a more complicated relation to feminism than some of the others examined in this book. These letters are crucial politically, as forms of women's self-representation, and as insights into how feminism as a social movement was being made-to-mean by so-called ordinary women as well as the feelings it provoked (Groeneveld 2018). Letters to the editor often appear motivated by intense emotions such as anger and disappointment (Groeneveld 2018, p. 159), something evidenced by these particular epistolary texts (and those in the previous chapter). In these letters, the anti-fan sentiment was initially directed at *McCall's* itself and the editor who had permitted such a deplorable feminism to sully the pages of their favourite text.

As self-professed regular readers or fans of *McCall's*, many wrote to the editor to complain about the decision to include Greer's writing, suggesting that the book's ideological position was fundamentally inconsistent with what they expected and found valuable in the magazine. For example, pathologising Greer as many do, this reader-writer (undated, unsigned) tells *McCall's* there will be commercial consequences for publishing such troublesome work: 'Are you kidding? This is an <u>article</u> for the Village Voice, not McCall's. Miss Greer is a sick, sick "woman". That you should even take enough interest in her bogwash theories shocks me. (I've cancelled my subscription.). Adios'.[3] Such a threat, of withdrawing monetary support, was routinely made in these letters to the editor. For example, another writer from Arizona, who describes the book as 'ghastly', likewise threatens to cancel her subscription (14 March) – similarly, *Cavett v*iewers who objected to Greer's feminism threatened to stop watching the show.[4] The decision to publish the extract, therefore, alienated and potentially jeopardised the magazine's core readership. Through such 'antifannish practices', we can gain some insight into 'what the text's best self should be according to the fan(s), and hence what has gone wrong' (Gray 2019, p. 31). Here, 'what has gone wrong' is *McCall's* inclusion of Greer's questionable feminism.

Many argue that because Greer's perspective fails to resonate with their audience, *McCall's* have misjudged, and let down, their loyal readers. In this

138 Germaine Greer, Celebrity Feminism and the Archive

respect, they are not just Greer anti-fans but *McCall's* anti-fans as well. As is common, another reader-writer suggests that the decision to put such material into print reflected extremely poorly on the magazine and its leadership: 'immoral and communistic…It could do much harm to the thinking of many women. It has lowered my opinion very much of *McCall's* magazine' (C.K., undated). Here, *McCall's* 'brand' is to seen to have been damaged by its inclusion of Greer and her purportedly destructive feminist propaganda; conversely, in the previous chapter, we saw that many *Playboy* readers thought its public image was improved. Likewise, a letter from a New York reader (F.H., 29 March) begins:

> I am appalled that you would waste the paper to print, "The Female Eunuch"…What we need are articles that encourage women to use their intelligence and opportunities – or to make opportunities, to better themselves and conditions around them – not some gal crying in her coffee.

In a common criticism, this reader-writer remarks that Greer has failed to offer any useful suggestions for women's empowerment. Other writers also dismiss Greer's contribution: 'McCall's has outdone itself for absolute nonsense' (D.C., 4 March) and 'McCall's, I'm shocked and disappointed in you' for publishing 'such drivel' (R.B., 11 March, Wisconsin). Seeing feminism as a social threat that needed to be curtailed, another reader-writer concludes: 'Articles like that do more damage to women than all the playboy clubs. Please in the future devote such space to constructive ideas' (place and date illegible). With such interventions, these writers attempt to shape the magazine's future engagements with women's liberation.

For the following woman from Ohio, *McCall's*, through its publication of Greer's writing, is failing to adequately represent its readers:

> As a woman I do not think that you are showing a true picture of what all women feel in a very disturbed time of identity. I am happily married… and it would take a lot more than a biter [sic] woman's recommendation to make me want to revolt in my role and claim I am my husband's equal in all matters.
>
> (K.S., undated; see also B.S, 6 March, PA)

In referring to a 'very disturbed time of identity', this reader-writer invokes feminist-inspired shifts in women's subjectivities – shifts she clearly laments. Signed 'I remain, sincere in my womanhood, and dedicated to my husband and my home', this letter also exemplifies one of the other key ways of critiquing Greer and her blockbuster: as an unfair, and unwarranted, attack on happy American housewives. In order to defend themselves, however, these

'Miss Greer is the most pathetic eunuch of all' **139**

writers sought to reposition Greer as the problem; it was she, they argued, who was living a lamentable life.

'She (Miss Greer) sounds a bit castrated herself': Pathologising Greer

Debates about the kinds of women granted the cultural legitimacy to speak as celebrity feminists, facilitated by online platforms and the publics they help constitute, have been visibly staged over the past 5-10 years (Hamad and Taylor 2015). However, these letters illustrate both that many women have historically had a hostile relationship with the feminists attempting to speak on their behalf and that they have chosen to publicly communicate such affective responses via the available channels (in this instance, the letter to the editor form). Moreover, the kind of antagonism favoured by *McCall's* reader-writers is echoed by feminism's contemporary online opponents, revealing not just that feminism has always provoked intense (dis)identifications but that textual vehicles for the public expression of such disdain have long appeared in various guises (Jane 2016, p. 17).

Although most letters lack the intensely misogynistic character of more recent online attacks on celebrity feminists, including Greer herself (as the following chapter demonstrates) and others such as Australian author Clementine Ford (Brady 2021), they do represent a troublesome attempt to regulate and police the bounds of gender (as Greer herself has appeared to do via her transphobic commentary). In contrast to the more positive response from women discussed in Chapter 2, who saw Greer as the model of a new kind of gendered subjectivity which they hoped to emulate, the criticisms from readers of *McCall's* are predicated on assumptions about femininity and Greer's failure to embody it in an appropriate fashion. Indeed, most see this as being the source of her misguided feminism: that she has become alienated from her 'true' womanhood (an accusation also levelled by the Steve Irwin emailers discussed in the following chapter). Greer, therefore, was characterised as being out of touch with the women she addressed.

Many engaged in personal attacks on the celebrity author, which Greer has endured throughout her public career. For example, one unsigned, and undated, postcard reads:

It is shocking to read such a radical viewpoint – not controversial by any means – just plain horrible. Is this the work of a former mental patient? A dike? A bitter, ugly old woman? Her thoughts are truly inspired – every word the work of the devil.

140 Germaine Greer, Celebrity Feminism and the Archive

Such a vitriolic characterisation of feminists, of course, has a long history, with which this framing is consistent (Tomlinson 2010); nor is positioning women with radical ideas, and a desire to publicly articulate them, as 'ill' a modern phenomenon (Showalter 1998). This equation of feminism-as-illness with lesbianism also has an extensive history in public discourse, as the women's liberationist came to be repeatedly figured as 'a fanatical and irrational pervert' (Hesford 2013, p. 77). Moreover, in this example, the pathologisation is entirely unsubtle, as this reader-writer conjectures that Greer may be a 'mental patient'.

In a letter entitled 'Rebuttal of The Female Eunuch', one reader-writer dismisses Greer's concerns as 'individual hangups' (J.R.W., undated, Oklahoma). Likewise, attempting to individualise and thus neutralise Greer's critique of patriarchal capitalism, another – whose words appear in this chapter's title – remarks:

> Miss Greer is the most pathetic eunuch of all. She should solve her own problems before advising others. Who, in heaven's name…would <u>want</u> to be liberated from the glories of being a true <u>woman</u>. I detect some sarcastic jealousy on Miss Greer's part.
>
> (unsigned and undated, original emphasis)

Women's liberation here is figured as an entirely undesirable aim, one that is at odds with an essential femininity – an assumption that marks nearly all the *McCall's* letters. The following reader-writer similarly locates Greer's dissatisfaction in the author herself and reinscribes the opposition between feminists and 'ordinary' women familiar in anti-feminist discourse:

> only a woman who is chained by her own inadequacies would write such an article…So let the Women's Lib frantic proponents go on screaming while the happily fulfilled continue to quietly build homes which have been and always will be the backbone of our country as God intended that it should be.
>
> (G.L.V., undated, Missouri)

Here, the role of women is further naturalised by the invocation of God, and Greer is rendered aberrant.[5]

After referring to her disparagingly as 'Germaine Queer', one writer continues: 'Miss Greer is no more qualified to talk about "maternal feelings" or mother-child relationships than an idiot or pathetic moron' (E.K., 19 March, New York). Here, Greer's ability to speak authoritatively is compromised by her personal 'failure' to adopt the normative feminine roles of wife and mother (as we also see in the Irwin emails). This reader-writer's gesture of positioning Greer's feminist discontentment as an individual malady attempts to

'Miss Greer is the most pathetic eunuch of all' **141**

depoliticise it. Moreover, Greer's apparent 'queerness' is a disease that only 'true' womanhood can cure. In this vein, a writer from Kentucky (M.A., 23 March), in a lengthy critique, notes with exasperation: 'I'm sick of reading articles written by "sick" women who are afraid to be women'. This discursive strategy mirrored news reports of the time, which 'often implied that feminists' violation of gender norms stemmed from their deviant personal psychologies rather than their politics, making their femininity – their credibility as women – the issue' (Dow 2014, p. 17). Such a shift patently occurs in these letters.

In and through their anti-fan practices, these women are exercising their agency, revaluing their ways of doing femininity through problematically devaluing Greer's. Along these lines, another reader-writer celebrating the apparent 'joys' of domesticity proclaims: 'Life for Germaine Greer must be a grim and bitter business, indeed!' (D.S., 5 March, Missouri). Greer is therefore coded as a miserable woman – or what Sara Ahmed (2010) would call a 'feminist killjoy' – who certainly does not speak for this readership: 'You have done your readers a grave disservice in implying that Geraldine [sic] Greer represents liberated women everywhere' (L.R., undated, Ohio). Similarly, a writer from New York (19 March, original emphasis) dismisses Greer's blockbuster as

> an atrocity; an insult to womankind; a sacrilegious [sic] slap-in the face of motherhood; the sad distortion of all that society holds to be decent. Miss Greer, who claims to seek freedom, will <u>never</u> be free! She is chained to her <u>fears</u> of being a <u>WOMAN</u>, a mate, a mother, an individual who can function in the natural male-female realm.

Freedom is again refigured through the invocation of essentialist language; choosing to accept, rather than rally against, innate gender difference represents the true path to liberation. Greer, unlike these readers, is seen to fear her 'natural' social positioning. Through such rhetoric, Greer becomes isolated from those readers she is seeking to reach with her polemical text. While Chapter 2 has shown that for other women, including housewives, Greer was commonly seen to admirably embody the kind of woman she urges others to become in her blockbuster, for these readers it is such embodiment that makes her so problematic.

Continuing in this vein, a number of these reader-writers express pity for Greer, whom they see as effectively missing out on the many pleasures of 'authentic' womanhood. A writer from Tennessee (K.N.C., 15 March) also finds Greer's work abhorrent and distinctly at odds with the form in which they are articulated: 'The article by Germaine Greer in March *McCall's*, contains the most revolting ideas I've read in a woman's magazine. If she believes what she writes, I'm glad I don't know her. But I am sorry for her'. Another likewise expresses pity for Greer, noting that after reading the extract she 'first felt angry, then sorry that any woman would be so unhappy...What she doesn't understand is that most women don't consider caring for her husband and babies slavery' (place and date illegible). Accusing Greer of a fundamental misinterpretation, the majority of reader-writers refuse to accept her argument that marriage and motherhood are something from which women need, and should want, to be liberated.

As we have seen, the *McCall's* extract featured *The Female Eunuch*'s argument that women should forego marriage in their quest for liberation; it was this point which *McCall's* readers found most troublesome, and they saw such a rejection as neither viable nor desirable. Though heavily criticised, Greer's lack of prescriptiveness can be seen as one of her text's virtues, with its conclusion placing the responsibility for change back on its readers: 'What *will* you do?' (1970, p. 331, original emphasis). Greer was, more than once, taken to task for a perceived failure to offer a manifesto, both at the time of publication and in subsequent reassessments of its impact: 'what women need now is not further analyses but programs for revolutionary change, and of these Germaine Greer offers little' (Kempton 1971; see also Tillyard 1999). These sentiments are also found in the *McCall's* letters. A number of these correspondents see no alternative available to women: 'What should I run from, to? What is better? What more fulfilling?' (M.A., undated, Indiana). Similarly, an Iowa reader-writer argues that Greer's disavowal of marriage is not a workable option for women, and she criticises her for not 'offer[ing] any proposals that any reader would seriously consider' (10 May).

For others, the suggestions that Greer does offer for personal transformation are dismissed as ludicrous. Although proclaiming herself a strong supporter of women's liberation, one reader-writer remarks that Greer's 'suggestions that women should not marry, and that all married women should leave their husbands is both neurotic and ridiculous [underlined in red pencil]. The goal of women's lib is not to destroy family life' (L.R., undated, Ohio, original emphasis). We can read these letters as attempts at refiguring marriage and motherhood, in a context where they were being largely devalued – especially by feminists. Moreover, these are the kind of women that the anti-feminist Phyllis Schlafly would mobilise in her campaign against the Equal Rights Amendment, represented most recently in the 2020 HBO television series *Mrs America* ('Motherhood is freedom, Jill', Schlafly tells republican feminist Jill Rickelhaus, in episode 6, 'Jill'; see Henderson and Taylor 2023).

These women refuse Greer's efforts to hail them as victims of either patriarchy in a macro sense or their husbands in a more micro sense; taking up their pens to contest such positioning is a significant act of self-representation. As one reader puts it, taking issue with Greer's framing of domesticity as imprisonment: 'Miss Greer and Women's Lib you may do what you want with your lives but please do not be so naïve as to think that every woman wants to be liberated because we are not all prisoners' (J.R.W., undated,

Oklahoma). This woman is not necessarily anti-feminist but she is, like the others, pro-housewife. Clearly, these reader-writers feel as though Greer mischaracterises them as dupes, something they seek to refute through these epistolary forms of re-presentation. They argue that they are not victims of the false consciousness that Greer seeks to attribute to them, and they categorically refuse her attempts to position them as subordinate: 'Why must we have as much Women's Lib forced upon us?...We are not *all* bored, subjugated by our husbands' (M.S., 14 March, New York, original emphasis). Here, it is women's liberation, not marriage and motherhood, that is being 'forced upon' women.

For another woman, heterosexual fulfilment is seen as antithetical to the emancipatory agenda proffered by Greer: 'Take your freedom lady, I'll take love!' (S.J., Iowa, original emphasis). Here, opposing 'freedom' to 'love', feminism becomes the enemy of heteronormative intimacy and should be resisted on such grounds. One reader-writer (3 March), like many others, also figures Greer's approach as fundamentally 'selfish': that failure to attend to the needs of others, especially in a domestic context, lamentably renders feminists like Greer self-centred. Therefore, as a single, childfree woman, Greer is seen as not having reached proper adulthood, a familiar critique of women without partners and especially without children. One writer dismisses Greer's as 'an immature viewpoint' (W.S., 14 March), an immaturity, she implies, that is the result of her perceived failure to become a full citizen through matrimony and motherhood (Taylor 2012).

Defensive housewives 'choosing their choice'

Within second-wave feminism, the idea that housewives were 'sentenced to everyday life' (Johnson and Lloyd 2004) was prevalent, and this was certainly a position that Greer herself sought to advance with her understanding of marriage and domesticity as akin to servitude. As Lesley Johnson and Justine Lloyd (2004, p. 2) argue, 'feminists during the first decades of second wave feminism constituted "the housewife" as "Other" to themselves as they sought to elaborate a speaking position for feminists and the feminist intellectual in particular' (see also Brunsdon 2000). The second-wave feminist critique of the 'unhappy housewife' in America began with Friedan's *The Feminine Mystique* (1963). For Friedan, women needed to be liberated from the domestic drudgery of suburban life. In her work on postfeminism, Stephanie Genz suggests that for both Friedan and Greer the housewife became 'an instantly identifiable figure that epitomizes everything that is wrong with patriarchy...she was seen simplistically and one-sidedly as a nonfeminist' (2008, p. 52; see also Munford and Waters 2014).

As a result of such positioning, housewives commonly felt alienated from the women's liberation movement, an alienation upon which anti-feminist

144 Germaine Greer, Celebrity Feminism and the Archive

celebrities such as Schlafly capitalised (Henderson and Taylor 2023). There were, as Marjorie Spruill argues, 'two women's movements' in America that need to be factored in when attempting to come to terms with 'the legacy of 1970s feminism' (2018, p. 40). She suggests that as

> feminists lobbied for policies they saw as fitting "today's realities" including the massive movement of wives and mothers into the labor force, women committed to traditional gender roles opposed them in an effort to preserve a way of life they saw as under attack and endangered.
>
> (Spruill 2018, p. 40)

These letters to *McCall's*, while perhaps not written by anti-feminist activists, were certainly consistent with this 'second' women's movement, which rallied against the women's liberation movement's disdain for the housewife.

While feminists have rightly problematised the deployment of the servitude trope in first- and second-wave polemic due to the US's history of slavery and racial oppression (Stevenson 2019), *McCall's* reader-writers also opposed this dominant second-wave view but on different grounds. These women explicitly reject the dominant feminist trope of slavery as a way of derogatorily characterising the housewife and her labour. For example, a wife and mother of two, who is 'incensed' after reading Greer's piece, contests the idea of enslavement: 'I certainly don't feel I'm a slave' (S.J., Iowa). They argue that they are not forced into their roles within the home by the patriarchy but willingly embrace and even find joy in them. In a postfeminist representational environment, we have seen a similar (re)valorisation of women's involvement in domesticity as well as the phenomenon of 'retreatism' (Vavrus 2007; Genz 2008; Negra 2009). Such retreatism, where harried working mothers forego the frantic space of work in favour of the relative calm and tranquillity of the home, manifests more recently in the figure of the 'trad wife' (Proctor 2022; Sykes and Hopner 2024). Retreatism, of course, reveals the 'class bias' in postfeminism, as 'only middle-class mothers who have some nonwork means of support (i.e., a working husband/partner) could, theoretically, make such a "choice" between work and family' (Projansky 2001, p. 79) – such privilege is also elided in these letters.

In critical accounts, 'choice' is positioned as a fundamentally postfeminist (and neoliberal) way of reacting against feminism and refiguring one's relationship to domesticity, thus foreclosing the possibility of such a discourse having been similarly deployed at other cultural moments. Through the *McCall's* letters, we can see that such a rhetorical manoeuvre dates back at least five decades and has acted as a way for these comparatively privileged women to push back against feminist claims of gender-based subordination. More recently, 'choice feminism' (Budgeon 2011) has seen the reframing of any choice a woman may make – no matter how regressive – as a feminist one. Like many other *McCall's* reader-writers, and later feminist scholars, a woman from Iowa (J.M., 26 February, original emphasis) takes personal offense at Greer's contemptuous attitude towards housewives and deploys a rhetoric of choice: 'those of us who FREELY chose to be housewives should not be condemned by the professional ladies'. To give some context to her critique, this reader-writer concludes: 'I went the career lady route and hated every minute of it. Now, I'm liberated'.

This letter, in particular, is echoed in postfeminist retreatist narratives, wherein a 'freely' chosen return to the home is figured as an act of liberation. In an earlier form of what Elspeth Probyn (1990) dubbed the postfeminist 'new traditionalism' of the late 1980s and early 1990s, '[t]he domestic sphere is rebranded as a domain of female autonomy and independence, far removed from its previous connotations of drudgery and confinement' (Genz 2008, p. 54; McRobbie 2009). This rebranding, however, may be entirely strategic. For Bonnie Kreps, writing in 1968, 'economic discrimination against the working woman is highly conducive to her seeing marriage as a liberation from ill-paid drudgery' (as cited in Rhodes 2004, p. 2). In this way, reader-writers' alternative framing, and celebration, of domesticity itself could be seen as a product of their own awareness of women's ongoing subordination rather than a refusal to concede its existence.[6] However, as women who presumably did not *have* to work outside their homes, these self-constructions significantly downplay their economic advantages – which are inextricable from their racial and class privilege – and the way in which it permits them to discursively constitute domesticity in this rather utopian manner.

Like *Sex and the City*'s (1998–2004) quintessentially postfeminist character, the upper-class, immensely privileged, white Charlotte York, they effectively 'choose their choice' and demand that feminists – here exemplified by Greer – respect them for it. As one of the published writers suggests, Greer

> failed to convince me in the least that, as a housewife, I'm missing out on all of the best things in life…Women's Liberation in the true sense should be the freedom of each woman to make the choice as to what type of life she would like to lead; those of us who prefer the role of the housewife should not be pressured by our peers into abandoning that which, to us, represents fulfilment in the truest sense of the word.
>
> (R.C.F., 2 March, Connecticut)

These women actively resist the feminist interpretive framework that Greer has applied to their lives, offering a counter-narrative of personal satisfaction and contentment. Given when these correspondents were writing, it is nevertheless clear that 'choice' does operate differently in this context, where many of these women simply had no choice but to choose live as wives and mothers (Giddens 1991) – while, conversely, many other less privileged women had no choice but to work outside the home.

146 Germaine Greer, Celebrity Feminism and the Archive

Many reader-writers, like the one above, contest the idea that happiness cannot be found within the domestic context, suggesting that, contra Greer's patronising claims of servitude, 'marriage and motherhood is an exhilarating, satisfying challenge' (16 March, Colorado). Overwhelmingly, the roles of wife and mother are significantly romanticised, as reader-writers represent them as liberatory, fulfilling 'choices': 'The freest and most liberated person on the face of the earth, regardless of race, creed or color, is a happily married woman with a loving husband and respectful children' (M.A., 23 March). Here, racial and class differences are clearly flattened as women's experiences are universalised. In the process, this reader-writer ignores the intersectional factors that would prohibit all women from conceptualising domesticity in this way. That is, such reframing represents a clear form of a class and racial privilege which goes unacknowledged by these middle-class American women, many of whom would likely have employed women of colour to make this 'chosen' domestic labour more manageable.

Conclusion

The *McCall's* letters reveal that white, middle-class American women in the early 1970s, especially housewives, were seeking to validate their way of being in the world through recourse to a feminist-informed vocabulary of choice. That is, while they were clearly resisting second-wave feminism, they were ironically relying upon its rhetoric to bolster their more conservative arguments and modes of being. Therefore, these women are not *choosing* domesticity over the public sphere – as those middle- and upper-class women in postfeminist retreatist narratives do – but they are positioning themselves agentically to contest feminist assumptions about their lives and subjectivities. What they are 'choosing', then, is to reject Greer's feminism via these acts of anti-fandom.

Although there is no record of Greer replying to these actual letters, elsewhere the provocative author was unsympathetic to arguments like those made by the *McCall's* readers. For example, in the Indian women's magazine *Eve Weekly*, she made her contempt clear:

> Too many people connive at their own oppression, and frankly, I have no time for them...There's the woman who claims "well, I have a loving husband and three beautiful children, what I do need to be liberated from?" This argument is as absurd as saying that if a slave has a good master he should remain a slave all his life. I find this type of woman a damn bore because she just refuses to look beyond her nose.
>
> ('Germaine Greer in India', 1979)

Here, Greer reinscribes her problematic equation of domesticity with slavery, condemns women for their short-sightedness, and demonstrates her impatience with the kind of argument mounted by these letter writers.

'Miss Greer is the most pathetic eunuch of all' **147**

This analysis of *McCall's* reader-writers from 1971 has foregrounded women's often complicated reactions to Greer's calls for their liberation. Although these anti-fans have attempted to take Greer to task for discrediting their own ways of being, such attempts are problematically reliant upon the invocation of an essentialised femininity to which Greer fails to adhere. That is, while they strongly criticise Greer for seeking to circumscribe the kinds of femininities they (choose to) inhabit, they do so through reinscribing the same rhetorical gesture: judging *her* for her 'failure' to marry or mother. They appropriate feminist-inspired rhetoric about freedom of choice for their own more conservative purposes and in the process undermine Greer's personal life decisions.

However, in writing such letters, these privileged middle-class housewives were seeking to intervene in contemporary debates about women's liberation and to have their voices heard, using one of the only forms at their disposal. Importantly, their challenge to Greer's discursive construction of domesticity as imprisonment, and through which they seek to reposition themselves as active, empowered agents, is itself echoed in later feminist critiques of the second wave's contempt for housewives. The inclusion of such epistolary texts in the archive enables us to reconsider the women often marginalised by second-wave feminism and to ensure that their contributions to contemporary debates are acknowledged. These letters therefore necessitate a level of nuance often missing from accounts of the impact of women's liberation, especially as they were not simply anti-feminist but not pro-feminist either.

Overall, the unpublished *McCall's* letters – like others across this book – underscore that women's complex responses to celebrity feminism, as well as the public articulation of these responses, have a much longer history than is sometimes conceded. These letters, as I have argued, reveal much about the historical and cultural milieu in which they were produced, an argument that Greer makes about the whole archive (that it is 'about the moment' [2017]). The women writers in this chapter seek to publicly discredit Greer and her feminism, something that has persisted across her career. In the next chapter, I continue this focus on more hostile responses to Greer. In 2006, her public commentary on the death of celebrity environmentalist Steve Irwin elicited masses of intensely misogynistic, hateful emails from those who perceived Greer to be imperilling both Australian masculinity and the Australian nation itself. The authors of these outward-facing letters, as I will show, attempt to curtail the threat that Greer as an outspoken, ageing feminist is seen to pose.

Notes

1 In contrast to the responses examined here, Le Masurier (2009, p. 111) notes that when *Cleo* published an article in 1973 – entitled 'Strike One Against Women's Lib' – featuring 'women who were opposed to Germaine Greer and were happy in their dependent married roles...the letters page erupted [in support of Greer]'. In terms of how readers impacted the magazine's content, Le Masurier observes,

148 Germaine Greer, Celebrity Feminism and the Archive

'*Cleo* editors took note and there was no strike two' (2009, p. 111). The magazines' different addressees would undoubtedly have been a factor in these reactions; *Cleo*'s implied reader was a young, employed, sexually empowered woman (Henderson and Taylor 2020) rather than a housewife whose identity was being called into question by prominent second-wave feminists like Greer.

2 Greer was asked to write for the inaugural issue of *Ms* in July 1972 (a piece called 'Notes from Abroad: Down with Panties' [Greer 1972]), so Carbine's editorship may go some way to explaining how Greer's extract actually made it into *McCall's*.

3 Original spelling and punctuation have been preserved in quotations from these letters.

4 For example, a Vermont woman viewer suggested that the Greer episodes were 'simply awful' and pledged to 'quit watching' (16 June, F.J.O., 2014.0044.164).

5 As Spruill notes, 'Most of the women disturbed by feminist gains were devoutly religious and believed in innate, indeed divinely created differences between women and men that mandated traditional gender roles, patriarchal families, and differential treatment of the sexes under the law. Feminism appeared to them as a dire threat not only to the security and happiness of American women, but to the survival of the nation—which drew its strength from the strength of the American family' (2018, p. 42).

6 This position was put forth by Australian anti-feminist activists such as Nance Cotter of the Women's Action Alliance (formed in 1975), for whom 'liberation meant the freedom to be a wife and mother at home, for it was workplace drudgery, not domesticity, that was oppressive' (Arrow 2021, p. 340).

References

Ahmed, S. (2010) *The Promise of Happiness*, Durham: Duke University Press.

Arrow, M. (2021) '"How Much Longer Will We Allow This Country's Affairs to be Run by Radical Feminists?" Anti-Feminist Activism in Late 1970s Australia', *Australian Historical Studies*, vol. 52, no. 3: 331–347.

Banet-Weiser, S. (2018) *Empowered: Popular Feminism and Popular Misogyny*, Durham: Duke University Press.

Brady, A. (2016) '"Taking Time Between G-String Changes to Educate Ourselves": Sinead O'Connor, Miley Cyrus, and Celebrity Feminism', *Feminist Media Studies*, vol. 16, no. 3: 429–444.

Brady, A. (2021) 'Clementine Ford, Online Misogyny, and the Labour of Celebrity Feminism', in A. Taylor and J. McIntyre (eds.), *Gender and Australian Celebrity Culture*, London: Routledge, pp. 91–108.

Bruns, A. (2008) *Blogs, Wikipedia, Second Life, and Beyond: From Production to Produsage*, Bern: Peter Lang.

Brunsdon, C. (2000) *The Feminist, The Housewife, and Soap Opera*, Oxford: Oxford University Press.

Buchanan, R. (2018) 'Foreign Correspondence: Journalism in the Germaine Greer Archive', *Archives and Manuscripts*, vol. 46, no. 1: 18–39.

Budgeon, S. (2011) *Third Wave Feminism and The Politics of Gender in Late Modernity*, Basingstoke: Palgrave.

Click, M. ed. (2019) *Anti-Fandom: Dislike and Hate in the Digital Age*, New York: New York University Press.

Coffin, J. (2020) *Sex, Love, and Letters: Writing Simone de Beauvoir*, New York: Cornell University Press.

Deem, M. (2003) 'Disrupting the Nuptials at the Town Hall Debate: Feminism and the Politics of Cultural Memory in the USA', *Cultural Studies*, vol. 17, no. 5: 615–647.

Dever, M., Newman, S., and Vickery, A. (2009) *The Intimate Archive: Journeys through Private Papers*, Canberra: National Library of Australia.

Dow, B. J. (2014) *Watching Women's Liberation 1970: Feminism's Pivotal Year on the Network News*, Urbana: University of Illinois.

Farrell, A.E. (1998) *Yours in Sisterhood: Ms Magazine and The Making of Popular Feminism*, Chapel Hill: University of North Carolina.

Fish, S. (1978) *Is There is a Text in this Class?*, Cambridge: Harvard University Press.

Friedan, B. (1963) *The Feminine Mystique*, New York: Penguin.

Genz, S. (2008) '"I Am Not a Housewife, but…" Postfeminism and the Revival of Domesticity', in S. Gillis and J. Hollows (eds.), *Femininity, Domesticity and Popular Culture*, London: Routledge, pp. 49–62.

Germaine Greer Archive. Early Years, 2014.0044, University of Melbourne.

Germaine Greer Archive. Correspondence with Publishers, 2014.0052, University of Melbourne.

Germaine Greer versus the USA (1971), dir. Brigid Segrave, Germaine Greer Archive, 2014.0041.00258, Audiovisual recordings produced and received by Greer, University of Melbourne.

'Germaine Greer in India' (1979), *Eve's Weekly*, 10–16 February: 38–39, Germaine Greer Archive, Major Works, 2014.0045.00032, University of Melbourne.

Giddens, A. (1991) *The Transformation of Intimacy*, London: Polity.

Gill, R. (2016) 'Post-postfeminism? New Feminist Visibilities in Postfeminist Times', *Feminist Media Studies*, vol. 16, no. 4: 610–630.

Gray, J. (2003) 'New Audiences, New Textualities: Anti-fans and Non-fans', *International Journal of Cultural Studies*, vol. 6, no. 1: 64–81.

Gray, J. (2019) 'How Do I Dislike Thee? Let Me Count the Ways', in M. Click (ed.), *Anti-fandom: Hate and Dislike in the Digital Age*, New York: New York University Press, pp. 25–41.

Green, B. (2012) 'Complaints of Everyday Life: Feminist Periodical Culture and Correspondence Columns in The Woman Worker, Women Folk and The Freewoman', *Modernism/Modernity*, vol. 19, no. 3: 461–485.

Greer, G. (1969) 'The Female Eunuch Editorial', Germaine Archive, University of Melbourne, accessed via: http://hdl.handle.net/11343/42289

Greer, G. (1970) *The Female Eunuch*, London: Paladin.

Greer, G. (1971) 'The Female Eunuch', *McCall's*, March, pp. 92, 144–147.

Greer, G. (1972) 'Notes from Abroad: Down with Panties', *Ms*, vol. 1, no. 1.

Greer, G. (2017) 'Germaine Greer meets the Archivists', 9 March, YouTube, accessed via: https://www.youtube.com/ watch?v=LOcMazsj6OQ.

Groeneveld, E. (2018) 'Letters to the Editor as "Archives of Feeling": *On Our Backs* Magazine and the Sex Wars', *American Periodical Studies*, vol. 28, no. 2: 53–167.

Grossberg, L. (1992) 'Is There a Fan in the House? The Affective Sensibility of Fandom', in L. Lewis (ed.), *The Adoring Audience*, New York: Routledge, pp. 50–68.

Hamad, H. and Taylor, A. (2015) 'Introduction: Feminism and Celebrity Culture', *Celebrity Studies*, vol. 6, no. 1: 124–127.

Hamilton, M. (1971) 'The Enraged Feminist', *San Francisco Examiner*, May 13, Germaine Greer Archive, Early Years, 2014.0044.00171, University of Melbourne.

Harman, S. and Jones, B. (2013) 'Fifty Shades of Grey: Snark Fandom and the Figure of the Anti-fan', *Sexualities*, vol. 16, no. 8: 951–968.

Hemmings, C. (2012) 'Affective Solidarity: Feminist Reflexivity and Political Transformation', *Feminist Theory*, vol. 13, no. 2: 147–161.

Henderson, M. and Taylor, A. (2020) *Postfeminism in Context*, London: Routledge.

Henderson, M. and Taylor, A. (2023) 'A Prosthetic Popular Feminism in Postfeminist Times: *Mrs America*'s Cool Feminism and Anti-Feminist Celebrity', *Signs: Journal of Women in Culture and Society*, vol. 48, no. 4: 1015–1039.

Hesford, V. (2013) *Feeling Women's Liberation*, Durham: Duke University Press.

Hills, M. (2002) *Fan Cultures*, London: Routledge.

Jane, E. (2016) *Misogyny Online: A Short (and Brutish) History*, London: Sage.

Jenkins, H. (2006) *Convergence Culture: Where Old and New Media Collide*, New York: New York University Press.

Johnson, L. and Lloyd, J. (2004) *Sentenced to Everyday Life: Feminism and the Housewife*, London: Berg.

Jones, B. (2015) 'My Little Pony, Tolerance is Magic: Gender Policing and Brony anti-fandom', *Journal of Popular Television*, vol. 3, no. 1: 119–125.

Kempton, S. (1971) 'Little Patience With and Much Advice for Her Own Victimized Class', *New York Times*, 25 April, accessed via: https://archive.nytimes.com/www.nytimes.com/books/99/05/09/specials/greer-eunuch.html

Lawson, C. (2023) *Just Like Us: Digital Debates on Feminism and Fame*, New Brunswick, NJ: Rutgers University Press.

Le Masurier, M. (2007) 'My Other, My Self: *Cleo* Magazine and Feminism in 1970s Australia', *Australian Feminist Studies*, vol. 22, no. 53: 191–211.

Le Masurier, M. (2009) 'Desiring the (Popular Feminist) Reader: Letters to *Cleo* During the Second Wave', *Media International Australia*, vol. 131: 106–116.

McCall's, Letters to the Editor (1972), Germaine Greer Archive, General Correspondence, 2014.0042.00547, University of Melbourne.

McRobbie, A. (2009) *The Aftermath of Feminism: Gender, Culture and Social Change*, London: Sage.

Moskowitz, E. (2001) *In Therapy We Trust: America's Obsession with Self-Fulfilment*, Baltimore: Johns Hopkins University Press.

Mrs. America (2020). Television series, Hulu, Santa Monica, CA. Directed by Anna Boden and Ryan Fleck.

Munford, R. and Waters, M. (2014) *Feminism and Popular Culture: Investigating The Postfeminist Mystique*, London: I.B. Tauris.

Murray, S. (2004) *Mixed Media: Feminist Presses and Publishing Politics*, London: Pluto.

Negra, D. (2009) *What a Girl Wants: Fantasising the Reclamation of Self in Postfeminism*, New York: Routledge.

'NY Town Hall Transcript' (1971), Germaine Greer Archive, Early Years, 2014.0044.00175, University of Melbourne.

Pinkowitz, J.M. (2011) '"The Rabid Fans that take *Twilight* Much Too Seriously": The Construction and Rejection of Excess in *Twilight* Antifandom', *Transformative Works and Culture*, vol. 7.

Probyn, E. (1990) 'New Traditionalism and Post-feminism: TV Does the Home', *Screen*, vol. 31, no. 1: 147–159.

Proctor, D. (2022) 'The #Tradwife Persona and the Rise of Radicalized White Domesticity', *Persona Studies*, vol. 8, no. 2: 7–26.

Projansky, S. (2001) *Watching Rape: Film and Television in Postfeminist Culture*, New York: New York University Press.

Rhodes, J. (2004) *Radical Feminism, Writing, and Critical Agency From Manifesto to Modem*, New York: State University of New York Press.

Roxon, L. (1971) 'A literary bombshell', *Sydney Morning Herald*, 10 April, Germaine Greer Archive, Early Years, 2014.0044.00171, University of Melbourne.

Scott, L.M. (2000) "Market Feminism: The Case for A Paradigm Shift," in M. Catterall, L. Stevens, and P. MacLaren (eds.) *Marketing and Feminism*, London: Routledge, pp. 16–38.

Sex and The City (1998–2004), Television series, HBO, New York. Created by Darren Star.

Sheehan, R.J. (2016) '"If we had more like her we would no longer be the unheard majority": Germaine Greer's Reception in the United States', *Australian Feminist Studies*, vol. 31, no. 87: 62–77.

Showalter, E. (1998) *Hystories: Hysterical Epidemics and Modern Media*, New York: Columbia University Press.

Silver, S.J. (1976) 'Then and Now: Women's Roles in *McCall's* in 1964 and 1974', *The Annual Meeting of the Association of Education in Journalism*, Baltimore: Association of Education in Journalism Conference, accessed via: https://files.eric.ed.gov/fulltext/ED124985.pdf

Smith, S. and Watson, J. (2010) *Reading Autobiography: A Guide for Interpreting Life Narratives*, Minneapolis: University of Minnesota Press.

Spruill, M. (2018) 'Feminism, Anti-Feminism, and The Rise of a New Southern Strategy in the 1970s', in A. Maxwell and T. Shields (eds.), *The Legacy of Second-Wave Feminism in American Politics*, New York: Palgrave Macmillan, pp. 39–69.

Stanley, L. (2004) 'The Epistolarium: On Theorizing Letters and Correspondences', *Auto/biography*, vol. 12: 201–235.

Steuer, L. (2019) 'Structural Affects of Soap Opera Fan Correspondence, 1970s–80s', *Transformative Works*, no. 30, accessed via: https://journal.transformativeworks.org/index.php/twc/article/download/1735/2209?inline=1

Stevenson, A. (2019) *The Woman as Slave in Nineteenth-Century American Social Movements*, London: Palgrave Macmillan.

Sykes, S., & Hopner, V. (2024) 'Tradwives: Right-Wing Social Media Influencers', *Journal of Contemporary Ethnography*, accessed via: https://doi.org/10.1177/08912416241246273

Taylor, A. (2004) 'Readers Writing *The First Stone* Media Event: Letters to the Editor, Australian Feminisms and Mediated Citizenship', *Journal of Australian Studies*, vol. 83: 75–87.

Taylor, A. (2012) *Single Women in Popular Culture: The Limits of Postfeminism*, Basingstoke: Palgrave Macmillan.

Taylor, A. (2016) *Celebrity and the Feminist Blockbuster*, Basingstoke: Palgrave Macmillan.

Thomas, S. (2014) 'Celebrity in the "Twitterverse": History, Authenticity and the Multiplicity of Stardom: Situating the 'newness' of Twitter', *Celebrity Studies*, vol. 5, no. 3, pp. 242–255.

Thompson, B. (2002) 'Multiracial Feminism: Recasting the Chronology of Second Wave Feminism', *Feminist Studies*, vol. 28, no. 2, pp. 336–360.

Thompson, J. (2010) *Merchants of Culture: The Publishing Business in the Twenty-First Century*, London: Polity.

Tillyard, S. (1999) 'Germaine Greer', *Prospect Magazine*, 20 April, accessed via: https://www.prospectmagazine.co.uk/magazine/germainegreerWallace

Tomlinson, B. (2010) 'Transforming the Terms of Reading: Ideologies of Argument and the "Trope of the Angry Feminist" in Contemporary US Political and Academic Discourse', *Journal of America Studies*, vol. 44, no. 1: 101–116.

Vavrus, M. (2007) 'Opting Out Moms in the News: Selling New Traditionalism in the New Millennium', *Feminist Media Studies*, vol. 7, no. 1: 47–63.

'Woman Leaves *Look* to Become Editorial Director of *McCall's*' (1970), *New York Times*, 22 August, accessed via: https://www.nytimes.com/1970/08/22/archives/woman-leaves-look-to-become-editoril-director-of-mccalls.html.

6

'STEVE IS TWICE THE AUSSIE ICON YOU WILL EVER BE'

Nationalistic Misogyny and the Irwin Hate Email

Introduction

Germaine Greer, as the previous chapters have clearly demonstrated, has elicited intense emotional responses from audiences across her career. In relation to the young woman who held her hostage at her Essex home in April 2000, she remarked: '"Ever since I published *The Female Eunuch* there's been an off chance that some nutter is going to pick me off, judging by the hostility in the letters"' (Smith 2000).[1] Here, Greer may seem to exaggerate, for effect, the more troublesome correspondence she has received over her career, but the emails examined in this chapter suggest that her comments were not hyperbolic. Of course, outspoken women, and especially feminists, have long been subject to attempts to discipline them and curtail their voices (Beard 2017; Kay 2020). The kind of feminism Greer prosecutes, and herself personally embodies, is deeply threatening to dominant patriarchal imaginaries, making the outspoken Australian expatriate the target of some vicious attempts to silence her. In Chapter 4, we saw some hostilities directed towards Greer in response to select newspaper and magazine articles published earlier in her career, and Chapter 5 examined the letters to the editor of *McCall's* from disgruntled housewives who felt their way of being in the world was being denigrated by the bestselling author. However, particularly as she ages, the cultural legitimacy of Greer's voice has come under increased strain; it is one such instance upon which this chapter focuses.

In September 2006, Greer wrote a controversial article in response to the death of celebrity wildlife presenter Steve 'the Crocodile Hunter' Irwin, who was killed by a stingray barb while filming his iconic television series on Australia's Great Barrier Reef. While the piece itself is not about gender,

DOI: 10.4324/9781315179841-7

sexuality, or feminism – Greer has published much more widely, especially over the past few decades, including on the environment – the reaction it provoked is indivisible from her status as a celebrity feminist. In the piece, entitled 'That sort of self-delusion is what it takes to be a real Aussie larrikin' (Greer 2006a) and originally published in the *Guardian*, Greer concluded that 'the animal world has finally taken its revenge on Irwin'. For hundreds and hundreds of Australian readers, Greer's public response to the untimely demise of a purported national 'hero' represented a symbolic assault not just on the 'Crocodile Hunter's' grieving family but on the nation itself. Following the article's appearance, Greer's agents – Gillon Aitken Associates, based in England – received copious hate emails directed towards the iconoclastic feminist. As Millicent Weber and Rachel Buchanan remark, 'Although Greer had written many columns where her views were contentious and strongly opposed to the mainstream thought, none attracted this sort of response' (2019, p. 238).

These archived emails, like the unpublished anti-fan letters to the editor discussed in the previous chapter, provide important insights into audience affective responses to this polarising figure. Moreover, as noted in Chapter 1, in the Greer archive the Irwin emails are filed alongside a clipping of the opinion piece in the Print Journalism series, representing a marked deviation from her practice of alphabetising reader correspondence and filing letters and journalistic pieces separately (Buchanan 2018, p. 26). This variation in her 'usual system of arrangement', which effectively directs researchers towards it, signals that Greer saw the piece and the response it provoked as culturally significant and worthy of critical attention (Buchanan 2018, p. 26). Although Greer told curator Buchanan that she did not personally read the emails, her curatorial practices suggest that she recognised their importance for scholars (2018, p. 26; Glanville 2018). With these emails, we also see a shift in communicative practices; much shorter than some of the letters considered earlier, they anticipate the kind of truncated comment culture we have seen develop with the rise of social media platforms, including their misogynistic tendencies (Banet-Weiser and Miltner 2016; Ging and Siapera 2019).

The intense, visceral responses from these emailers suggest just how much is at stake in Greer's challenge to dominant ways of framing the nation in twenty-first-century Australia. Tightly policing the boundaries of what constitutes 'Australian-ness' as well as mobilising problematic assumptions about the 'correct' way of publicly doing femininity, these emails call into question Greer's authority to speak publicly not just about this matter but about any issue at all. In so doing, these emails – which include threats of violence – demonstrate that the vitriolic, misogynistic hate speech commonly directed towards vocal women in the contemporary mediasphere (especially via platforms such as Twitter/X) has a history that extends far beyond these platforms. Against the representation of Irwin as the model Australian, Greer is dismissed not just as a 'bad' woman but as a 'bad' citizen (Cloud 2009).

These emailers, as I foreground, are Irwin fans and Greer anti-fans. Accordingly, this chapter considers both the kind of 'Greer' and the kind of 'Irwin' being discursively constructed in these emails and how the mutually constitutive discourses of misogyny and nationalism were deployed in these attempts to marginalise and silence Greer and to mourn and celebrate Irwin.

The expatriate Greer and Australia

Although the archive reveals that Greer has been formally designated an Australian National Living Treasure,[2] allocated a plaque on the Circular Quay Writer's Walk in Sydney, and featured on an Australia Post commemorative stamp,[3] her relationship with the country of her birth has been fraught. She left Australia in 1964 to undertake further postgraduate studies at Newnham College, University of Cambridge, and until recently has spent the majority of her life in England. Greer is the only woman amongst a coterie of Australian expatriates (including Clive James and Barry Humphries) who created successful public lives in Britain, and her celebrity and its reception cannot be easily separated from her expatriot status. As Stephen Alomes (2000, p. 14) notes, 'The postwar experience of expatriation to London is a chapter in Australia's cultural history. It tells the story of the tensions and the difficulties of creators, performers and writers who felt intense ambivalence about Australia and about Britain' (see also Britain 1997). It appears, too, that this ambivalence went both ways, something that Greer overtly reflects upon in a letter regarding the promotion activities surrounding her biography of her father, *Daddy, We Hardly Knew You* (1989).

Greer writes that marketing the book in Australia will be a waste of time, energy, and money: 'The case of Germaine Greer, unrepentant expatriate, v Australia has a long and bitter history, of which the people who want to arrange this tour know nothing' (28 December 1988, Stump Cross, 2014.0052.00013). Along these lines, during Greer's 1972 Australian book tour to promote *The Female Eunuch*, she received a much more hostile response than she had in the US the previous year (Lilburn et al. 2000; Sheehan 2016; O'Neill 2019). In addition to scathing book reviews (Thelma Forshaw's 'Yen for feminist grizzle' [1972] and Joan Lowson's 'The Female Unique' [1972] are the most noteworthy), some Australian media outlets were less than welcoming. For example, the *Sunday Telegraph* had purchased the rights to serialise *The Female Eunuch*, but the paper's owner, Sir Frank Packer, 'was outraged by the book's sexual content' and the serialised book was therefore pulled (Wallace 1997, p. 256).

Relatedly, as mentioned in the previous chapter, the ABC, owing to her apparent media 'overexposure', refused to air the Sydney abortion debate. As Greer tells a Victorian woman, while in Australia she was 'under a virtual press ban' and 'couldn't really do any more useful work' (to M.L., undated, 2014.0042.00511). In Greer's press conference when she left Australia, the

156 Germaine Greer, Celebrity Feminism and the Archive

typed notes of which appear in the archive, she complained about the treatment she received from the Australian press: 'You could say I'm leaving for my health. One more day of Australian newspapers and I'll have a plastic bag instead of a colon' (1972). Following her harsh treatment by the Australian press, many concerned citizens wrote to check in on Greer and to reassure her that she had made a difference to their lives.[4] In an archived article from the *Sunday Telegraph*, John Radovan (1989) reports that Greer offered to work for the Australian Labor Party after Prime Minister Gough Whitlam's infamous sacking but was told to '"kindly desist and not make any statements on their behalf. That's my relationship with Australia. I may love them, but they don't love me."'[5] While this longer history of Australian disdain for Greer could be seen as a manifestation of the 'tall poppy syndrome', as I discuss shortly, the challenge posed by the feminist subjectivity she has so publicly and unapologetically inhabited for decades clearly informs these kinds of responses.

The 'back story' of online misogyny

The key themes of the emails, all sent within a day or two of the publication of Greer's *Guardian* article, are that her comments were the result of publicity hunger; she is not an 'Australian' and has no right to speak on, or even to return to, her homeland; she should have died instead of Irwin, and, relatedly, she deserves some form of physical and/or sexual punishment for her transgressions; and she fails to embody femininity and sexuality in the 'correct' ways (Butler 1990). All of these criticisms are, of course, deeply gendered. Unfortunately, it is not unique for feminists to be subjected to the kind of attacks directed at Greer in the hundreds of emails she received in the days after her controversial piece was published. Indeed, such speech has proliferated and intensified as a result of digital media, and misogynistic vitriol is part and parcel of any feminist intervention online. Although these texts were not expressly written for public consumption, the tone of this correspondence undoubtedly mirrors the kinds of online misogyny mapped by Emma Jane (2014, 2016).

While new media may have amplified this kind of misogyny, it did not create it, requiring us to place such hate speech in the wider historical context of public woman-hating (Dworkin 1974; Richardson-Self 2021). As Jane argues, intensely misogynistic discourses proliferate in the new media environment, and for women – who experience this vitriol far more than men – such insults are overwhelmingly of a sexual nature: 'If you're not being called ugly, fat, and slutty on the Internet, odds are you're a man' (2016, p. 12). As she continues, 'misogyny online has become so pervasive and has received so much media coverage that it can be difficult to remember a time when the

'Steve is twice the Aussie icon you will ever be' **157**

Internet didn't seem to be made out of rape threats' (Jane 2016, p. 17). However, as Jane puts it, 'this discourse did not suddenly appear in recent years, but has a back story pre-dating social media' (2016, p. 17) – some examples of which we saw in response to Greer's *Playboy* article.

This 'back story' is particularly important as these emails to Greer predate the widespread take-up of social media platforms yet clearly exist on a continuum with these later forms of technologically mediated hate speech. Such 'gendertrolling', as Karla Mantilla argues, needs to be seen as the most recent manifestation of 'long-standing patterns of misogyny', which attempts to 'inhibit and shame women from fully participating in public spheres' (2015, p. 132). In this sense, the emails received by Greer are part of this important 'back story' of misogyny, and thereby they must be considered in the broader historical context of vocal women in the public sphere being disciplined via deeply misogynistic discourses (Kay 2020). I want to emphasise, though, that in Australia this 'back story' is inextricably linked to mythologies around nationhood that are, as I will discuss, predicated upon the exclusion of women as citizens (Holland and Wright 2017).

As a feminist strategy, this chapter follows Jane's (2014) call for the exposure of explicit material directed towards women, which 'must be spoken in its unexpurgated entirety' (p. 81). Readers should therefore be aware that the material analysed over the course of this chapter is violently misogynistic and disturbing. For Jane, rendering visible such objectionable material is an important political gesture for feminists, and it is in this spirit that I cite and critically engage with these emails here. Through including these texts in the archive, Greer makes such noxious material available for public analysis and scrutiny, thereby deploying the kinds of tactics that Jane advocates regarding the public exposure of gendered hate speech directed towards publicly outspoken women – and especially towards feminists. While not written in response to an article dealing with an overtly feminist issue, authors of these deeply unpleasant missives, like others discussed in this book, seek to discipline her not just for her apparent disrespect of Irwin but for her years of promulgating feminist positions in the media.

The celebrity conservationist and the celebrity feminist

While my focus here is on the emails following the publication of Greer's Irwin article, it is important to place this discussion both in the context of celebrity culture more broadly and in a consideration of Irwin's and Greer's respective statuses as celebrity environmentalist and celebrity feminist. Both figures represent a form of overtly political celebrity. Although he had appeared on various local television programmes since the early 1990s, Steve Irwin first came to international public attention through his long-running

158 Germaine Greer, Celebrity Feminism and the Archive

wildlife documentary series, *Crocodile Hunter* (1996–2007), a persona with which he was to become conflated. He was frequently positioned as 'the larrikin celebrity environmentalist' (Northfield and Macmahon 2010, p. 415), but debate about his efficacy – in terms of any conservation efforts – has been pronounced. Nonetheless, his public persona traded on a number of key tropes around Australian masculinity that appeared to publicly resonate. As Margaret Gibson (2007, p. 2) remarks:

> Steve Irwin embodied a mythology of Australian working-class masculinity; the image of the true blue (patriotic) Australian who presents himself honestly, without deception or dissimulation. He tapped into a part of the Australian psyche, which reveres the 'down-to-earth' straightforward, straight-talking bloke. People did assume that the public persona that was Steve Irwin was pretty much the same as the private person of Steve Irwin and, because of this, many people really did believe that they lost someone known to them.

This conflation – of the 'Crocodile Hunter' persona and Irwin himself – is important for understanding the affective response to his death. In these emails and in posthumous media coverage, Irwin, like many television personalities, is overwhelmingly seen to just 'be himself' (Bennett 2010); thus, the labour of persona building and self-branding is obscured, and an 'authentic', genuine self is presumed to be discernible. Moreover, it is on these grounds that we see the email authors referring to Irwin as someone they knew and needed to staunchly defend.

Following his death, Irwin was seen to embody traits that all Australians purportedly venerate. In this regard, on Irwin's death the hyper-masculine Australian actor Russell Crowe (Redmond 2021) reportedly remarked that '"he was the Australian we all aspire to be"' (Rayner 2007, p. 115). If this was the case, then Greer was comparatively framed, including by women, as the Australian we most definitely did *not* wish to be. Such was the intensity of public support for Irwin that the National Portrait Gallery in Canberra even replaced a portrait of Greer with one of Irwin and a circus elephant in response (Buchanan 2018, p. 26), a move which – as Greer (2007) reflected in the *Guardian* – 'pumped new life into the carcass of this forlorn controversy'. As evidence of his resonance with audiences, 'Steve Irwin was almost perceived as a martyr following his death in 2006, a status never witnessed in wildlife circles' (Northfield and MacMahon 2010, p. 415; see also Brockington 2008; Carman 2010). While affective investment in Irwin as a celebrity is important to these responses, of as much – if not more – importance is Greer's status as a renowned Australian feminist.

Greer can always be relied upon for a controversial headline; as I have flagged, she has made offensive comments about trans women and, even more

'Steve is twice the Aussie icon you will ever be' **159**

recently, about the #MeToo movement and the viability of penalties for rape. It is with this in mind, presumably, that the *Guardian* approached Greer, and paid her GBP£1000 (T.L., 4 September 2006), to write an opinion piece following Irwin's death in September 2006. Although the *Guardian* did not launch in Australia until 2013, readers could have accessed the UK version online. For other readers, the *Sydney Morning Herald* reprinted the piece, albeit in a condensed form (Greer 2006b). This piece, like many across Greer's career, was subjected to unsolicited and unwelcome editorial intervention. A woman from the agency representing Greer writes to the *Herald* (20 September 2006): 'We are very concerned that Germaine's article on Steve Irwin was edited without her consent…we need an explanation as to why changes were made without consent' (though the edits are unclear). After the editor replies that he presumed everything had been approved, Greer writes back to her representative:

> I think what this means is that all future requests from *Sydney Morning Herald* for syndication rights will be refused. We cannot do business with editors and publishers who treat contractual agreements in so cavalier a fashion. Incompetence is no excuse. We certainly don't need to be put to so much hassle for such a trifling amount of money.
>
> (22 September 2006, 2014.0046.01067)

The archival inclusion of such material, which makes clear Greer's frustrations at having her work interfered with, provides crucial insights into the difficulties of maintaining an 'authentic' voice as a freelance journalist, as well as the additional professional burden to either contest or rewrite material following these unwelcome editorial interventions. As briefly canvassed in Chapter 4, Greer's push-back, too, also reveals a degree of privilege; she can afford to take on the editors of large, international publications as her celebrity (or, perhaps more aptly, notoriety) ensures that there will always be other opportunities. The suggestion elsewhere in the archive that she would demand 'kill fees' for any withdrawn piece (Buchanan 2018; Weber and Buchanan 2019) also implies that, unlike other precarious workers lacking her high degree of attention capital, she often has little to lose financially in withdrawing the product of her labour. It was the overall tone of the original piece, however, not these seemingly unapproved edits that rendered it so objectionable to many Australian readers.

'The animal world has finally taken its revenge': Greer on Irwin

Before moving on to the hostile reception it received, we need to briefly engage with Greer's article and its key arguments. In contrast to predominant ways of figuring Irwin, Greer sought to reposition him from celebrity conservationist to a kind of environmental vandal, mining – and mishandling – the

160 Germaine Greer, Celebrity Feminism and the Archive

natural world for commercial ends. Irwin, Greer argues, physically intervened in various habitats in a highly disruptive fashion and thereby could not, and should not, be celebrated as an environmental advocate:

> What Irwin never seemed to understand was that animals need space. The one lesson any conservationist must labour to drive home is that habitat loss is the principal cause of species loss. There was no habitat, no matter how fragile or finely balanced, that Irwin hesitated to barge into, trumpeting his wonder and amazement to the skies. There was not an animal he was not prepared to manhandle. Every creature he brandished at the camera was in distress. Every snake badgered by Irwin was at a huge disadvantage, with only a single possible reaction to its terrifying situation, which was to strike.
>
> (Greer 2006a)

For Greer, Irwin's death was seen as an inevitable consequence of his mistreatment of the animals he opportunistically captured on film, and in this respect her article went 'completely against the prevailing discourse in Australia at the time' (Hanusch 2009, p. 33). Greer's comments themselves also have a troublesome air of elitism, as she comes to position herself above the 'popular' figure in whom audiences were seen to wrongly affectively invest (a position, of course, which fails to acknowledge her own celebrity). Greer's assumption, too, that she is the 'real' defender of the environment in opposition to the caricatured television environmentalist, further works to set up her defence of the environment as more 'real' or authentic than Irwin's. Greer (2006a) concludes the article with what came to be seen as its most controversial, and offensive, statement: 'The animal world has finally taken its revenge on Irwin'. Unsurprisingly, Greer's implication here that Irwin was being rightly punished was seized upon by those who celebrated his work and, more significantly here, his persona.

Media responses to Greer's article worked to buttress the pro-Irwin memorialising discourses that had characterised the coverage of his death, and 'the media had to deal with the interjection in the mythologising process and it needed to silence this alternative perspective' (Hanusch 2009, p. 33). Central to this process was the discursive construction of Greer as an out-of-touch elite who 'represented everything that Steve Irwin and other "ordinary Australians" stood against' (Hanusch 2009, p. 34). This treatment is indicative of a gendered manifestation of 'tall poppy' syndrome, wherein successful Australians are effectively punished for their success, especially when they are seen to have deserted their country of origin. As John Montgomery remarks in an article identifying its most famous expats (Humphries, James, and Greer) via this trope, 'Australia has never come to terms with the "cultural cringe" and loves to bring elitists, artists and intellectuals down' (2008, p. 34). Moreover, the elevation that is part and parcel of celebrification itself undermines the long-held, egalitarian mythologies which presume that all citizens are on the same level (Taylor and McIntyre 2021). As I argue, Greer is seen to need disciplining because of her very embodied challenge to the ideal Australian citizen.

Although, as mentioned, parts of the article were republished in the *Sydney Morning Herald*, many Australian readers – and certainly those considered here – accessed Greer's comments only through tabloid newspapers. In fact, it was Sydney's uber-conservative *Daily Telegraph* that was responsible for the influx of hate email since – in an article entitled 'Germaine, try this muzzle on for size: Grieving nation urges Greer to shut up' (McIlveen 2006, p. 5) – it published the contact details of Greer's agent on its front page and urged readers to 'give Greer a gobful' and 'tell the vicious old cow what you think of her'. In this respect, the *Daily Telegraph* acted to 'dox' Greer, a term that signals the way private details, such as physical addresses, are released to invite the transfer of victimisation from the virtual to the 'meat' world (Jane 2016). An email from Greer's agents (Gillon Aitken, 12 September 2006) notes:

> We are still receiving awful emails from Australia. I posted a batch of 200 or so to you yesterday. We've kept everything, but do please let me know if you want me to stop forwarding them. They don't make for pleasant reading.
>
> (2014.0046.01067)

While it is commonly thought that the anonymity of digital forms of communication enables hate speech and emboldens correspondents in their vitriol, these emails are in most instances signed.

Given that the hundreds of responses were sent within a day or two of the newspaper's call to arms and the publication of Greer's agent's email address, and given that they reinscribe the paper's discursive construction of Greer, we can presume that those who penned these deeply troublesome epistles were indeed *Daily Telegraph* readers. However, it was not only tabloid newspapers who reacted hostilely to Greer. *The Age*, a Victorian broadsheet, cited a number of prominent Australian political figures, including soon-to-be Labor Prime Minister Kevin Rudd, who – in language remarkably similar those of the hate email authors – told reporters that Greer should '"stick a sock in it"' ('Greer draws anger over Irwin comments', 2006). In the next section, I consider the persistent Australian national mythologies that informed these emails. (For the sake of accuracy, original spelling and punctuation have been retained in all the forthcoming email quotations.)

162 Germaine Greer, Celebrity Feminism and the Archive

The 'un-Australian' Greer as 'bad citizen'

Within this correspondence, Greer was overwhelmingly coded as someone with no right to speak on this issue – and especially no right to speak 'as an Australian'. A number of historians and cultural critics have sought to lay bare the politics undergirding dominant myths about Australian-ness, or what Graeme Turner dubs its 'national fictions' (1993; see also White 1981), including their exclusion of women (Summers 1975). As Kay Schaffer (1989) notes, 'When critics and commentators set out to define Australian culture and construct a national mythology which would mark the country's distinctive difference from England, they scarcely registered the presence of women' (p. 28). She continues that although 'there have always been feminist challenges to the masculine myth of Australian culture' (Schaffer 1989, p. 31), their success has been by no means guaranteed. Later studies, including Catriona Elder's (2007) *Being Australian*, have attended to the complex ways in which such narratives continue to circulate, to the active exclusion of alternative histories and modes of being – which is especially problematic in a country founded on the dispossession of its Indigenous people. In relation specifically to gender, Jack Holland and Katherine Wright (2017, p. 594) have shown how these enduring white national fictions – predicated upon masculinist concepts and tropes such as mateship, the bushman, the Aussie 'battler', and the Anzac 'digger' – worked in the public 'disciplining' of Julia Gillard, Australia's first woman Prime Minister: 'The difficulty of being a woman leader is particularly acute in Australia, due to the interweaving of gender expectations with foundational and exclusionary national identity narratives'. Though made of women politicians, these comments are also relevant to the reaction against Greer mapped here.

While many emails characterised Greer's comments as 'totally unAustralian' (C.H., 8 September), none specifies what an 'Australian' actually is, implying this is something we all just *know*, a self-evident truth which Greer seeks to wrongly contest. Furthermore, there is a shared assumption being invoked that the public criticism of a 'good Aussie bloke' represents an act of cultural treachery. For example, 'all REAL AUSTRALIANS have a love and respect for him [Irwin] that she could never understand' (G.W., 11 September) and 'You're a disgrace and you're sure as hell not an Australian' (H.R., 8 September). Elder notes that the 'term un-Australian has become a way of trying to define what are seen as the limits of unacceptable behaviour in the Australian nation' (2007, p. 2). She continues, 'the term is often used as both an insult and a disciplining expression' (Elder 2007, p. 3). Along these lines, the disavowal of Greer's very 'Australian-ness' marks almost all of these vitriolic responses, and they position themselves as arbiters of authentic national identity; as one tells her, 'we disown you' (T., 8 September).

However, in the case of these missives against Greer, it is not simply that she is discursively constituted 'un-Australian' but that she is 'unwomanly'. The frame of 'traitor to the nation' has been explored by D.L. Cloud in her analysis of hate mail that she personally received as a vocal critic of American responses to terrorism. Given that Greer, like Cloud herself, is a woman who is problematising dominant nationalist mythologies, the email writers position her as 'doubly traitorous' (Cloud 2009, p. 471). These texts make clear 'that to be a woman critical of the nation is to be both a bad woman and a bad citizen' (Cloud 2009, p. 466). Greer's compounded transgressions are seen as grounds for her to be silenced. As one woman writes, 'she has only proven to be a thorn in Australia's side as well as an embarrassment to the women from our nation' (C.M., 8 September). Described as a 'pathetic excuse for a woman' (N.W., 8 September), Greer – given her refusal to dutifully support, or indeed venerate, Irwin as an exemplary Australian – is seen to be deviant in terms of both national identity and gendered identity.

Like the above example, a number of the emails calling Greer's femininity into question are from those with names coded feminine, suggesting that misogyny is not only the province of men. For example, one remarks, 'What have you done in your life????????? Just a pathetic rebel woman without a cause. You are an imbarrassment to the rest of us women' (S.K., 6 September). Another woman similarly invokes the term 'embrassment' to describe Greer, adding that it is not just failed womanhood she embodies but failed Australianness: 'You are an embarrassment to all women and especially the great country of Australia' (M.C., 6 September). In this respect, as Cloud has observed, 'the authors of [Greer's] hate mail stand as righteous representatives of the "people" and the arbiters of acceptable masculine and feminine roles and behaviour' (2009, p. 473). These women position themselves as able to speak on behalf of all Australian women in a way that Greer, they believe, simply cannot. For one writer, Greer's relegation to a traditionally feminised domestic space will ensure her silence: 'I suggest you go back to the kitchen where you belong and keep your Un-Australian, incompassionate feelings and thoughts to your twisted mind' (L.B., 8 September). As Kay presciently argues,

> When women's voices are heard within the public sphere, they are symbolically registered as being *out of place* – as irredeemably tainted by an association with the domestic, which also serves as a misogynistic reminder that the domestic is where they belong.
>
> (2020, p. 102, original emphasis)

These emailers seek to restore the contested gendered division of public/private spheres by demanding Greer's relegation to the latter.

Patrolling literal and symbolic Australian borders

In addition to her apparent gendered transgressions, Greer's ability to speak with any authority on Australia is seen to have been compromised by her

164 Germaine Greer, Celebrity Feminism and the Archive

expatriate status. While in the letters to *Harper's* editors we saw US-based correspondents challenge Greer's ability to speak because she was not American, here Greer's migration to the UK is seen as a betrayal of her place of birth. In this respect, in the Irwin emails much was made of Greer's apparent 'outsider' status, which became central to these calls for her silence, once again invoking judgements about 'real' Australians who do not abandon their country of origin. In this vein, the *Herald Sun* (2005) suggested, '"Greer's self-appointed role as a feminist warrior has long withered and she has become shrill and sour, criticising targets in the homeland she turned her back on"' (as cited in Hanusch 2009, p. 35). For emailers too, Greer's lack of geographical proximity as a long-time resident of the UK is seen to disqualify her from speaking about matters Australian: 'You abandon your right to comment on Aussie's when you abandon our shores for the UK' (R.B., 10 September). Similarly, another irate email – using the derogatory Australian slang term for a sexually active woman, 'mole' (an insult deployed throughout these texts) – reads, in upper case for emphasis: 'DONT EVEN GIVE OPINIONS ON AUSTRALIANS IF YOU DON'T EVEN LIVE HERE YOU OLD MOLE' (G.R., 8 September). For the majority of these writers, Greer's comments about Irwin work to further prevent her from claiming any affiliation with her birthplace. In these emails, a particular story of what constitutes Australian-ness is clearly being told, and the authors of this hate mail position themselves, as well as Irwin himself, as ideal citizens against Greer as transgressor of such ideals.

The recalcitrance of the exclusionary nationalistic mythologies discussed earlier is evidenced by these emails and the wider hostile discursive environment from which they emerged. The writers' hatred is directed towards Greer as an embodied threat to their collective identity/way of life, and itself cements these bonds: '*Together we hate, and this hate is what binds us together*' (Ahmed 2004, p. 118, original emphasis). The defensiveness that underpins such hatred is not merely for Irwin but for what he represents: a white, patriarchal, conservative, exclusionary Australia for which they nostalgically long. As Andrea Whaling (2019, p. 27) observes, despite Australia's diverse population, 'the White, iconic ideal has continued to be representative both of Australian men and what it essentially means to be "Australian"'. Though written nearly a decade after Australia's populist politician Pauline Hanson (of the anti-immigration, xenophobic 'One Nation' party) emerged as a divisive public figure (Henderson and Taylor 2020), their rhetoric of an authentic 'Australian-ness', which is maligned, disrespected, and under threat clearly aligns with Hanson's. (More recently, of course, such nationalist populism has found voice in figures such as Donald Trump in the US.)

Moreover, these writers police not just symbolic borders but actual borders, with the overwhelming majority expressing a desire to prevent Greer from returning to Australia. As Ahmed observes, 'Hatred is a negative attachment to an other one wishes to expel, an attachment that is sustained through

'Steve is twice the Aussie icon you will ever be' **165**

expulsion of the other from bodily and social proximity' (2004, p. 55). The following comments, among many more, are indicative of this sentiment: 'The best thing you ever did for Australia is leave' (M.A., 8 September), 'your kind isn't welcome here anymore' (L. and M.C., 8 September), and 'Germaine don't bother coming back to Oz, no one wants you here' (D. and A., 8 September). What is also important here is the political and discursive context in which such texts were written; the conservative Howard Government (1996–2007) throughout its tenure sought to introduce extreme border protection measures, turning back refugees seeking to access Australia by boat (Devetak 2004). That is, such rhetoric of protectionism and border policing – commonly linked to paternalism and misogyny – was widely circulating when these emails were written.

Defending a 'top Aussie bloke'

While themselves failing to actually address the substance of Greer's comments and why they may be misplaced, these emails reveal ongoing, deeply held assumptions about Australian masculinity (and, relatedly, femininity as its devalued Other). As previously mentioned, much has been written on how the Australian national imaginary has relied upon a series of tropes and narratives about masculinity that continue to endure. Summarising Russell Ward's (1958) 'Australian legend' in his article on Irwin, Hanusch (2009, p. 31) remarks that he is 'the bushman who is down to earth and close to nature, willing to try out anything, non-religious, egalitarian and anti-elitist, independent and against authority (a "larrikin") and who proves himself a good mate'. Hanusch further notes that 'while most Australians would not subscribe to Ward's description of the typical Australian, a number of those aspects still circulate in public discourse today' (2009, p. 31). In particular, so deeply intertwined is Irwin with these ideas about 'larrikinism' that Australian cultural historian Melissa Bellanta begins her book-length study of how the meanings of this term have shifted over time with an anecdote about the Crocodile Hunter's death: 'Among the deluge of sorrowful comments and obituaries one phrase was repeated continually. Irwin, it was said, was "a true blue Australian larrikin"' (2012, p. xi).

As in media coverage, the ideal citizen that emerges from these emails is a 'natural', down-to-earth Aussie bloke, whom these authors presume to know personally, representing a failure to concede that Irwin's public persona – that of the 'Crocodile Hunter' – is in itself a performance (Bennett 2010). Significantly, it is not his environmentalism, such as it is, that they celebrate but his Australian-ness which shores up a type of admirable masculinity that (feminist) figures like Greer threaten. Indeed, his apparent conservation efforts are rarely even mentioned by these correspondents; it is instead his embodiment of ostensibly quintessential Australian traits, as

166 Germaine Greer, Celebrity Feminism and the Archive

well as the ways in which he has represented Australia on the international stage, that drives them to defend him. For example, one writer (D., 8 September) tells Greer, 'Steve's done so much more for promoting us in the international community than you could ever hope to achieve, so stick it, bitch'. This kind of nationalistic misogyny becomes the default response of these emailers.

Celebrating Irwin as a 'top Aussie bloke', this email elucidates the sexualised nature of the symbolic violence characterising the majority of these responses:

> fuck u you skanky slut u r a fuckin mole steve irwin is a top bloke I back him all the way u r a stuck up old tart who should stick your head up ya twat and wake up to ya self or no better still go and curl up in a ball and rot in hell for all i care once again fuck u!!! steve is a legend!!
>
> (T.B., 11 September)

Here, the word 'stuck up' further invokes this struggle as one between 'everyday' Australians and elites like Greer. She is dismissed as publicity hungry, a criticism which many commentators have levelled at the ageing feminist (as we saw in Chapter 3) and which itself reveals familiar anxieties about women who seek fame (York forthcoming). For example, she is dubbed 'an evil, washed up, media hungry jealous piece of trash' (S.M., 7 September) and 'a bitter, twisted publicity whore' (D.G., 8 September). In contrast, Irwin's global 'Crocodile Hunter' fame is seen to be warranted. As one emailer remarks, and as featured in the title of this chapter, 'Steve is twice the aussie icon you will ever be' (L. and M.C., 8 September).

Across the emails, Greer, as someone characterised as the antithesis of the Australian 'working class man' – a woman and an intellectual – comes to embody a threat to these dominant ways of making sense of the Australian nation. As Elder emphasises, 'stories of being Australian are always made *in relation to* other ways of being that are marked as similar or different' (2007, p. 10, original emphasis). Through her comments on Irwin, Greer appears to hit a nerve, provoking anxieties around where the lines of 'Australian-ness' are being drawn. These email writers, therefore, call for the silencing of this aberrant citizen: 'Keep your ugly, devil mouth shut! Piss off, dog!' (M.C., 8 September). Such speech, according to Cloud, 'establishes its target as monstrous, rendering the letter author as a human pitted against an inhuman enemy, thus warranting violence against the monstrous' (2009, p. 469). For example, one asserts, 'fucken dog hope you get what you deserve a bashin' (M., 8 September), and another warns Greer, 'Polute this world with your fucked up garbage once more and ill shit down ya throat. No bullshit,

I would fucking enjoy it' (J.G., 8 September). As one viciously writes, speaking on behalf not just of Australians but of global citizens:

> Look, your just a used up old slut. I hate you, my friends hate you, Australia hates you and the world hates you. Hurry up and walk in front of traffic so I will never have to look at your disgusting old face again... well apart from your headstone which I would gladly piss on. Get fucked.
>
> (B.L., 8 September)

Such epistolary texts slip from symbolic violence to threats of literal violence and a desire for the ultimate form of silencing: death. Most stop short of actually threatening to kill Greer, but nevertheless express an eagerness for her death: 'I hope you get hit by a bus you turd' (A., 8 September) and 'Bugger off and die you pathetic bitch' (T.C., 8 September).

Irwin's seemingly earnt, enduring iconicity and 'legendary' status are seen as grounds for the intense public mourning following his passing, something emailers bitterly suggest will elude Greer. For these writers, Greer's life, unlike Irwin's, is seen as unworthy of mourning; she is constituted as an ungrievable subject (Butler 2009): 'I can assure you, when you die, nobody will mourn you' (M.C., 6 September) and 'When you die I will not grieve, I will not miss you and Australia will certainly be a better place without your dribble' (T.R., 8 September). Another suggests: 'STEVE WILL LIVE ON & WE MOURN HIM AND WILL PROTECT HIS FAMILY – MS GREER WILL PASS ONE DAY – [we can't bloody wait]' (J.P., 7 September). For many, given this unmournability and the affront she has made to the country, several argue that Greer should have died instead of a 'decent' Aussie bloke like Irwin. Many gleefully suggest that compared with the national mourning precipitated by Irwin's death, Greer's passing will be the source of great celebration for Australians:

> This bitter man hating old woman is so sexist that she can not even acknowledge a man who has obviously been a great benefit to the animal KINGdom. When Greer dies, it should have on its tombstone 'The wicked witch is dead' and there will be much rejoicing.
>
> (K.B., 8 September)

As the ultimate symbol of a powerful woman whose speech must be curtailed (Kay 2020), the trope of the witch surfaced in another email that, like others, welcomed the prospect of Greer's death: 'That mole is an oxygen theif. if I saw her crossing the road i would not brake, i can't wait to see if she dares to show her witch of a head down under again' (R.D., 8 September).

Not much later in the same decade, of course, Australia's first female Prime Minister, Julia Gillard, would be subject to some of the most intense vitriol

168 Germaine Greer, Celebrity Feminism and the Archive

and misogyny ever seen in Australian public discourse, and the language was remarkably similar to that used to (attempt to) discipline Greer. For example, at an anti-carbon tax rally in 2010, protesters held placards using terms like 'bitch', while one read, 'Ditch the witch'. In the same year, infamous Sydney radio shockjock Alan Jones suggested that the then Prime Minister should be '"thrown into a chaff bag"' and taken '"far out to the sea"' (Summers 2013, p. 141). As these comments exemplify, public Australian women like Greer and Gillard have been subject to an 'extraordinary torrent of hatred and hostility' (Summers 2013, p. 20). In a book of the same name, Summers classifies the 'misogyny factor' in Australia as 'an entrenched system of attitudes and practices that are designed to exclude women or to demean them if they do succeed in gaining entry' (2013, p. 21). Both Greer and Gillard have been subject to such disciplinary measures.

Summers also makes clear that the attacks on Gillard, like those on Greer, were not merely sexist but also sexual (2013, p. 115). For example, one email appeared with the subject heading: 'SUCK MY BALLS' (D.N., 8 September), while throughout Greer is referred to as 'bitch', 'whore', or 'slut': 'you're a fucking whore. i wish you'd got the fucking barb through you, you ugly old dirty hag' (D.H., 8 September). One particularly offensive example reveals the way in which sexualised violence is being mobilised in an attempt to discipline Greer; in upper case, it reads, 'THIS OLD FUCKING BITCH NEED TO TAKE A BIG FAT METAL STICK AND SHOVE IT UP HER FUCKING ARSE!' (M.A., 8 September). The authors of sexual threats and those more generally threatening to Greer's bodily integrity clearly wield 'violation as the ultimate correction to female insurrection' (Cloud 2009, p. 470). As Jane (2014, 2016) has shown, one of the central elements of 'e-bile' is the threat of often sexualised violence against women, something also evidenced by these emails.

Disciplining Greer: Anti-feminism, heteronormativity, and ageism

As part of this defence of Irwin/Australian national mythologies, and the anti-feminism that is at the heart of their anti-fandom, emailers recurrently deploy a number of familiar tropes about feminists. Greer is characterised as a 'hateful and a sad pathetic femmi-nazi' (Y.M., 11 September) and 'a man hateing woman...nothing but a ball breaking man hater' (unsigned, 7 September 2006). Her response to Irwin is not perceived to be a legitimate critique but the product of an irrational form of (feminist) hate: 'the pathologizing discourse foils [Greer] as irrational, not only to discredit [her] point of view but also to give shape to the writer's own identity as a rational citizen' (Cloud 2009, p. 469). Here, Greer's own affective response to Irwin's death is discounted, while their own is privileged as the rational, 'reasonable' reaction to the passing of a celebrated Australian. Of course, the trope of the feminist as a bitter,

'Steve is twice the Aussie icon you will ever be'   **169**

man-hating lesbian has long done significant political and cultural work in the attempt to publicly discipline feminists (Bulbeck 2005; Hesford 2013), and these emails appear to be no exception. As Barbara Tomlinson argues, 'This "trope of the angry feminist" is designed to delegitimize feminist argument even before the argument begins' (2010, pp. 101–102). The persistent invocation of such a trope, or what Ahmed (2010) dubs the 'feminist killjoy', works to foreclose any possibility of debate or dialogue and functions to normalise anti-feminist sentiment: 'Its incessant repetition constitutes part of a cultural training program that makes anti-feminism and misogyny a routine element in everyday speech and written argument' (Tomlinson 2010, p. 102).

Describing Greer as a 'vile leso' and using the same language as the *Daily Telegraph*, one email reads: 'Such a disgraceful bitter and twisted old woman is an embarrassment to the entire universe and should be muzzled' (P.W., 8 September). These calls for Greer's 'muzzling' work in tandem with those hoping for her death; that is, both rely upon the assumption that Greer simply needs to shut up. The following quotation – not insignificantly from a woman – is indicative in this regard: 'You are nothing but a vicious, cruel, heartless and extremely stupid bitch. How about doing us all a favour by PUTTING A SOCK IN YOUR DRIBBLING MOUTH AND A BAG OVER YOUR HEAD' (T.R., 8 September). In these missives, Greer's very manlessness (she has no male partner) is seen as a central part of her pathology, and her 'abnormality' as a woman is perceived as the source of her attack on Irwin and Australian masculinity itself. Her misguided criticism of Irwin is thereby seen to emerge from her own failure to effectively perform normative femininity and heterosexuality, something the *McCall's* housewives discussed in the previous chapter also presumed.

The fact that Greer is neither a wife nor a mother renders her an especially threatening figure who must be muted. In a letter that is signed off, 'A true Aussie woman', one author remarks, 'I was around in your hey day even then you were known as a loud mouth bitch with no in site into a real loving relationship' (R.B., 10 September). As I have previously argued (Taylor 2012), single women, despite early-2000s claims of their newfound cultural affirmation, have continued to function as anxiety-provoking figures, subject to various forms of regulation and management. That Greer has failed – for it is very much positioned as a personal failure – to marry, or reproduce, is seen to make her even less representative. One explicitly dismisses Greer on these grounds as 'bitter – old – pathetic – *barren* – saggy' (J.P., 7 September, emphasis added). The majority of emailers idealise Irwin as a family man, celebrating his success in reproducing the patriarchal nuclear family, while Greer is denigrated as the aberrant childless, single woman. In 2007, prior to her tenure as PM, Julia Gillard was derogatorily referred to as 'deliberately barren' by a conservative Senator, while a 2009 newspaper profile featuring a photograph of an empty bowl on her dining table – read as a metaphor for

170 Germaine Greer, Celebrity Feminism and the Archive

her childlessness – reignited public attention to her purported reproductive 'failure' (Taylor 2015). Such coverage indicates the persistence of these anxieties about the childfree woman around this time (if not beyond).

While Greer is throughout referred to as a 'slut' or a 'whore', this assumption co-exists with the idea not that Greer is having too much sex – as these appellations suggest – but that she is not having enough, something that is framed as the cause of her bitter attack on Irwin and, by extension, hegemonic Australian masculinity. That is, as is common in vitriol directed towards feminists, the solution to Greer's 'bitterness' is seen to be a penis: 'Will you just get a dick in you and relax you scornful man wannabe...Shave your armpits!!!!' (D.I., 8 September). For others, it is Greer's 'failure' to be sexually desirable that is seen as the source of her unreasonable criticisms of men:

> You are a stupid fat leso bitch. No one is interested in your man hating, feminist dopey comments you poisonous bitch...Don't take it out on men, just because you are so ugly that no man wants to fuck you. Go and get fucked you fat leso.
>
> (S.W., 8 September)

Through the repeated use of the homophobic slur 'leso', these emails call into question Greer's heterosexuality. Moreover, in these epistolary attacks, it is clear that 'as in physical publics – the body is the locus of abuse' (Sobieraj 2017, p. 1701). It is also significant, and perhaps unsurprising, that ageism is central to these misogynistic attacks.

The question of celebrity, gender, and ageing has been the subject of much critical work, with commentators drawing attention to the regulatory gaze being directed towards older women celebrities (Whelehan and Gywnne 2014; Holmes and Jermyn 2015). Indeed, Greer herself critically interrogated the problematic discursive construction of ageing women in *The Change* (1991). As Greer argued, the woman who dares to age publicly is heaped with scorn and ridicule. Over time, Greer herself has become the object of the kind of ageist, misogynistic caricatures she has long exposed. These emails merely serve to buttress her already convincing argument about the prevalence of ageism and misogyny, including in Australia, and the fact that Greer is an ageing woman yet active in the public sphere clearly provokes much ire. Her age is persistently mobilised as a gendered insult; so deep is the fear of a woman ageing that it features in almost all of these disciplinary texts. One email, over a page long, merely repeats the words: 'YOU'RE AN OLD STOOPID SLUT' over and over, in capital letters (R.B., 8 September). She is variously referred to as a 'twisted old bitch' (K.M.c., 7 September), a 'HORRIBLE OLD COW' who should 'SHUT UP AND GET STUFFED' (R.W., 8 September), and a 'FAT OLD SAGGY LOUDMOUTHED SKANK' (W.T., 8 September). There is, these emailers suggest, nothing more objectionable than an ageing woman who dares to remain publicly visible and who has a voice that continues to publicly resonate.

Conclusion

The emails sent to Greer after her response to Irwin's death in 2006 suggest that those who call into question a particular Australian national imaginary are intensely anxiety-provoking figures. They reveal deeply held investments in nationalistic sentiments, along with entrenched sexist assumptions about masculinity and authority and public femininities and their (il)legitimacy. The concerted attempts to discipline Greer in these emails presume an ideal, and idealised, masculinity, which is valorised over a pathologised, aberrant femininity. In addition to his whiteness, cis-gender status, and heterosexuality, the ideal Australian, then, continues to be gendered masculine. These emails, too, pre-empt the form of misogynistic nationalism, populism, and anti-elitism we now see celebrity political figures such as former US President (and current Presidential nominee) Donald Trump embodying. Aggression towards Greer, like the public vitriol directed at Trump's 2016 opponent, Hillary Clinton, suggests that misogynistic and nationalistic discourses in Australia (as elsewhere) are co-constitutive. Greer, seen to embody a challenge to such mutually reinforcing frames, constitutes a threat that must be curtailed. Such attempts by these anti-fans to silence Greer, however, were by no means successful, and she continues to speak publicly on all manner of topics. Nevertheless, speaking publicly as a woman continues to have substantial risks, both materially and symbolically (Kay 2020). This analysis has also destabilised assumptions about the newness of the toxicity now commonly practiced online (Bacon 2022).

While the public disciplining of women is routine in the online environment, the feminist especially has always been – and continues to be – a figure against which such deeply offensive attacks are levelled. For example, Australian feminist journalist and author Clementine Ford experiences daily threats of rape and death via Facebook, Twitter/X, and email, which she routinely reposts on her own social media (Brady 2021). Moreover, prominent women who mount a challenge to dominant national mythologies mapped here also continue to be subject to disciplinary measures. For example, on Anzac Day (Australia's public holiday in remembrance of veterans) in 2017, Yassmin Abdel-Magied, a 26-year-old Muslim Australian journalist who then worked for Australia's public broadcaster (the ABC), wrote a Facebook post suggesting that all deaths resulting from war should be remembered. The backlash was fierce, and Abdel-Magied was seen to be attacking deeply held 'Australian values'; indicative of interlocking oppressions, sexism and racism worked together in this public castigation of a young Muslim woman who implicitly challenged the fictions upon which Australian nationhood, including the glorification of military action, is based

172 Germaine Greer, Celebrity Feminism and the Archive

(Kay 2020). While there are significant differences between Greer and Abdel-Magied, they are united in their refusal to endorse the key mythologies upon which Australian national identity continues to be predicated.

Finally, these digital epistolary texts reveal the success of Irwin's persona-building and branding, as the authors of this hate email presume no distinction between the 'Crocodile Hunter' and the person whose death they mourn. As Irwin fans, they mount a defence of this 'top bloke' and 'Australian legend', performing a type of parasocial connection even after death. Undoubtedly, such defences are about much more than one particular celebrity; they are part of the ongoing labour involved in sustaining gendered national fictions, ones that continue to position women at best on the periphery, at worst as having no authority to speak on, for, or even about the nation. In making the hundreds of Irwin emails publicly available, Greer gives researchers an opportunity to examine the ways in which the authority of celebrity feminists has been called into question, as well as the kinds of ideological, cultural, and disciplinary work that the twin discourses of nationalism and misogyny continue to do in twenty-first-century Australia. In the conclusion, I reflect upon the kind of 'Greers' we have come to know through audience letters, the ways in which archived material can help come to terms with how celebrity feminism has functioned socially and politically over time, and how we might use the Greer archive to further our understanding of this iconic feminist's work in the public sphere.

Notes

1 The university student who broke into Greer's Essex farmhouse and reportedly held her hostage was framed in media coverage as a 'teen stalker'. This incident provided the impetus for Joanna Murray-Smith's 2008 play, *The Female of the Species* (Taylor 2018).

2 In 1997, she was designated one of a hundred National Living Treasures by the Australian National Trust (2017.0028.00005), alongside Olympian Cathy Freeman, country singer Slim Dusty, poet Les Murray, former PM Paul Keating, Indigenous Judge Pat O'Shane, playwright David Williamson, former PM Gough Whitlam, actor Judy Davis, and writer Colleen McCullough, amongst others.

3 On 20 January 2011, a 60c stamp postage stamp featuring Greer was issued by Australia Post, under the 'Advancing Equality' series. The three other women in the series were Women's Electoral Lobby co-founder and activist Eva Cox, former Whitlam advisor Elizabeth Evatt, and journalist and author Anne Summers. The Australia Post material accompanying the stamps notes: 'The recipients of the 2011 award each rose to prominence during the 1970s, the period in which second-wave feminism flourished, challenging the status quo. The progressive thinking, passionate commitment and tireless work of our four recipients have confronted fundamental issues of gender inequality, allowing for profound changes to reshape the public and private experiences of all Australians. Many of the rights we enjoy and take for granted today have been achieved through advocacy, counsel and efforts' (2017.0028).

'Steve is twice the Aussie icon you will ever be' **173**

4 For example, a woman from Toorak, a suburb in Melbourne, wrote to reassure her, 'I wanted to write at once and tell you that I feel sure that you have made a big impact on a great many people here in Australia' (26 March 1972, 2014.0042.00508). A man (P.O., Victoria, 20 April 1971) told her: 'I feel saddened by the response you received in Australia and angered by the appalling press and television coverage that you endured'. Greer replied: 'Just a note to let you know how grateful I was for your letter of the 20th of April. In fact, when I left Australia, I found a great many loving and encouraging letters waiting for me when I got back to England' (8 June 1972, 2014.0042.00648).
5 This article was sent to Greer with a bunch of clippings by then Returned Services League President Bruce Ruxton, with whom Greer appeared to form an unlikely friendship.

References

Ahmed, S. (2004) *The Cultural Politics of Emotion*, Edinburgh: Edinburgh University Press.

Ahmed, S. (2010) *The Promise of Happiness*, Durham: Duke University Press.

Alomes, S. (2000) *When London Calls: The Expatriation of Australian Creative Artists to Britain*, Cambridge, UK: Cambridge University Press.

Bacon, S. ed. (2022) *Toxic Cultures*, Bern: Peter Lang.

Banet-Weiser, S. & Miltner, K.M. (2016) '#MasculinitySoFragile: Culture, Structure, and Networked Misogyny', *Feminist Media Studies*, vol. 16, no. 1: 171–174.

Beard, M. (2017) *Women and Power: A Manifesto*, London: Profile Books.

Bellanta, M. (2012) *Larrikins*, St Lucia: University of Queensland Press.

Bennett, J. (2010) *Television Personalities: Stardom and the Small Screen*, London: Routledge.

Brady, A. (2021) 'Clementine Ford, Online Misogyny, and the Labour of Celebrity Feminism', in A. Taylor and J. McIntyre (eds.), *Gender and Australian Celebrity Culture*, London: Routledge, pp. 91–108.

Britain, I. (1997) *Once an Australian: Journeys with Barrie Humphries Clive James, Germaine Greer and Robert Hughes*, Oxford: Oxford University Press.

Brockington, D. (2008) 'Celebrity Conservation: Interpreting the Irwins', *Media International Australia*, vol. 127: 96–108.

Buchanan, R. (2018) 'Foreign Correspondence: Journalism in the Germaine Greer Archive', *Archives and Manuscripts*, vol. 46, no. 1: 18–39.

Bulbeck, C. (2005) '"Women are exploited way too often": Feminist Rhetorics at the End of Equality', *Australian Feminist Studies*, vol. 20, no. 46: 65–66.

Butler, J. (1990) *Gender Trouble: Feminism and the Subversion of Identity*, New York: Routledge.

Butler, J. (2009) *Frames of War: When Is Life Grievable?*, London: Verso.

Carman, L. (2010) 'Sacrificing Steve: How I Killed the Crocodile Hunter', *Cultural Studies Review*, vol. 16, no. 2: 179–193.

Cloud, D.L. (2009) 'Foiling the Intellectuals: Gender, Identity Framing, and the Rhetoric of the Kill in Conservative Hate Mail', *Communication Culture and Critique*, vol. 2, no. 4: 457–479.

Crocodile Hunter (1996–2007), Animal Planet, Silver Spring, MA. Created by John Stainton and Steve Irwin.

Devetak, R. (2004) 'In Fear of Refugees: The Politics of Border Protection in Australia', *The International Journal of Human Rights*, vol. 8, no. 1: 101–109.

174 Germaine Greer, Celebrity Feminism and the Archive

Dworkin, A. (1974) *Woman-Hating*, New York: Dutton.

Elder, C. (2007) *Being Australian: Narratives of National Identity*, Sydney: Allen & Unwin.

Forshaw, T. (1972) 'Feminist yen for a grizzle and a bit of rough', *The Age*, 15 January, Germaine Greer Archive, Early Years, 2014.0044.00201, University of Melbourne.

Germaine Greer Archive. General Correspondence, 2014.0042.00760, University of Melbourne.

Germaine Greer Archive. Print Journalism, 2014.0046, University of Melbourne.

Germaine Greer Archive. Correspondence with Publishers, 2014.0052, University of Melbourne.

Germaine Greer Archive. Honoris Causa and Recognition, 2017.0028, University of Melbourne.

Gibson, M. (2007) 'Some Thoughts on Celebrity Deaths: Steve Irwin and The Issue of Public Mourning', *Mortality*, vol. 12, no. 1: 1–3.

Ging, D. and Siapera, E. eds. (2019) *Gender Hate Online: Understanding the New Anti-Feminism*, London: Palgrave Macmillan.

Glanville, L. (2018) 'The End of Reckoning – Archival Silences in the Germaine Greer Archive', *Archives and Manuscripts*, vol. 46, no. 1: 45–48.

'Greer draws anger over Irwin comments' (2006), *The Age*, 6 September, accessed via: https://www.theage.com.au/national/greer-draws-anger-over-irwin-comments-20060906-gdoc0r.html

Greer, G. (1972) 'Australian press conference notes', *Germaine Greer Archive, Print Journalism*, 2014.0044.00198, University of Melbourne.

Greer, G. (1989) *Daddy, We Hardly Knew You*, New York: Random House.

Greer, G. (1991) *The Change*, London: Hamish Hamilton.

Greer, G. (2006a) 'That sort of self-delusion is what it takes to be a real Aussie larrikin', *The Guardian*, 5 September, accessed via: https://www.theguardian.com/world/2006/sep/05/australia

Greer, G. (2006b) 'The animal world got its revenge', *The Sydney Morning Herald*, 6 September, accessed via: https://www.smh.com.au/national/the-animal-world-got-its-revenge-20060906-gdobwy.html

Greer, G. (2007) 'When your face doesn't fit', *The Guardian*, 20 February, accessed via: https://www.theguardian.com/commentisfree/2007/feb/20/australia.comment

Hanusch, F. (2009) '"The Australian we all aspire to be": Commemorative Journalism and the Death of the Crocodile Hunter', *Media International Australia*, vol. 130: 28–38.

Henderson, M. and Taylor, A. (2020) *Postfeminism in Context*, London: Routledge.

Hesford, V. (2013) *Feeling Women's Liberation*, Durham: Duke University Press.

Holland, J. and Wright, K. (2017) 'The Double Delegitimation of Julia Gillard: Gender, the Media and Australian Political Culture', *Australian Journal of Politics and History*, vol. 634: 588–602.

Holmes, S. and Jermyn, D. (eds) (2015) *Women Celebrity and Cultures of Ageing*, Basingstoke: Palgrave Macmillan.

Irwin hate mail (2005), Germaine Greer Archive, Print Journalism, 2014.0046.01067, University of Melbourne.

Jane, E. (2014) '"Your a ugly, whorish, slut": Understanding E-bile', *Feminist Media Studies*, vol. 14: 531–546.

Jane, E. (2016) *Misogyny Online: A Short (and Brutish) History*, London: Sage.

Kay, J.B. (2020) *Gender, Media and Voice: Communicative Injustice and Public Speech*, London: Palgrave Macmillan.

Lilburn, S., Magarey, S., and Sheridan, S. (2000) 'Celebrity Feminism as Synthesis: Germaine Greer, *The Female Eunuch* and the Australian Print Media', *Continuum*, vol. 14, no. 3: 335–348.

Lowson, J. (1972) 'The Female Unique', *The Australian*, 15 January, Germaine Greer Archive, Early Years, 2014.0044.00201, University of Melbourne.

Mantilla, K. (2015) *Gendertrolling: How Misogyny Went Viral*, Santa Barbara: Praeger.

McIlveen, L. (2006) 'Germaine, try this muzzle on for size – Grieving nation urges Greer to shut up', *The Daily Telegraph*, 8 September, p. 5.

Montgomery, J. (2008) 'The Strange Tale of the Lucky Country, the Cultural Cringe and the Flight of the Tall Poppies', *Art Monthly Australia*, no. 215: 32–35.

Northfield, J.K. and MacMahon, C.R. (2010) 'Crikey! Overstating the Conservation Influence of the Crocodile Hunter', *Science Communication*, vol. 32, no. 3: 412–417.

O'Neill, V. (2019) 'When Greer came home: January – March 1972', 5 June, accessed via: https://blogs.unimelb.edu.au/librarycollections/2019/06/05/when-greer-came-home-january-march-1972-save-us-from-shaggy-germ-o-man/

Radovan, J. (1989) 'Snubbed in Australia, Germaine complains', *The Sunday Telegraph*, 27 August, Germaine Greer Archive, General Correspondence, 2014.0042.00760, University of Melbourne.

Rayner, J. (2007) 'Live and Dangerous? The Screen Life of Steve Irwin', *Studies in Australasian Cinema*, vol. 1, no. 4: 107–117.

Redmond, S. (2021) 'The Manly Whiteness of Russell Crowe', in A. Taylor and J. McIntyre (eds.), *Gender and Australian Celebrity Culture*, London: Routledge, pp. 39–54.

Richardson-Self, L. (2021) *Hate Speech Against Women Online*, New York: Rowman & Littlefield.

Schaffer, K. (1989) *Women and The Bush: Forces of Desire in the Australian Cultural Tradition*, Cambridge: Cambridge University Press.

Sheehan, R.J. (2016) '"If we had more like her we would no longer be the unheard majority": Germaine Greer's Reception in the United States', *Australian Feminist Studies*, vol. 31, no. 87: 62–77.

Sobieraj, S. (2017), '"Bitch, slut, skank, cunt": Patterned Resistance to Women's Visibility in Digital Publics', *Information, Communication and Society*, vol. 21, no. 11: 1700–1714.

Smith, J. (2000) 'When heroine worship turns sour', *The Independent*, 30 April, accessed via: https://www.independent.co.uk/voices/commentators/joan-smith/when-heroine-worship-turns-sour-281142.html

Summers, A. (1975) *Damned Whores and God's Police*, Sydney: Allen & Unwin

Summers, A. (2013) *The Misogyny Factor*, Sydney: Allen & Unwin.

Taylor, A. (2012) *Single Women in Popular Culture: The Limits of Postfeminism*, Basingstoke: Palgrave Macmillan.

Taylor, A. (2015) 'Behind Every Great Woman: Celebrity, Political Leadership and the Privileging of Marriage', in S. Cobb and N. Ewen (eds.), *First Comes Love: Power Couples, Celebrity Kinship, and Cultural Politics*, London: Bloomsbury Academic, pp. 169–187.

Taylor, A. (2018) '*The Female of The Species*, Celebrity Feminism and Generationalism', unpublished paper presented at the *Crossroads in Cultural Studies conference*, 12–15 August, Shanghai University.

Taylor, A. and McIntyre, J. (2021) 'Introduction: Gendering Australian Celebrity', in A. Taylor and J. McIntyre (eds.), *Gender and Australian Celebrity Culture*, London: Routledge, pp. 1–20.

Tomlinson, B. (2010) 'Transforming the Terms of Reading: Ideologies of Argument and the "Trope of the Angry Feminist" in Contemporary US Political and Academic Discourse', *Journal of America Studies*, vol. 44, no. 1: 101–116.

Turner, G. (1993) *National Fictions: Literature, Film and the Construction of Australian Narrative*, Sydney: Allen & Unwin.

Wallace, C. (1997) *Germaine Greer: Untamed Shrew*, Melbourne: PanMacMillan.

Ward, R. (1958) *The Australian Legend*, Melbourne: Oxford University Press.

Weber, M. and Buchanan, R. (2019) 'Metadata as a Machine for Feeling in Germaine Greer's Archive', *Archives and Manuscripts*, vol. 47, no. 2: 230–241.

Whaling, A. (2019) *White Masculinity in Contemporary Australia: The Good Ol' Aussie Bloke*, London: Routledge.

Whelehan, I. and Gywnne, J. eds. (2014) *Ageing Popular Culture and Contemporary Feminism: Harleys and Hormones*, Basingstoke: Palgrave Macmillan.

White, R. (1981) *Inventing Australia: Images and Identity, 1688–1980*, Sydney: Allen & Unwin.

York, L. (forthcoming) 'Unseemly Affects: Gender, Celebrity, and the Policing of Fame Hunger', in J. McIntyre and A. Taylor. (eds.), *The Routledge Companion to Gender and Celebrity*, London: Routledge.

CONCLUSION

'Messages in a Bottle': Reframing Greer's Legacy

In her 1992 *Independent* article 'Strangers in the Mail', as mentioned in the Introduction, Greer laments her overflowing mailbox. Letters held in the archive, however, indicate that she routinely shows her appreciation to those who have taken the time to communicate how she has moved them. To a Norwich woman who wrote to say how stimulating and affirming she found *The Change* (1991), Greer affectionately replied: 'Thank you so much for writing! It does me a power of good to read a letter like yours. Writers never know whether their message in a bottle has reached land until we get one back! Love, Germaine Greer' (to A.B., 8 April 1992, 2014.0042.00055). The archived reader and viewer letters analysed here suggest that Greer's 'message' – or rather messages – certainly did 'reach land'. The process, however, was much more complicated than the linear communication model implied in Greer's comment; as I have demonstrated, this is not a reception history in any simple sense. Greer's audiences did not just passively imbibe her feminist 'message' from 'a bottle'; rather, they took it and incorporated it into their own 'mattering maps', making it mean in ways that connected to their lived experiences and needs (Grossberg 1992).

Greer, as I have emphasised throughout, has been far more than just an author of lightning rod polemics – though she was (and is) certainly that. Her celebrity feminism, across multiple media forms, allowed her to enter people's loungerooms, kitchens, dorms, and offices, sometimes in unexpected ways that they welcome, at other times uncomfortably problematising their worldviews and ways of being. Greer, like other celebrities, plays a crucial part in terms of whether or how audiences come to identify with feminist reimaginings of gender, and these letters tell us much about such identifications (or disidentifications). This book, the first to critically reflect upon this

DOI: 10.4324/9781315179841-8

often polarising figure, has shown that Greer has always elicited complex affective responses from audiences. Across her decades-long career, Greer has mediated audience understandings of and emotional responses to feminism in profound ways. That is, Greer and her work stimulate in audiences a range of emotions, some of which they have been able to articulate in epistolary form. While digital media might currently be where audiences share such responses, these written traces of how Greer and her feminism made readers and viewers think and *feel* are important historical sources in terms of the cultural, ideological, and affective work that celebrities do in the world.

Although there are multiple ways of responding to Greer and her feminism, there is no doubt that many 'ordinary' women (and indeed men) have been radically transformed after consuming Greer's books, after hearing her rehearse her feminist arguments on the small screen, or after reading her polemical journalistic writing. The different forms through which they come to access Greer and her feminism shape these affective processes in significant ways. For many, too, their intertextual knowledge of Greer-as-celebrity informs their responses, with some suggesting that while Greer did not appeal to them in one form she 'wins them over' through others – as with some of the *Cavett* viewers and indeed the *Playboy* readers. In this respect, we see the importance of this cross-media strategy in her efforts to reach as many viewers and readers as possible. Claims about the transformative nature of Greer's bestsellers and other forms of cultural production (and indeed Greer herself) are not hyperbole; it is in these very terms that many audiences describe their impacts. That said, as my analysis has made clear, there is not a singular Greer reader or viewer. Such is the complexity of the work she did and still does as a celebrity feminist and how she assists audiences in 'making sense of the world' (Turner et al. 2000, p. 15) – including in gendered terms.

The 'Greers' that emerge from these letters (i.e., how their writers represent her and her feminism) vary. For some, she is a brave trailblazer, who has given them the tools to imagine their lives *otherwise*; a life-changing role model (often described as their 'heroine'); and a skilled, 'authentic' television host who transforms their understandings of women's liberation. For more hostile correspondents, she is a misguided woman who regrettably and selfishly rejects normative gender roles. Motivations for writing to the controversial celebrity, then, vary: They write to tell her how much she means to them, expressing their love and heartfelt thanks for her eye-opening bestsellers. They write to tell her how she has helped in their very personal struggles, whether an unhappy marriage or medical treatments for menopause. They write to offer their support, fearing she is encountering undue criticisms. They write in fear of how her feminism threatens their identity and/or way of life. They write to silence and discipline her.

Some use their letters to contest Greer's authority to speak by positioning her as an outsider, whether literally (as an Australian expatriate) or symbolically.

Conclusion **179**

While this positioning may be why she can astutely comment on other countries, for many it renders her unqualified to speak beyond her own cultural context. We saw instances of this in both the *Harper's* letters, where writers questioned Greer's intervention into domestic US politics, and the Irwin emails, where writers saw Greer's 'desertion' of Australia as disqualifying her from intervening in local debates. Many use the epistolary form to engage in dialogues over the meanings of feminism, with Greer or those who are responsible for providing her the platform to articulate her feminist vision (i.e., newspaper or magazine editors). In contrast, most notably for the *Playboy* letter writers, Greer's critique of what we might now call 'toxic masculinity' deeply resonated and inspired many men to shamefully reframe their prior sexual behaviour as assault and commit to change. In terms of *The Female Eunuch*, although some feminists lamented Greer's failure to tell women what to do, readers found this energising, with many feeling reassured after reading the book that they were already agentically working towards liberation.

These letters, as I have shown, offer important insights into historical fandoms (and anti-fandoms) that are often overlooked. Many explicitly identify as Greer fans, though not without an often self-reflexive ambivalence, as we saw especially with the blockbuster fan mail. For others, Greer and her feminism evoke feelings of anger and resentment; this is especially the case with the *McCall's* letters and Irwin emails. Even her fans are not afraid to tell her when they think she has failed in her feminist work, as with *The Last Word* viewers and their critique of the series' lack of diversity, in terms of the chosen panellists, and Greer's failure to attend to intersectional factors. From 'their' Greer, they expected better. While there was not a second series, Greer did promise letter writers she would address their criticisms if one were to go ahead. At other times, Greer is heartened by support from fans, such as when she departed *The Big Brother* house early and more broadly when they reassure her that her media work is having an impact. For some, especially those who write in response to her blockbusters and her television work, we have seen that their Greer fandom continues along the life course. There is much more work to be done in terms of what constitutes feminist fandom, how it might function as a form of activism, and the role that archives can play in helping us to better understand these kinds of fan attachments. This form of fandom – of a celebrity feminist – is overtly political in ways that some others may not be. That is, as I have suggested, fans of feminists are feminist fans, making this an especially rich area for further investigation. Conversely, anti-fans, as we saw in both the *McCall's* and the Irwin instances, appear repelled by both Greer and the feminism she so publicly embodies; they perform their anti-feminism through their anti-fandom, especially in the latter case.

Therefore, in terms of Greer's correspondents, there is a wide spectrum, from those who overtly identify themselves as fans and celebrate her publicly performed feminism and the change in consciousness it can precipitate, to those at the other extreme whose misogynistic hostility is clearly indicative of the obstacles that feminists have faced – and continue to face – as they seek to disrupt and supplant dominant patriarchal imaginaries and structures. On the other hand, there are those who sit between these two extremes, exhibiting neither the emotional intensities of the fans who credit Greer with utterly transforming their worldviews nor the intense disdain of those whose identities and ideologies Greer puts under profound strain. The kinds of discourses used by letter writers in their responses to Greer's feminism, the alternative ideological frameworks which shape some of these reactions, the written selves they bring into being and how, and the emotions that drive them to write in the first instance suggest much about the periods in which the letters were written. Many, as we saw, write as if they knew her, with the 'presumed intimacy' (Rojek 2015) that feeds celebrity culture. The level of intimacy they seek or suppose varies according to the particular letter form; for example, the often confessional texts in response to *The Female Eunuch* differ in tenor from some of the more detached outward-facing letters which seek to discredit Greer's arguments.

Germaine Greer, Celebrity Feminism and the Archive has been able to offer this reassessment of Greer's considerable legacy, and analysis of her celebrity feminism as a crucial form of activism that has reverberated widely, because of the material that she personally collected and curated for her archive (not to mention the immense institutional support she received from the University of Melbourne in this endeavour). As Joan Scott remarks, 'the archive is a provocation; it contents offer an endless resource for thinking and rethinking' (2011, p. 147). Across this book, I have used the extensive Greer archive to critically reflect upon her celebrity feminist labour as well as its effects. Through her work as an archivist, Greer directs researchers towards specific material, including that produced by audiences, and thereby actively shapes the uses we make of her collection. However, I have shown that via her own curatorial practices, she does not aim to create a universally celebrated 'Greer' but offers a more complex picture, not censoring those more judgemental voices but in many ways foregrounding them (as is especially the case with the deeply egregious Irwin emails). In this way, she illustrates how celebrity feminists, in their disruptions to gender certainties and orthodoxies, are intensely anxiety-provoking figures who face opposition and hostility throughout their careers. Through this work, I have also been able to reflect upon the methodologies used in feminist celebrity and fan studies, demonstrating how archives enable us to significantly reframe famous figures (Stead 2021) and 'unsettle' what we think we know of them (Buchanan 2018) and their lengthy careers in the limelight.

Although previous critics have focused on Greer's early career and its impact, this book has underscored not just that she has continued this sort of work in the public sphere until relatively recently but that to do so she has turned to a variety of media forms and genres with a commendable agility. For nearly six decades, Greer has maintained and extended her feminist celebrity capital. At times quite a problematic figure, especially more recently, Greer has had remarkable longevity as a celebrity feminist (rivalled only by Gloria Steinem). While Greer came to fame during a tumultuous period, that fame has endured – because of how she captured audiences across decades, continents, classes, and genders through her iconoclasm. She has subverted dominant social norms and refused to be silenced. Dissident voices such as Greer's are crucial to precipitating, and making sense of, social and political change. The letters audiences wrote to her make that abundantly clear. We can also see how celebrity feminists have functioned as consciousness-raisers, bringing feminism to those who may not otherwise have accessed it and stimulating them to thought and sometimes feminist action, through the archives of other famous feminists, such as Gloria Steinem and Betty Friedan. It is vital, as I have suggested, that we maintain a sense of historical consciousness, emphasising that celebrity and popular feminism – and audience contests over their meanings – are by no means recent phenomena (as some critics appear to presume).

Second-wave feminists often saw feminism and celebrity as antithetical (and indeed anxieties over celebrity feminism persist in the present). Greer, as my analysis has shown, had no faith in unsustainable notions of ideological purity, resulting in the kind of cultural reach that has eluded many other feminists. Feminist work in the media, including by those who have become its key celebrities, has always represented a central way through which attachments to feminism come to be formed by a broad section of the populace. This is the power and vitality of celebrity feminism, as Greer recognised. While the cultural moment that produced celebrities like Greer has passed, there are now many ways of becoming highly visible as a feminist. In the present, the women who have come to be defined as celebrity feminists are predominantly those whose renown stems from their achievements in a specific field (acting, music, comedy, and politics) and who later come to be seen as representatives of particular forms of feminism – *celebrity* feminists as opposed to celebrity *feminists* (Taylor 2016). Most notably, the seemingly global mania around the recent Taylor Swift 'Eras' tour, including in Australia, and audience investment in her (white, neoliberal) feminism suggest that this other form is playing an increasingly important role in the lives of audiences.

In addition, micro-celebrities such as influencers emerging from TikTok or Instagram also appear to be mobilising audiences and informing the kinds of feminisms in which they might invest and through which diverse, intersectional, and more inclusive feminisms are performed. Digital feminisms more broadly have expanded the forms of feminism that come to circulate publicly, and various platforms have facilitated this greater diversity (Parsons-Clarke 2022; Casey and Watson 2023). In other respects, of course, digital media has

182 Germaine Greer, Celebrity Feminism and the Archive

resulted in toxic forms of 'networked misogyny' that must temper any more celebratory claims about these spaces (Banet-Weiser and Miltner 2016); in Sarah Banet-Weiser's (2018) terms, popular feminism and popular misogyny are co-constitutive, and the kind of abuse that Greer experienced via email is now routinely directly at celebrity feminists online (Brady 2021). The work that high-profile feminists do is difficult and perhaps thankless but also essential to the ongoing struggle to create futures that are more equitable for all genders. However, we know relatively little about the ways in which celebrity feminists more overtly intervene in political processes and help precipitate legislative or policy change. #MeToo and the celebrity-led Time Up's movement (Lawson 2023), as well as recent celebrity anti-trafficking activism (Majic 2023), demonstrate both the possibilities and limitations of celebrity interventions into these processes. At the current conjuncture, therefore, it is both forms (celebrity *feminism* and *celebrity* feminism), and how audiences engage with them, that require much further consideration.

In many respects, much of Greer's feminism, especially her popular writing on consent and sexual assault, is highly relevant in the present. While women's anger may have publicly emerged in the wake of #MeToo and through feminism's newfound visibility (Gill 2016; Kay 2019), anger has always been at the heart of Greer's public feminist interventions, as has humour. The combination of these two affective registers has produced a writing style – and indeed wider style of public performances – that ensures her ongoing if at times contentious cultural resonance. Greer has a long public history as an 'unruly woman' (Taylor 2016; see Rowe 1995), doggedly pushing back against the attempts to constrain or contain her. Such 'unruliness' has been and continues to be at the heart of Greer's celebrity persona. She has, however, more recently become a deeply divisive figure for feminism; her offensive anti-trans commentary as well as attacks on other high-profile women such as former Australian Prime Minister Julia Gillard and the former Duchess of Sussex, Meghan Markle, must certainly be condemned. At the time of writing, Greer is 85 years old. For Monica Dux, '[p]art of the uncomfortable legacy of *The Female Eunuch* is that its author has not only grown old but has refused to go away, keep quiet or even to mellow' (2010, p. 11). As an ageing feminist who refuses to be silenced (Bueskens 2020), Greer continues to be an iconoclastic figure.

Although research into Greer and her feminism has been remarkably sparse for a figure of this stature, her importance to the history of modern feminism cannot be overstated, not least because of how she provided the tools for women (and men) to change their lives and embrace different modes of femininity and masculinity – as befitting her countercultural origins. Beginning with the publication of the book responsible for her initial celebrification, *The Female Eunuch* (1970), Greer has persistently advocated revolution over reform, challenged normative gender ideals, critiqued patriarchal capitalism and commodity culture, dismissed domesticity and marriage and the nuclear

Conclusion **183**

family itself, and promoted the reclamation and celebration of women's sexuality (what became known as 'sex positivity') and bodily autonomy (Taylor 2019). This book has revealed that she has also personally served as a model for the alternative kind of subjectivity she advocated for women, as indicated in countless letters praising her for bravery in contesting dominant understandings of femininity. While Greer has remained wedded to her radical form of feminist politics alongside her libertarianism, some accuse her of a lamentable transformation in terms of her feminist commitments; for others it is her consistency that is noteworthy (Bueskens 2020, p. 285).

Greer's feminism and its public articulation have taken many forms over her decades in the limelight. As a celebrity feminist activist, Greer exhibited a unique prescience in terms of her strategic use of the media. Various digital platforms – including social media – have become even more vital as activist tools in feminist work that remains unfinished (Henderson and Taylor 2020). However, Greer has problematised the idea that visibility in the contemporary era is entirely contingent upon the effective management of digital media or digital self-branding. In contrast, the non-digital Greer continues to use analogue methods to do her feminist work in the public sphere. (As I was finishing this book, however, the famous feminist was interviewed by television personality Louis Theroux in a podcast episode which itself received extensive media coverage, focusing on one of Greer's ostensibly more noteworthy comments: 'Germaine Greer tells Louis Theroux why women should marry truck drivers' [Harris 2024]). Television, in particular, has been how the twenty-first-century Greer has maintained a public presence – and an increasingly controversial one (North 2012) at that (though since the COVID-19 pandemic, and owing to her own health issues, this has markedly declined). One can imagine the kinds of tweets and hashtags that Greer may have inspired had she a digital footprint; such forms, with their limited characters and 'idioms of practice' (Gershon 2010), would also make the kinds of longer, self-reflexive epistolary texts that I have examined here difficult (as the Irwin emails made clear).

This lengthy celebrity career also tells us much about the changing relationship between feminists and various forms of Anglo-American media across time. In particular, Greer complicates a number of dominant critical narratives about the feminism–media relationship, including that it was invariably one of hostility and antagonism, especially (but not only) in the 1970s. While many second-wave feminists may have heavily criticised Greer's approach to the media and feared that her feminism would be compromised, her reception – as both Rebecca Sheehan (2016, 2019) and Megan Le Masurier (2016) have shown – suggests that such criticisms were misdirected. Greer successfully destabilises the idea that radicality and popularity are fundamentally incompatible; the dilution of her liberation feminism, I have established, was *not* a condition of her celebrification. Always forthright and irreverent, she threw metaphorical bombs into the mainstream, whether in the form of books, newspaper articles, or television shows. Furthermore, despite attempts to 'fix' this iconic figure in the second-wave moment, Greer's decades-long media interventions significantly complicate the 'waves' model which continues to dominate feminist historiography (Henry 2004). We have also seen the often taxing labour of remaining publicly visible as a feminist; while much recent work on digital platforms has attended to this often precarious work (McRobbie 2016; Duffy 2017), a much longer history needs to be taken into account, as Greer's archival material on 'unmade' creative projects in particular renders visible.

In terms of the difficulties of classifying Greer's feminism, Natalya Lusty's comments regarding that of anarchist Emma Goldman are apposite: it 'defies ready-made feminist categories, then and now' (2019, p. 268). In light of such complexity, Greer's feminist philosophy deserves deeper analysis, particularly in terms of the citational politics theorised by scholars such as Claire Hemmings (2011) and through which Greer appears to have been largely written out of feminist histories. Greer's archive makes possible this kind of scholarship, including in terms of her first blockbuster. As Isobelle Barrett Meyering observes, *The Female Eunuch*, despite its immense cultural reverberations, has (like Greer herself) 'remained on the outer edge of academic feminism' (2016, p. 19). Given its role in launching her onto the international stage, *The Female Eunuch* – in terms of its argumentation, literary techniques and structure, and how it became such an immense international bestseller (i.e., its publication and promotional history, work begun by Marilyn Lake [2016]) – needs to be further considered as a groundbreaking literary and cultural phenomenon. Indeed, all of her popular feminist books, including *The Change* (1991) and *The Whole Woman* (1999), could benefit from such attention using thus far under-examined archival material.

When I started working on this book, I did not imagine that audience letters would take the prominence they ultimately have. However, as researchers working with archival fonds, we have to be open to where the archive might take us, even if it diverts us from our imagined path (Jacobs 2006, p. 18). In addition to revealing the immense feminist labour of Greer herself, the archive has led me to the many voices of readers and viewers, voices that have demonstrated her enormous and long-lasting impact. Considering the extent of both her career and her archive, it is impossible to map her complicated legacy fully in one volume. Indeed, engagement with the archive itself is inevitably partial: 'You know that you *will not finish*, that there will be something left unread, unnoted, untranscribed' (Steedman 2002, p. 18, original emphasis). The archive has grown over the years that I have been using it, and it will continue to do so, as those of living figures invariably do. But it is my hope that I have firmly

Conclusion **185**

repositioned Greer within feminist history and laid the groundwork for future work on all aspects of her public career. The archive's vastness, and indeed its richness, will hopefully ensure that reassessments of one of modern feminism's most formidable figures continue well into the future.

References

Banet-Weiser, S. (2018) *Empowered: Popular Feminism and Popular Misogyny*, Durham: Duke University Press

Banet-Weiser, S. & Miltner, K.M. (2016) '#MasculinitySoFragile: Culture, Structure, and Networked Misogyny', *Feminist Media Studies*, vol. 16, no. 1: 171–174.

Barrett Meyering, I. (2016) 'Germaine Greer's "Arch Enemy": Arianna Stassinopoulos' 1974 Australian Tour', *Australian Feminist Studies*, vol. 31, no. 87: 43–61.

Brady, A. (2021) 'Clementine Ford, Online Misogyny, and the Labour of Celebrity Feminism', in A. Taylor and J. McIntyre (eds.), *Gender and Australian Celebrity Culture*, London: Routledge, pp. 91–108.

Buchanan, R. (2018) 'Foreign Correspondence: Journalism in the Germaine Greer Archive', *Archives and Manuscripts*, vol. 46, no. 1: 18–39.

Bueskens, P. (2020) 'Germaine Greer's *On Rape* Revisited: Clarifying the Long-standing Relationship Between Rape and Heterosexual Pleasure in Greer's Work', *Hecate*, vol. 45, no. 1–2: 268–288.

Casey, S. and Watson, J. (2023) *Hashtag Feminisms: Australian Media Feminists, Activism, and Digital Campaigns*, Bern: Peter Lang.

Duffy, B. (2017) *(Not) Getting Paid to Do What You Love*, New Haven, CT: Yale University Press.

Germaine Greer Archive. General Correspondence, 2014.0042, University of Melbourne.

Gershon, I. (2010). *The Breakup 2.0: Disconnecting Over New Media*, Ithaca, NY: Cornell University Press.

Gill, R. (2016) 'Post-postfeminism?: New Feminist Visibilities in Postfeminist Times', *Feminist Media Studies*, vol. 16, no. 4: 610–630.

Greer, G. (1970) *The Female Eunuch*, London: Paladin.

Greer, G. (1991) *The Change*, London: Hamish Hamilton.

Greer, G. (1999) *The Whole Woman*, London: Doubleday.

Greer, G. (1992) 'Germaine Greer on Strangers in the Mail', *The Independent*, 4 April, Germaine Greer Archive, Print Journalism, 2014.0046.00287, University of Melbourne.

Grossberg, L. (1992) 'Is There a Fan in The House? The Affective Sensibility of Fandom', in L. Lewis (ed.), *The Adoring Audience: Fan Culture and Popular Media*, New York: Routledge, pp. 50–68.

Harris, R. (2024) 'Germaine Greer Tells Louis Theroux why women should marry truck drivers', *Sydney Morning Herald*, 13 March, accessed via: https://www.smh.com.au/world/europe/germaine-greer-tells-louis-theroux-why-women-should-marry-truck-drivers-20240311-p5fbgb.html

Hemmings, C. (2011) *Why Stories Matter: The Politics Grammar of Feminist Theory*, Durham: Duke University Press.

Henderson, M. and Taylor, A. (2020) *Postfeminism in Context*, London: Routledge.

Henry, A. (2004) *Not My Mother's Sister: Generational Conflict and Third Wave Feminism*, Bloomington: Indiana University Press.

Jacobs, J. (2006) 'The Television Archive: Past, Present, Future', *Critical Studies in Television*, vol. 1. No. 1: 13–20.

Kay, J. B. (2019) 'Introduction: Anger, Media, and Feminism: The Gender Politics of Mediated Rage', *Feminist Media Studies*, vol. 19, no. 4: 591–615.

Lake, M. (2016) '"Revolution for the hell of it": The Transatlantic Genesis and Serial Provocations of *The Female Eunuch*', *Australian Feminist Studies*, vol. 31, no. 87: 7–21.

Lawson, C. (2023) *Just Like Us: Digital Debates on Feminism and Fame*, New Brunswick, NJ: Rutgers University Press.

Le Masurier, M. (2016) 'Resurrecting Germaine's Theory of Cuntpower', *Australian Feminist Studies*, vol. 31, no. 87: 28–42.

Lusty, N. (2019) 'Women Modernists and the Legacies of Risk: An Introduction', *Australian Feminist Studies*, vol. 34, no. 101: 267–276.

Majic, S. (2023) *Lights, Camera, Feminism: Celebrities and Anti-trafficking Politics*, Berkeley: California University Press.

McRobbie, A. (2016) *Be Creative: Making a Life in the New Culture Industries*, London: Wiley.

North, A. (2012) '4 Wildly Controversial Things Germaine Greer Has Said', *Buzzfeed*, 28 August, accessed via https://www.buzzfeed.com/annanorth/4-wildly-controversial-things-germaine-greer-has-s

Parsons-Clarke, R. (2022) *Networked Feminism: How Digital Media Makers Transformed Gender Justice Movements*, Los Angeles: University of California Press.

Rojek, C. (2015) *Presuming Intimacy: Parasocial Interaction in Media Society and Celebrity Culture*, London: Polity.

Rowe, K.C. (1995) *The Unruly Woman: Gender and the Genres of Laughter*, Austin: University of Texas Press.

Scott, J. (2011) *The Fantasy of Feminist History*, Durham: Duke University Press.

Sheehan, R.J. (2016) '"If we had more like her we would no longer be the unheard majority": Germaine Greer's Reception in the United States', *Australian Feminist Studies*, vol. 31, no. 87: 62–77.

Sheehan, R.J. (2019) 'Intersectional Feminist Friendship: Restoring Colour to the Second-Wave Through the Letters of Florynce Kennedy and Germaine Greer', *Lilith*, 25: 76–92.

Stead, L. (2021) *Reframing Vivien Leigh: Stardom, Gender, and the Archive*, Oxford: Oxford University Press.

Steedman, C. (2002) *Dust: The Archive and Cultural History*, Manchester: Manchester University Press.

Taylor, A. (2016) *Celebrity and the Feminist Blockbuster*, Palgrave Macmillan: Basingstoke.

Taylor, A. (2019) '"Equality is a profoundly conservative aim": Germaine Greer and the Radical Possibilities of Popular Feminism', unpublished Conference Paper, Cultural Studies of Australasia Conference, 4–6 December, University of Queensland.

Turner, G., Bonner, F. and Marshall, P.D. (2000) *Fame Games: The Production of Celebrity in Australia*, Sydney: Cambridge University Press.

INDEX

Pages followed by "n" refer to notes.

Abdel-Magied, Y. 171–172
abortion 15, 76, 79–80, 96, 114–120, 130; *see also* reproductive freedom/ rights
'Abortion: Right or Wrong?' debate 114
Abortion Reform Society 114
activism 7, 47; celebrity 9, 180, 182
affective dis-investment 2, 11, 16, 135–136
affective dissonance 45, 56
affective investment 11, 135–137
affirmative consent 110
The Age 123, 161
ageing women/ageism 35, 59, 91, 95, 147, 168, 170–171, 182
agency 10, 25–26, 34, 64, 95, 120, 130, 141; sexual 46, 112, 117–118; situated 24, 26
Ahmed, S. 8, 11, 47, 52, 59, 93, 116, 141, 164–165, 169
Alomes, S. 155
Amis, M. 36, 38
Ang, I. 79
anger 52–53, 179, 182
anti-fandom 4, 13, 15–16, 130, 136–137, 179; anti-feminism and 168–171, 179
anti-feminism 116, 140–144, 147, 148n6
Anzac Day 171

archival methodologies 3, 14, 24–25, 39
archival studies 2–3, 14, 24, 39
archives/archival practices: 'archiving "I"' 24, 32–33, 39; celebrity 23, 29, 37–39; content and composition 23; and feminist celebrity studies 25, 29, 39; as spaces of privilege and exclusion 29; *see also* Greer archive
Arrow, M. 48
attention capital 2, 29, 34, 36–37, 74, 159
Atwood, M. 36
audiences 1–16, 23, 27–28, 34, 36, 38, 46, 54, 61, 67, 73–75, 77–95, 104, 123, 129–135, 137, 153–154, 158, 160, 172, 178, 180–182, 184
Australia 153–171; borders 163–165; cultural cringe 160–161; expatriates 155, 163–164, 178; masculinity 147, 158, 165, 169–171; national mythologies 157–158, 160–164, 168, 171; press 155–156; 'un-Australian' 162–163
Australia Post 172n3
Australian National Living Treasure 155
Australian Women's Weekly 62, 123
authenticity 3, 15, 29, 32, 58, 73, 82–83, 96, 141, 178
autobiography 32, 51–52
Azbug, A. 120

188 Index

Banet-Weiser, S. 182
Barker-Plummer, B. 6
Barrett Meyering, I. 184
BBC 74, 83–84, 87
Beatty, W. 36
Beauvoir, S. de 12, 62, 115, 132–133
Being Australian (Elder) 162
Beins, A. 64–65
Bellanta, M. 165
Bennett, J. 74, 82
'Betty Friedan's Notebook' (*McCall's* column by Friedan) 133–134
Bleakley, P. 92
biographies/biographers 16n1, 32
Bonner, F. 73, 77, 85
Borges, M. J. 45
Brown, S. 34
Buchanan, R. 14, 24–25, 27–29, 32, 36, 39, 97n7, 103, 114, 154
bullying 90

Carbine, P. 133
Cardiff University 16n4
Cavett, Dick 76, 95
celebrity archives 23, 29, 37–39
Celebrity Big Brother 15, 35, 74, 76, 84, 90–95, 179
celebrity culture 4, 6, 10, 49, 105, 107, 157, 180
celebrity feminism 16, 23, 177, 180; as activism 9, 180, 182; debates about 2, 17n7, 130, 139; definition 9; labour and function of 9–11, 25, 184; as political resource 6, 9
celebrity studies 3–4, 14, 16, 24, 28, 39
The Change (Greer) 14, 59–62, 66, 68n5, 170, 177, 184
childlessness 169–170
Chisolm, S. 120
choice 129–130, 143–146; choice feminism 144–145
class 8, 12, 15, 30, 89–90, 129–130, 133, 144–147, 158, 166, 181
Cleo 123, 147, 147n1
Clinton, H. 171
Cloud, D. L. 163, 166
Coffin, J. 12, 62
commodified activism 9
commodity capitalism 103, 134
consciousness-raising (CR) 6, 23, 47–48, 78, 123, 179, 181
consumer culture 134
Coombs, A. 33

COVID-19 pandemic 3, 30, 183
Crocodile Hunter (documentary series) 158
Crowe, R. 158
Cvetkovich, A. 6

Daddy, We Hardly Knew You (Greer) 16n3, 155
Daily Mail 91, 94
Daily Telegraph 6, 161, 169
Daphne Productions 95
Dean, K. 30
Deller, R. 92
Democratic Convention in Miami (1972) 118–119
Dennis, E. 103
Dever, M. 12, 17n12, 27–28
diaries 3, 8, 11, 23, 129
The Dick Cavett Show 13, 15, 36, 51, 74, 76–83, 88–89, 91, 93, 96, 130, 137, 178
Didion, J. 118
digital media 13, 178, 183; affordances 131; inclusive feminism 89
digital remediation 49
domesticity 143–146; celebration of 141, 145; critique of 134, 182; freedom 135, 141–143, 145, 147; as imprisonment 142–143; slavery trope 135, 142, 144–146
Douglas, J. 26–27, 33–34
Douglas, K. 12
Dow, B. J. 77
doxing 161
Drake, P. 84
Driessens, O. 92
Dux, M. 91, 182
Dyer, R. 25, 68n2

editors 4, 13, 15, 25, 27, 36, 96, 96n2, 103–107, 111–118, 120, 123, 129–139, 147n1, 148n2, 153–154, 159, 164, 179
Edwards, K. 16n4
Eichhorn, K. 28
egalitarianism 161, 165
Elder, C. 162, 166
emotions 5, 11–13, 52, 106, 116, 137, 153, 178, 180; history of 45
environment 16n3, 154, 158, 160
Equal Rights Amendment (ERA) 120
Esquire 32, 107, 119
Evans, H. 114
Evans, K. 87

Index **189**

fan studies 49, 180
fans/fandoms 179–180; artifacts 49; belonging 57; collective identity 49; critical engagement 13; definitions 49; diversity 12–13; feminist identity work 57; identification 13, 52, 68; imagined community 46, 49, 57, 68, 131; mail 13, 45–68; pathologisation of 49; political 13, 68, 179; practices 13, 17n11, 46, 49–50; self-reflexivity and 48–51
Farrell, A. E. 131
Fear of Flying (Jong) 47
Featherstone, L. 109
Fellini, F. 36
Felski, R. 52, 54–55, 58
The Female Eunuch (Greer) 1–2, 16n3, 45–48, 50, 52–58, 60–68, 75, 77, 81, 102, 104, 109, 111, 114, 122, 129–147, 153, 155, 182, 184; book tours 106, 131; cultural reverberations of 65–67; eunuch metaphor 46–47, 60; *McCall's* extract 134–135; promotion of 46, 81, 131–132; reception in Australia 155–156; research 68n1; US publication 130
The Female of the Species 172n1
The Feminine Mystique (Friedan) 48, 132, 135, 143
femininity 15, 56, 95, 129, 134–135, 140–141, 147, 154, 156, 163, 165, 169, 171
feminism: affective engagements with 45; attachments to 13, 46, 61, 181; choice 144–145; micropolitics 59; as hope 53, 56, 58–60; intersectional 86, 90; liberal 8; neoliberal 181; online opponents of 139; pathologised 140, 169, 171; popular health 61–62; radical 2, 8, 17n8, 105, 108–109; self-discovery 54–55; vernacular 59, 89; *see also* anti-feminism; second-wave feminism; popular feminism; women
feminist blockbusters 2, 45–47, 52–53, 57, 61, 65–67, 75, 84, 93, 96, 102, 111, 121, 133, 135, 137, 141, 179, 184
feminist killjoy 93, 141, 169
feminist periodicals 103
feminist reflexivity 45, 56
field migration 103

Firkus, A. 49
The First Stone (Garner) 59
Ford, C. 139, 171
Four Corners 114
Friedan, B. 5, 26, 53, 132–135, 145, 181
The Friends of Gondwana Rainforest 30

Garner, H. 59–60
gender 1–2, 4–5, 12, 14–16, 26, 35, 38–39, 48–49, 51, 53–54, 57, 62, 74, 79, 86, 89, 92, 95–96, 102, 105, 109, 112–113, 116, 122–123, 130, 139, 141, 144, 148n5, 153, 156–157, 160, 162–163, 165, 170–171, 172n3, 177–178, 180–182, 184
gendered 'biomythological' framing 48–49
gendered insults/hate speech 154, 156–157, 161–162, 164, 170–171
gendertrolling 157
General Correspondence series 3–4, 13, 36, 45, 48, 67, 78, 91, 104, 111, 131
Genz, S. 143
'Germaine Greer Meets the Archivists' event 32, 34–35
'Germaine Greer on why the Abortion Act is a calamity' 15, 103, 115–116
'Germaine Greer on Strangers in the Mail' (Greer) 6, 177
The Germaine Greer Show 77, 84, 95
Germaine Greer versus the USA 131
Gibson, M. 158
Gilbert, S. 37
Gillard, J. 2, 16n4, 162, 167–170, 182
Gillon Aitken Associates 154
Glanville, L. 31, 34, 36, 48, 76
Goldman, E. 24, 184
Gordon, L. 117
Gray, J. 136–137
Green, B. 52
Greer, Germaine: academic work 37, 106; as a consciousness-raiser 5, 47, 67, 81, 93; celebrity, political use of 2, 6, 9–11, 180, 183; cross-media feminism 2–3, 10, 23, 178; disavowal of celebrity 6, 17n11, 34–35; expatriate 16n3, 155–156, 164; fan incident 153, 172n1; as a freelance journalist 106; hate mail against *see* hate emails; legacy 1–2, 177–185; on Irwin *see* Irwin, S; journalistic writing *see* journalism; labour 1–3, 6, 9–10, 14–15, 23, 25–31, 34, 36–38,

190 Index

63, 73–74, 95, 102, 106, 123, 159, 180, 184; libertarianism 63, 106; marriage, critique of 8, 15, 46, 130, 132–135, 142; media pragmatism 6–9; misogyny directed at 153, 157, 161–162, 168, 171; public persona 4–5, 7, 10, 14, 23–24, 34, 52, 59, 62, 67, 74, 77–78, 82–83, 94, 158, 160, 182; as a role model 59, 81; sex positivity 8, 110, 183; singleness 10, 143, 169; women's movement, outsider status 5, 81, 120
Greer archive 14–15, 23–38; archivists 3, 14, 24, 27–28, 30, 32, 34, 36–37, 39; audio diary entries 29–30; authority of 31–34; conditions of access 3, 23; content and composition 23, 36–38; curation and curatorial practices 3, 14, 23, 25, 31, 33, 35–37, 39, 45, 154, 180; diary cassette tapes 32; Early years series 4, 78; feminist agency 26; letters in 3–6, 177–180; General correspondence series 3–4, 13, 36, 45, 48, 67, 78, 87, 91, 104, 131; Major works series 4, 31; management of files 38; recordkeeping 106; narratives about 34–38; omissions and silences 38, 76; origin story 28–31; Print journalism series 4, 104, 106, 124n3; prohibition of photographs 28, 30; purpose 31–32; sale of 29–30; scholarship 14, 37; Television series 4, 31, 76, 87
Groeneveld, E. 137
Grossberg, L. 11, 135
Guardian 16, 36, 93, 154, 156, 158–159
Gubar, S. 37

Habermas, J. 86
Hannell, B. 52
Hanson, P. 164
Hanusch, F. 165
Harker, J. 47
Harper's Magazine 15, 103, 118–119, 122, 164, 179
hate emails 16; misogyny 156–157, 161–171; themes 156; threats 154, 157, 167–168
Hefner, H. 111, 124n12
Heller, D. 86–87
Hemmings, C. 24, 56, 184
Henderson, M. 46

Herald Sun 84, 164
heteronormativity 143, 168
Hills, M. 49
historiography 2, 184
Hobbs, C. 32
Hodgetts, K. 32
Holland, J. 162
homophobia 169–170
hope 58–60
hostile letters 13; *see also* hate emails
housewives 130, 138, 141, 143–147, 147n1
Howard, J. 165
humour 182
Humphries, B. 155, 160

idolatry 61
Independent 6, 177
influencers 82, 181
interpretive community 118, 130
intersectionality 89, 146
intimacy 12, 28–29, 38, 46, 48, 60, 62, 68, 74, 82–83, 85, 94, 96, 105, 137, 143, 180
Irwin, S. 36, 147, 153; Australian-ness 154, 162, 164–166; celebrity status 157–158; conservationism 157–158, 160, 165; death and posthumous media coverage 16, 158; Greer on 159–161; larrikin 154, 165; masculinity 158, 165–167, 169–170; public support for 158; *see also* hate emails

Jackson, M. 84
Jacobs, J. 78
James, C. 155, 160
Jane, E. 156–157
Jenson, J. 49
Johnson, L. 143
Jolly, M. 12
Jones, A. 168
Jong, E. 47
journalism 15, 102–124, 178; cunt power 8, 108, 118; editorial interventions 32, 108, 159; freelance 106, 159; invitations and fees for 106–107; journalistic voice 105–106

Kay, J. B. 77–79, 163
Kennedy, F. 4
Kleinhenz, E. 16n1
Konchar Farr, C. 47
Kreps, B. 145

Ladies' Home Journal 132–133
'Lady Love Your Cunt' (Greer) 108
Lake, M. 184
The Last Word (BBC series) 15, 36, 74, 76, 79, 83–91, 179
Le Masurier, M. 133, 147, 147n1, 183
Lee, J. 84
Lee, K. 74
Lehrmann, N. 108
lesbians/lesbianism 140, 163
Leslie, A. 85
letters 3–6; as audience research 5, 11; autobiographical 51; epistolarity 4–5, 11–12, 28, 45–46, 51–52, 67, 74, 93, 96, 136, 143, 147, 178–179, 183; as historical sources 12; political and affective role 12; private 4, 12; out-ward facing 4, 13, 147, 180; Riot Grrrl archive 12; scholarly value 48; to the editor 4, 13–14, 36, 102–124, 129–147, 147n1, 148n2, 153–154, 179; writers 4–5, 46; *see also* General Correspondence series
Life 7, 81
Lloyd, J. 143
Loaded 107
Lusty, N. 184

MacNeil, H. 34
Mailer, N. 32, 132
Major Works series 4, 27, 31
man/men 4, 7, 10–11, 33, 48, 50–51, 54, 65, 81–82, 84–86, 88, 94, 102–104, 107–113, 117, 119–120, 122, 148n5, 156, 163–164, 166–170, 178–179, 182
Mantilla, K. 157
Marcus, S. 5, 10, 49
Markle, M. 182
marriage 8, 15, 46, 130, 132–135, 142, 178, 182
masculinity 85–86; Australian 147, 158, 165, 169–171; toxic 179
McCaig, J. 28
McCall's (magazine) 15, 47, 129–147, 153, 169, 179
McClure, D. 76–77
McDermott, P. 106
McGill, R. 24
McGovern, G. 119–120
'McGovern, The Big Tease' (Greer) 118–123
McGrath, A. 75

media literacy 90, 131
media pragmatism 6–9
menopause 61–62, 66, 178
#MeToo 2, 110, 159, 182
Millar, E. R. 115–116
misogyny 113; history of 157; networked 182; online 139, 156–157, 161–171; public discourse 168
Montgomery, J. 160–161
Moore, S. 85
Moran, C. 85
Morley, D. 79
Moskowitz, E. 135
mothers/motherhood 15, 53, 96, 118, 129–132, 134–136, 140–146
Mrs America 120, 142
Ms (magazine) 131, 133
Munro, A. 28
Murray, S. 46, 132
'My Mailer Problem' (Greer) 107

Nagouse, E. 16n4
national fictions 162
national mythologies 163–165, 171
National Portrait Gallery, Canberra 158
National Women's Political Caucus 119
nationalism 155, 162–167, 171
The Nationwide Audience (Morley) 79
networked misogyny 182
new journalism 106, 118–119
New York Post 75
New York Times 93
NOW (National Organisation for Women) 122

O'Donnell, K. 37, 61
On Rape (Greer) 8, 110
Ordone, C. 85
Our Bodies, Ourselves 47
Oz 103, 108

Packer, F. 155
parasociality 13, 172
paratexts 31, 62
Pearce, L. 48–49
Peck, J. 84
Pitzulo, C. 108–111
Playboy 15, 62, 102–103, 108–114, 123, 124n8, 133, 138, 157, 178–179
Plummer, K. 51
POL 107
'The Politics of Female Sexuality' (Greer) 108

192 Index

Poletti, A. 12
Pollock, G. 24
popular feminism 2, 5, 9, 14, 29, 35, 89, 107, 113, 123, 130–135, 181–182, 184; popular health feminism 61–62
Porter, J. S. 85
postfeminism 86, 129–130, 143–144
precarity/precarious work 159, 184
Probyn, E. 45, 56, 145

Q&A (television program) 16n4
Quinn, S. 7

race 12, 89, 130, 144–146
racism 171
Radovan, J. 156
rape 9, 109–113, 157, 159, 171; *see also* sexual assault
reader-writers 102, 104, 111–113, 116–118, 120–123, 129, 131, 137–147
recognition in reading 52
Reddy, H. 48
Redmond, S. 83
reformism 8, 105, 122
religious tropes 60–61
reproductive freedom/rights 114–115, 117–118
retreatism 144
'Right Now: A Monthly Newsletter for Women' (*McCall's* monthly section) 133
Riot Grrrl archive 12
Roe v Wade (US Supreme Court decision) 114–115
Rojek, C. 9
Rowlands, S. 46
Rudd, K. 161

salons, feminist 86–87
Schaffer, K. 162
Schickel, R. 82
Schlafly, P. 142, 144
Scott, J. 180
The Second Sex (Beauvoir) 132–133
second-wave feminism 1, 5, 47–48, 52, 109, 130, 133, 172n3, 181; abortion 115; anger 110; Anglo-America feminists 7; celebrities 10; collective memory 9; correspondence 12, 58; exclusions 88, 133; housewives and 143–147;

journalism 103; literary critics 37; media and 7–8, 15, 24, 106, 183; servitude trope 144; sisterhood 57, 60, 110, 119; television 77, 83, 88, 93; *see also* Women's liberation movement
'Seduction is a Four-Letter Word' (Greer) 108–114
self-reflexivity 6–7, 31, 34, 39, 48–51, 107
Serisier, T. 110
Sex and Anarchy (Coombs) 33
Sex and Destiny (Greer) 16n3
Sex and the City 145
sex positivity 8, 108, 183
sexism 47, 110, 171; *see also* misogyny
sexual agency 112, 117–118
sexual assault 8, 110, 113, 182
sexuality 2, 4, 8, 12, 15, 38–39, 46, 74, 95, 105, 109, 154, 156; heterosexuality 8, 35, 85–86, 90, 106, 143, 169–171
shame 112, 123, 179
Shattuc, J. 87–88
Sheehan, R. 7, 75, 78–79, 83, 109, 124n10, 183
Silver, S. 133
Simons, M. 38
sisterhood 57, 60, 110, 119
situated agency 24, 26
slavery 135, 142–144, 146
Smith, S. 52
social media 5, 154, 157, 171, 183
Spare Rib 115
Spender, D. 37
Spruill, M. 144, 148n5
Stanley, L. 131
Stead, L. 23, 25
Steedman, C. 105
Steinem, G. 5, 26, 35, 75, 103, 109, 118, 120, 122–123, 133, 181
Steuer, L. 57–58
The Story of Human Reproduction 77, 95, 96n1
The Structural Transformation of the Public Sphere (Habermas) 86
Suck 103, 108
Summers, A. 168, 172n3
Sunday Telegraph 155–156
Sunday Times 15, 93, 103, 114–118
Sydney Morning Herald 159, 161
Sydney Push 33, 108
Sykes, R. 4, 124n5, 124n10

tall poppy syndrome 156, 160
Taylor Swift 181
Telegraph 84
television (appearances and
performances) 8, 14–15, 73–96;
Celebrity Big Brother 15, 35, 74, 76,
84, 90–95, 179; *The Dick Cavett
Show* 13, 15, 36, 51, 74, 76–83,
88–89, 91, 93, 96, 130, 137, 178;
Greer's preference for 75; immediacy
75, 80; *The Last Word* 15, 36, 74,
76, 79, 83–91, 179; *Nice Times*
(comedy skit show) 75; *Strictly Come
Dancing* 75
Tharunka 33
Theroux, L. 183
Thompson, J. 133
Thompson, J. D. 124n2
Thornton, M. 17n12
Tillyard, S. 35
Time Up's movement 182
Tomlinson, B. 169
Town Hall debate 132
toxic masculinity 179
trad wife 144
trans commentary 2, 16n4, 139, 158,
182
Tribune 6
Trump, D. 164, 171
Turner, G. 10, 162
Twitter/X 154, 171

underground press 102, 106–107, 111
University of Melbourne 3, 23, 28, 30;
'Germaine Greer Meets the
Archivists' event 32, 34–35
University of New South Wales 33
US Supreme Court: Roe v Wade decision
114–115

vernacular feminisms 59, 89
victim-blaming 107, 113
Vogue 62, 133

Wallace, C. 16n1, 32
Ward, R. 165
Warwick University 106
Washington Post 7
Watching Dallas (Ang) 79
Watching Women's Liberation 1970
(Dow) 77
Watson, J. 52
Weber, M. 35, 154
Weinstein, H. 16n4
Whaling, A. 164
'What Turns Women On' (Greer) 107
White Beech (Greer) 16n3
whiteness 8, 13, 15, 30, 35, 85, 89–90,
129, 133, 145–146, 162, 164, 171,
181
Whitlam, G. 96n1, 156, 172n3
The Whole Woman (Greer) 16n3, 50,
65–67, 68n3, 184
Wicke, J. 25, 107
Wills, S. 114
Winant, C. 119
Winfrey, O. 84
women: agency *see* agency; authors of
non-fiction 48–49; domesticity 130,
132, 134–135, 141–146; life
writing practices 11–12, 46;
objectification 111; public
disciplining 171; self-representation
45, 48, 51, 53, 58, 67; sisterhood
57, 60, 110, 119; television
industries 77, 95; violence against
166–168; *see also* feminism
Women's Legal Defense and Education
Fund 113
Women's liberation movement/women's
liberationists 6–8, 10, 12, 25, 46–48,
65, 76–79, 81, 102, 106, 109, 114,
119–120, 129, 133, 137, 143–144;
see also second-wave feminism
Wright, K. 162

York, L. 26

Printed in the United States
by Baker & Taylor Publisher Services